# THE CONSTITUTION OF BANGLADESH

The book provides a comprehensive introduction to the Constitution of Bangladesh. It traces the sociopolitical and legal context of its birth in the aftermath of a violent Independence War, through to the seventeen amendments to date as Bangladesh evolved through military coups and dictatorships, shifting alliances between religious and political parties, and the emergence of development state. Aimed at readers who are keen to understand the underpinnings of the constitutional system, its evolution, and the politics behind the scenes, the book will explore the impact of political bargains and extra-legal developments on the evolution of the Constitution instead of treating it as a standalone doctrine. By focusing on the overall sociopolitical context up until 2020, the book departs from the dominant tendency in legal scholarship to restrict attention to the development of the Constitution from its inception to the modern day.

The volume will be of great interest to scholars and researchers of law, politics and South Asian studies.

**Arafat Hosen Khan** is a practicing Advocate at the Supreme Court of Bangladesh; also works as Senior Lecturer at the Department of Law, North South University, Dhaka, Bangladesh; and as Senior Researcher on Constitutional Law, Democracy and Contemporary Human Rights issues. He is a member of the Board of Trustees, Institute of Inclusive Policy (IIP), a leading research-based thinktank in Bangladesh; and partner at Apex Court Chambers, Dhaka. Following completion of his LL.B. (Hons.) at the University of Essex, UK, in 2008, he was successfully called to the English Bar by the Honourable Society of Lincoln's Inn in 2009. He also completed an MA in Global Ethics and Human Values at King's College London in 2013 with a Chevening Scholarship funded by the Foreign and Commonwealth Office (FCO), UK; and was awarded the O'Brien Fellows in Residence at the McGill Centre for Human Rights and Legal Pluralism, Faculty of Law, McGill University, Montreal, Canada.

# THE CONSTITUTION OF BANGLADESH

## People, Politics and Judicial Intervention

*Arafat Hosen Khan*

Routledge
Taylor & Francis Group
LONDON AND NEW YORK

Cover image: Getty Images

First published 2023
by Routledge
4 Park Square, Milton Park, Abingdon, Oxon OX14 4RN

and by Routledge
605 Third Avenue, New York, NY 10158

*Routledge is an imprint of the Taylor & Francis Group, an informa business*



*British Library Cataloguing-in-Publication Data*
A catalogue record for this book is available from the British Library

ISBN: 978-1-032-13093-4 (hbk)
ISBN: 978-1-032-42488-0 (pbk)
ISBN: 978-1-003-36300-2 (ebk)

DOI: 10.4324/9781003363002

Typeset in Bembo
by MPS Limited, Dehradun

# CONTENTS

# ACKNOWLEDGEMENTS

I was born and brought up in a political family in the southern part of Bangladesh. As a result, I had the privilege of observing political development from a very early age and subsequently recognized the need for democratic due process in society. My father, who is a freedom-fighter and is an Advocate of the Supreme Court of Bangladesh, is a well-regarded politician who has sacrificed a large portion of his life fighting for independence, democracy, and the rights of our people. He was actively involved in the mass upsurge of early 1969 that served as a catalyst for the liberation struggle of Bangladesh.

As an individual, I am proud of my identity and heritage and therefore, maintained focus on democratic process, rule of law, and human rights issues that plague Bangladesh, even during my tenure as a student in the United Kingdom as well as during my professional career. The continuous undermining of law, equality and justice in Bangladesh has been a grave cause of concern for me. As such, being inspired by my father, I have dedicated myself to contributing to democracy and human rights situation through legal empowerment. Therefore, I would like to dedicate this book to my father Khan Altaf Hossain Bhulu.

I would like to express a deep gratitude to my LL.B graduate students at the Department of Law of North South University, Dhaka Bangladesh namely Wasif Jamal Khan, Sabiha Mehzabin Oishee, Rizowan Ahmed, Shahriar Bin Wares, and Monisha Jahan Joya who helped in my research greatly as well as the motivation provided to make it to the end. I would also like to thank my very good friends Farah Huq and Qareena Khan for helping me with the proposal of this book. I would also like extend my thanks to Pritam Kumar Das, my dear friend Md Saimum Sadi, Barrister, and my sister in law Nowshin Noor Aysharzo for helping with the proofreading of this book. I would also like to show my appreciation for my mother Anowara Begum, wife Benajir Anjum, and daughter Anaya Ameerah Khan, for their endless support and encouragement throughout.

Writing a book is harder than I thought and more rewarding than I could have ever imagined. None of this would have been possible without my wife, Benajir Anjum Chandni. She stood by me during every struggle and all my successes. I would like to thank her for her constant support, for all the late nights and early mornings, and for keeping me sane during the time I was working on this book.

# 1

# INTRODUCTION: THE OPENING STATEMENTS

'A state without a constitution is like a boat without oarsman'—Bangabandhu Shaikh Mujibur Rahman.[1] The Constitution of Bangladesh, promulgated in 1972, earned plaudit from all quarters for its wide vision, democratic values, and secular ideas. The democratic spirit which the constitution displayed, and the speed at which it was framed, was praised by all, which was a great achievement for a newly independent country, just emerged out of a bloody war.

In 1971, the world saw the born of a new country unlike any that had come before. In an era of decolonization and initiating a new period in economic speculation, the new born Bangladesh constitution was a bold step away from the status quo. Our founding father Bangabandhu Shaikh Mujibur Rahman had a vision for a country ruled by the people that lived and worked in it rather than the people and families at the top of society. He had a vision of a nation that would be recognized as a torch-bearer for peace, democratic values, tolerance, courage, secularism, and, above all, harmony. With this idea, our constitution was written in 1972. The constitution was seen sceptically by our infant nation with many assuming that such idea or vision would crash and burn not long after it started. Our success as a country and rise to the status of world hegemon today proves that a country can in fact be successfully run on ideas of democracy and secularism.

The constitution, while reflecting many of the values of its time, was largely progressive in its orientation and vision, reflecting a democratic and secular spirit within the first years of it came into an effect. But with the passage of time, especially since the assassination of *Bangabandhu* Sheikh Mujibur Rahman and other pro-liberation leaders, the Constitution has immensely suffered in the hands of the successive military and semi-military governments, first by General Ziaur Rahman, and later, by General Ershad. The constitution, in its letter and spirit, was trampled down, and grossly distorted by different amendments. Even the elected governments did not lag behind in this process.

DOI: 10.4324/9781003363002-1

Since the independence of our country, the legislatures who are represented by the different political parties have shown their party focused attitudes in amending the constitution rather a *people-centric approach*. Amendments, which did not fit in at all with the spirit of the 1971 liberation war, and its outcome the 1972 constitution, were adopted through brute majorities in the parliament. These brought dominant debates on politicization of the constitution and constitutional amendments include secularization of the constitution, Islamization of the constitution, one-party government to multi-party democracy, basic structure doctrine, military intervention and martial law, provision to the referendum to amend the constitution, insertion and abolition of the caretaker government, appointment and impeachment of the SC judges. However, the Supreme Court of Bangladesh as a guardian of the constitution had intervened from time to time and had declared several amendments unconstitutional to uphold the spirit of the 1971 liberation war, and its outcome the 1972 constitution.

This book aims to narrate the journey of the Bangladesh constitution—how it was written, the making process, the vision and the experiences which constituted its framing, and how by repeated amendments, the constitution moved away from its original democratic and secular character, and also how it again tried to restore its original form by the intervention of the judiciary.

The political history of Bangladesh can be broadly divided into three eras: the era of populist authoritarianism (1972–1975), the era of military dominated rule (1975–1990), and the era of representative democracy (1991- to date). There were a number of constitutional amendments which occurred during different eras. There were 5 (1$^{st}$ to 5$^{th}$) constitutional amendments during 1972–1975, 4 (6$^{th}$ to 9$^{th}$) were constitutional amendments during 1975–1990, and 8 (10$^{th}$ to 17$^{th}$) constitutional amendments during 1990–2018. This research will cover all constitutional amendments till their inception.

This book will also focus, as it happened, and got reflected, in the chequered history of Bangladesh politics during the last four decades. This research will aim to document various key political and constitutional issues that, came across via different judicial intervention in the several amendments by conducting interviews of the parliamentarians and the legal experts who had written the constitution and also were involved in those landmark cases, social leaders and representatives of the religious and ethnic minorities who may have been affected due to the changes made, and also other stake holders.

## Background

Any modern state cannot be thought of without a constitution. The entire legislative, executive, and judicial functions of the state are guided and regulated by the constitution. The constitution and its development, as the supreme legal framework of a country, is a continuing process so that the hopes and aspirations of its populace can be accommodated along with socio-economic changes. Bangladesh is not an exception to this.

Since the emergence of Pakistan, Punjabi rulers of the West though the exploitation of the cycle exploited Bangladesh, the then East Pakistan economically and in some cases, socially. After 23 year of limitless exploitation, East Pakistan turned into a crematorium. Our Father of the Nation Bangabandhu Sheikh Mujibur Rahman mentioned multiple times the aspirations of the Bengali nation in his writings and speeches, which have been rationalized in the elections of 1970s. The historic victory of the Awami League in that election brought a threat to the plots of the Pakistani military junta.

Bangabandhu Sheikh Mujibur Rahman declared the independence of Bangladesh on 26 March 1971. On this call of the Father of the nation, within a fortnight, an independent government was formed on 10 April, 1971 and consequently led the way to the nine-month long bloody battle for freedom.

In this war of 1971, many women lost their dignity and thousands of lives were taken away brutally. More than 150,000 people of the East Pakistan were inhumanly tortured by the Pakistani juntas and their allies. More than 10 million people were forced to leave the country losing everything they had and took shelter as refugees in India. This statistics of sacrifice, murder, and torture for gaining freedom is still unmatched to any country in the world.

The war was not just a matter of marking territory or having a separate flag. People from all classes and professions participated in the war with dreams of liberation in every sector of the country and more importantly to establish the right to self-determination in their own terms.

The then Prime Minister Tajuddin Ahmad, during this war, explained several times the need for a secular democratic identity of the country. The demand for a non-communal Bengali nationalism was expressed through posters and manifestos distributed from Mujibnagar during the war. A notable poster during the Liberation War read, '*Hindus of Bengal, Christians of Bengal, Buddhists of Bengal, Muslims of Bengal - we are all Bengalis.*'

The liberation war portrayed the awareness and non-communal spirit of the people of this nation. Their stand was against the fundamentalists and communal evils. Bangabandhu Sheikh Mujibur Rahman called for a struggle that was not just for geographic freedom, that was the struggle against inequalities in social, political, and religious sectors.

The main feature of Bangali nationalism is their non-communalism. People from all religions and ethnicity hold this spirit in their hearts. The urge for freedom was more due to a long period of torture and exploitation the Bengalis had to undergo. Bangabandhu's inspiration of socialism, thus, fuelled the Bengalis spirit and people from all levels of the society jumped into the war without giving a second thought.

These desires and hopes were reflected for the first time in the constitution of 1972. The outline of the constitution was declared by Bangabandhu Sheikh Mujibur Rahman in the very first session of the Assembly on 10 April 1972. He remembered the sacrifice of 3 million martyrs on the day of drafting the Constitution. He said at the starting of his speech,

> *Mr. Speaker, you know that we have got this freedom in exchange for the blood of three million brothers and sisters. As members of this Constituent Assembly, we will remember and remember their sacrifice. We must remember that the blood we have got freedom for should not go in vain … .*

Bangabandhu's speech of 3 November 1972 was the most denotable because it had given a direction for the foundation of the constitution of Bangladesh. He, in this speech, defined 'democracy,' 'socialism,' and 'secularism' which are the main parts of the fundamental principles of the Constitution of Bangladesh.

After the partition of 1947, the 24 year long radical rule of Pakistan was a time of suppression and exploitation. Bangabandhu Sheikh Mujibur Rahman is not just a name; it is a dream and a philosophy that came like a ray of light after this long tormenting period in the lives of the Bengalis. Bangabandhu Sheikh Mujib, along with his associates, created the constitution of to give the newly born country a backbone.

Bangladesh declared its independence on 26 March 1971; which was achieved against the Pakistani Occupation Forces by the Liberation Forces of Bangladesh on 16 December 1971; in alliance with the Indian Defence Forces. In 1972, the 300 members who were elected in the Legislative Assembly of East Pakistan were made the members of the Bangladesh Constituent Assembly, and the law minister of the new government was enforced to draft the constitution of the new country by an all-party committee (except for the Islamic Parties) lead by Dr. Kamal Hossain.

An amendment to the constitution usually refers to the revision of the constitution of a nation or state. In many jurisdictions, the text of the constitution itself is altered; in others the text is not changed, but the amendments change its effect.

Most constitutions require that amendments cannot be enacted unless they have passed a special procedure that is more stringent than that required for ordinary legislation. Examples of such special procedures include supermajorities in the legislature, or direct approval by the electorate in a referendum, or even a combination of two or more different special procedures.

The special procedures for the amendment of some constitutions have proven to be so exacting that of proposed amendments either few, as in Australia, or none, as in Japan, have been passed over a period of several decades. In contrast, the constitution of the US state of Alabama has been amended over 800 times since 1901. From the period 1973 to 2019, 17 amendments have been made to the Constitution of the People's Republic of Bangladesh.

The constitution has been amended by Acts of the Parliaments and by the Marital Law Proclamation Orders as well. It is argued that in Bangladesh the constitution has been amended for the sake of narrow party interests. Even personal benefits encouraged to make amendments to the constitution. Almost all the amendments created serious political debates, antagonism, and crises in the country. The judiciary has also made their observations and decisions on some of the amendments. Their observations and decisions have received mixed reactions from the political parties, scholars, and elites. It is true that no constitution is static. One feature of all good constitutions is to accommodate the requirements of the time. To confront and adjust the necessity of time and new generations, all major constitutions had to go through amendments and reformations.

The Constitution of the People's Republic of Bangladesh is not an exception. However, with the change of the society and circumstances, except the fundamental structure of the constitution, amendment may be essential and such necessity is recognized and contemplated in article 142 of our constitution. So, in the following sections of this chapter an attempt has been made to: (a) depict an outline of the history and development of constitution, (b) define constitution from various points of view, and (c) explain amendments and process of amending the constitution.[2]

The term 'constitution' originates from the Latin word '*constitutio,*' used for regulations or order. In modern days 'constitution' refers to a set of rules and principles that define the nature and extent of government. Constitution is 'supreme' as the solemn expression of the people and sole authoritative symbol of … sovereignty.[3]

It is the embodiment of the supreme will of the sovereign people. It includes the fundamental objectives of the state and declares of the basic rights guaranteed to the people. There is no specific time frame of constitution's beginning. Some might say it began over 2500 years ago in the city-states of ancient Greece. Others might place its beginnings nearly three-quarters of a millennium back in the fields of Runnymede. Still others might say the constitution had its origins three centuries or so ago during the tumultuous years of the 17th-century English revolutions. Or others, more patriotic perhaps, might date the beginnings of the constitution from events in the Western Hemisphere, from the Mayflower Compact, the Massachusetts Charter of 1629, or from any number of charters and constitutional documents that the colonists resorted to during the 1st century and a half of American history.

San Marino, a sovereign nation, is still governed by the oldest written document. *The Leges Statutae Republicae Sancti Marini* consists of six books and it is written in Latin. With 62 articles, the first book establishes the power assigned to different institutions like courts, council and various executive officers. The rest of the books are concerned with judicial procedures, criminal and civil law and remedies. The document, which was written in 1600, was based upon the Statuti Comunali (Town Statute) of 1300. Codex Justinianus influenced itself, and it still remains in force today.

Fundamental Orders was adopted by the Colony of Connecticut in 1639 and it was the first North American constitution. It is considered the basis for every new Connecticut constitution since then and it is also the reason behind Connecticut's nickname, 'the Constitution State.'[4] Oliver Cromwell set up the English Protectorate after the English Civil War and it promulgated the first written constitution which was very detailed that was adopted by a modern state. It was known as the Instrument of Government. This created the foundation of government for the short-lived republic from 1653 to 1657 by giving a legal rationale for the increasing power of Cromwell, after Parliament continuously failed to govern effectively.[5] A state council consisting of 21 members was set up by the constitution while executive authority was given to the office of 'Lord Protector of the Commonwealth'; this position was originally nominated as a non-hereditary life appointment. As the basis of its authority, the Parliament refused to accept it and both the radicals and Royalists rejected it. Therefore, the Instrument had failed to gain widespread acceptance. In May 1657, though 'Humble Petition and Advice' replaced it for a short period of time, it met its end after the restoration and the death of Cromwell.

Thomas Hobbes, Jean-Jacques Rousseau, and John Locke, the philosophers of the Age of Enlightenment, developed 'enlightened constitution' model which is sometimes another name of the democratic constitution. In the model, it was proposed that constitutional governments should represent the people and be stable, accountable, adaptable, and open.

Ratified on 21 June 1788, The United States Constitution was influenced by the writings of Polybius, Montesquieu, Locke, and others along with the political system of the United Provinces and the British constitutional system. The document eventually became a benchmark both for the republicanism and codified constitutions which were written thereafter.

After that, there were the Polish–Lithuanian Commonwealth Constitution of 3 May 1791, and the French Constitution of 3 September 1791. On 19 March 1812 an enlightened constitution was ratified in Spain by a parliament gathered in Cadiz, the only Spanish continental city which was safe of French occupation. The Constitution of Spain worked as a model for other liberal constitutions of several South-European and Latin American nations like the Norwegian constitution of 1814, Portuguese Constitution of 1822, constitutions of various Italian states and the Mexican Constitution of 1824.

After Brazilian Independence, the option for monarchy was considered as a political system the Constitution of 1824 in Brazil. Portuguese prince Pedro I, elder son of the king of Portugal, was the leader of the national emancipation process. As first emperor of Brazil, Pedro was crowned in 1822. Until 1889, Constitutional monarchy ruled the country then the Republican model was finally adopted. As a result of the Napoleonic Wars, in Denmark, the absolute monarchy lost its personal possession of Norway to another absolute monarchy, Sweden. However, the Norwegians infused a radically democratic and liberal constitution in 1814, by adopting many facets from the American constitution and the revolutionary French ones; but they maintained a hereditary monarch which is limited by the constitution similar to the Spanish one. In 1811, the formulation of a proto-constitution happened following the Serbian revolution and a full-fledged Constitution of Serbia came into existence few decades later, in 1835.

On 1 July 1867, the Canadian constitution came into force as the British North America Act, an act of the British Parliament. The colonies of Canada West

(Ontario), Canada East (Quebec), New Brunswick and Nova Scotia were unified by the BNA Act into the self-governing Dominion of Canada. The BNA Act was brought back to the Canadian Parliament and supplemented with the Canadian Charter of Rights and Freedoms. Since then, while the original BNA Act is called the Constitution Act, 1867, the written constitution as a whole has been known as the Constitution Acts, 1867 to 1982. Canada's constitution also has unwritten elements based in common law and convention apart from the Constitution Acts, 1867 to 1982.[6]

Constitutionalism in Bangladesh has had a life of its own. The independence movements when invoking liberal values drew not only upon values transmitted from European sources, as elaborated in Anglo-American constitutional jurisprudence, but upon the aspirations and objectives of those who had actively engaged in those movements for political freedom, and for economic and social justice. This has been the common experience of women and men throughout the length and breadth of Bangladesh for most of the 20th century. The values set out in the preamble of the post-independent constitution in Bangladesh; reflects the objectives of the popular movements through which independence was attained. These values form the core of Bangladesh's constitution, and derive legitimacy from the fact that these represent aspirations cherished by all of the people, in whose name independence was claimed and won, and who engaged in struggles, involving sacrifice and suffering.

However, since its inception, the constitution and constitutional amendments (17 amendments till date) in Bangladesh have encountered multifarious controversies. However, as a guardian of the constitution, the Supreme Court (SC) under the constitutional mandates has tried to protect the sacred document emanated from the will of the people.

As of now, the Supreme Court of Bangladesh has declared five amendments out of the 17 (5th, 7th, 8th, 13th, and 16th) unconstitutional. The Constitution (Fifth Amendment) Act, 1979 validated all amendments, additions, modifications, substitutions, and omissions made in the constitution during the period between 15 August 1975 and 9 April 1979 by the Martial Law Authorities. However, this amendment was declared unconstitutional in 2005 by the High Court Division in *Bangladesh Italian Marble Works Ltd v Bangladesh* (2006) BLT (Special) (HCD) 1. Subsequently, the Appellate Division upheld the decision of the HCD in *Khondhker Delwar Hossain v Bangladesh Italian Marble Works Ltd and Others* (2010) 62 DLR (AD) 298. Furthermore, the Constitution (Seventh Amendment) Act, 1986 provided, among others, that all proclamations, proclamation orders, Chief Martial Law Administrator's Orders, Martial Law Regulations, Martial Law Orders, Martial Law Instructions, ordinances and other laws made during the period between 24 March 1982 and 11 November 1986 had been validly made. This amendment was also declared unconstitutional in *Siddique Ahmed v Bangladesh* (2011) 33 BLD (HCD) 84 by the High Court Division. Thereafter, the Constitution (Eighth Amendment) Act, 1988 has declared, among others, that Islam shall be state religion (Article 2A) and also decentralized the judiciary by setting up six permanent benches of the High Court Division outside Dhaka (Article 100). Change in the original Article 100 regarding the seat of the HCD was challenged and the Appellate Division in *Anwar Hossain Chowdhury v. Bangladesh* (1989) BLD (AD) (Special) 1 declared the amendment of Article 100 unconstitutional. The Constitution (Thirteenth Amendment) Act, 1996 introduced a non-party Caretaker Government (CtG) system which, acting as an interim government, would give all possible aid and assistance to the Election Commission for holding the general election. The vires of this amendment was questioned in *Saleem Ullah v Bangladesh* (2005) 57 DLR (HCD) 171, in which the HCD validated the CtG system. Subsequently, the decision was challenged in the Appellate Division which, in *Abdul Mannan Khan v Bangladesh* (2012) 64 DLR (AD) 1, decided against the HCD and by a four-to-three decision prospectively declared the Thirteenth Amendment unconstitutional. Finally, the Constitution (Sixteenth Amendment) Act, 2014 gave power to the parliament to remove superior court judges if allegations of incapability or misconduct against them are proved. The HCD declared this amendment unconstitutional in *Asaduzzaman Siddiqui and Others v Bangladesh* (Writ Petition No. 9989 of 2014; decision of 5 May 2016). The Appellate Division upheld the HCD's decision in *Government of Bangladesh and others v Advocate Asaduzzaman Siddiqui and others* (Civil Appeal No. 6 of 2017; decision of 3 July 2017).[7]

A book on this subject is long overdue, and will contribute to deepening the understanding of the legal and political developments that has catalysed changes in the framework for rights and governance. The research will be committed to reflecting diverse voices, including the critical ones on the evolution of the constitution to date.

## Notes

1 https://www.thedailystar.net/law-our-rights/bangabandhu-the-constitution-1307341
2 Ibid.
3 Quoted in Carl J. Friedrich, *Constitutional Government and Democracy*, Oxford & IBH Publishing Co., New Delhi, 1974, p. 155.
4 https://connecticuthistory.org/the-fundamental-orders-of-connecticut/ visited on 23.7.2020.
5 Ibid.
6 Ibid.
7 https://www.thedailystar.net/law-our-rights/unconstitutional-amendments-1487263

# 2

# RECOLLECTING THE TALES OF GLORY

## Part A

### *Prologue*

***P**olitical Background of what triggered the political process that resulted in an armed struggle for liberation.*

### *A Brief Overview of Political History from 1947–1971*

The process of having an independent Bangladesh began considerably earlier than attaining the independence itself in 1971. During the time of the partition in 1947, the decision to include East Bengal inside Pakistan, tentatively 2,500 miles away from the mainland Pakistan, was made with clear intentions to stir troubles in the future. Despite the wide array of cultural differences between the people of these two regions, it was religion which was arguably the only thing in common between the two regions that happened to bind them together under the same flag.

The people of (prior) East Bengal were largely Muslims and subsequently, were initially prone to the idea of establishing the Muslim State of Pakistan. Driven apart by bitter rivalry with the Hindus that developed during the colonial era, it was an idea well accepted by most. Though well aware of the massive difference between the two groups, not much heed was paid to the division it was bound to create in the foreseeable future. The West Pakistanis always perceived the East Pakistanis as being racially inferior to them. In addition, people of the West and their army also perceived them in a manner that deemed them as minority. A common perception among the people of the West was the 'Bangalis' are influenced by their significant Hindu neighbour and

DOI: 10.4324/9781003363002-2

therefore, cannot be equal to them.[1] Despite comprising 56% of the population, unfortunately, it was the people of East Pakistan who were not only deemed as politically inferior, but also religiously, culturally, and socially.

To add to these facts, very little defence (from a military perspective) was provided for East Pakistan, despite sharing 4,156 kilometres long border with their bitter rivals—India. As a testament to that, General Umair, who was posted in East Pakistan during the 1960s stated, *'There were no artillery force or tank regiment in East Pakistan. The Airforce had 6 planes only. According to him, the theory was that the defence of protection of East Pakistan lay in the West.'* A theory, which later turned out to be, nonsensical.

Economically, the East was stripped off the power to exercise its own regional economic rights, in an attempt to make it fully dependent on the West. For example, the entire region transferred its jute to the West. It was an unfair tactic that solidified any claims regarding the unfair distribution of national wealth.

Militarily, baring minimum Bangladeshi Officers were recruited in the Army. Those who managed to join, were never given significant postings due to their race. As a result, East Pakistani Officers could not reach significant positions in the military to exert any influence. The same was seen in the Bureaucratic sector.

## Ever-Lingering Political Upheaval in West Pakistan and its Subsequent Effect on the East

Pakistan was born on 14th August 1947—upon the partition of what was formerly Colonized India. Only a year and a month later, the founding and incumbent Governor-General and the President of the Constituent Assembly of Pakistan, Muhammad Ali Jinnah, passed away. From the day of inception, 14th August 1947, Khwaja Nazimuddin was appointed the Chief Minister of East Bengal. Upon the death of Jinnah, Khwaja Nazimuddin assumed the position of Governor-General of Pakistan. On 15 September 1948, Nurul Amin ML was appointed Chief Minister of East Bengal.

On 23rd June 1948, Maulana Abdul Hamid Khan Bhashani, Shamsul Huq, and Bangabandhu Sheikh Mujibur Rahman founded the Awami Muslim League (AML). On 8th December 1948, the students of Dhaka University demanded that 'Bangla' be made the national language of Pakistan. Unfortunately, on 24th March 1948, Governor-General Jinnah, in a speech in Dhaka, declared that Urdu will be the only national language of Bangladesh.

On 30th January 1952, Bengali students along with others from various walks of life, established the 'Bhasha Andolon' (language movement) to ascertain the recognition of Bangla as a national language of Pakistan. The then Governor-General of Pakistan, and Former Chief Minister of the East Pakistan, Khwaja Nazimuddin, despite being of Bengali origin himself, on 21st February 1952, declared Urdu to be the national language of Pakistan. This declaration was followed by a series of clashes between the students and the government defence and law enforcement agents that resulted in the death of 10 protestors. Nevertheless, on 29th February 1956, the Pakistan Constituent Assembly approved a new constitution that finalized the establishment of a new Pakistani Republic that enlisted Bangla and Urdu as official languages of the state.

Awami Muslim League (AML), along with Krishak Sramik Party (KSP), Nezam-e-Islami (NI), and Ganatantri Dal (GD), on 4th December 1953 formed the United Front (UF). This coalition government partook in the legislative election that was held in the East on 12th March 1954. They succeeded in attaining 223 of the possible 309 seats in the Provincial Assembly. Subsequently, A. K. Fazlul Huq was appointed Chief Minister of East Pakistan by the United Front. Unfortunately, the province of East Pakistan was dissolved in August 1955.

On 23rd March 1956, the Islamic Republic of Pakistan was established. Nevertheless, on 7th October 1958, President Iskandar Ali Mirza abrogated the 1956 constitution and, in its place, imposed the Martial Law. General Muhammad Ayub Khan was appointed as the Chief Martial Law Administrator. Soon after, on 27th October 1958, General Ayub Khan disposed of President Iskandar Mirza and in his place assumed in the position of Presidency. On 8th June 1962, he promulgated the new constitution. On 4th October of the same year, the National Democratic Front (NDF) was established.

The tension between the people of the East Pakistan and the Pakistani government escalated when General (then President) Ayub Khan denounced any movement for autonomy of East Pakistan. Subsequently, Bangabandhu Sheikh Mujibur Rahman was arrested on 18th April 1966. Protests and violence lingered right after the arrest, and resulted polices breaking up a riot by killing 10 people on 7th June of that year in Narayanganj.

It was in 1968, when the prospect of liberation started becoming tangible. On 6th January of 1968, the Pakistani government declared their suspicion of a secessionist conspiracy in East Pakistan. As a result, in less than two weeks, Bangabandhu Sheikh Mujibur Rahman, the current president of Awami League, was yet again arrested. 34 other political activists were also arrested at the same time, among whom 3 died in prison. Tension spiked once again in the December of 1968, when police fired upon demonstrators in Dhaka. Two demonstrators were reportedly killed in that attack. Between 24th January to 30th January of 1969, 16 more people were brutally killed by the police during a peaceful demonstration. Estimated 675 people were killed from 7th December 1968 to 30th January 1969.

On 25th March 1969, President Ayub Khan abrogated the 1962 Constitution and transferred the position of Presidency to General Agha Muhammad Yahya Khan. General Yahya Khan oversaw the legislative election that occurred on 7th December 1970. In that election, the Awami League, led by Bangabandhu Sheikh Mujibur Rahman, won 167 out of a possible 313 seats in the Pakistan National Assembly. In addition, the Awami League also won 288 seats out of the 300 seats in the Legislative Assembly of East Pakistan. As a result of their landslide victory, the Awami League proposed the transfer of power from Federal Government to State Government.

Ever since the Awami League's dominant victory, violence erupted all over East Pakistan. From the 1st to the 3rd of March, over 170 people were killed as a result of political violence only in Dhaka. Furthermore, 50 people were killed by the Pakistani forces in Jaydevpur on 19th March 1970. On 24th of March, violence erupted in Chittagong, Rangpur, and Syedpur and resulted in the death of reportedly more than 1,000 people. President Yahya Khan, perplexed by the unbroken will of the people of East Pakistan, declared a state-of-emergency in East Pakistan effective from 25th March, 1971. Later that night, the Pakistani troops launched Operation Searchlight—perpetrating the most heinous atrocities on the unaware and innocent people of East Pakistan.

## *Overview and Background of the Six-Point Movement*

On 5th and 6th of February 1966, a national conference of Pakistan's opposition parties was held in Lahore. Bangabandhu Sheikh Mujibur Rahman, on behalf of his party, Awami League, took part in the conference. Although Bangabandhu Sheikh Mujibur Rahman intended to iterate the demands in the conference, due to the reluctance displayed by the other opposition leaders present there, he had to announce the programme at a news conference.

> '***The six points are listed below:***
> *The constitution shall provide for a federation of Pakistan in its true sense on the Lahore Resolution, and the parliamentary form of government with supremacy of a legislature directly elected on the basis of universal adult franchise.*
>
> *The federal government shall deal with only two subjects: Defence and Foreign Affairs, and all other residuary subjects shall be vested in the federating states.*
>
> *Two separates, but freely convertible currencies for two wings should be introduced; or if this is not feasible, there should be one currency for the whole country, but effective constitutional provisions should be introduced to stop the flight of capital from East to West Pakistan. Furthermore, a separate reserve bank should be established, and a separate fiscal and monetary policy be adopted for East Pakistan.*
>
> *The power of taxation and revenue collection shall be vested in the federating units and the federal centre will have no such power on the issue. The federation will be entitled to a share in state taxes to meet its expenditures.*
>
> *There should be two separate accounts for the foreign exchange earnings of the two wings; the foreign exchange requirements of the federal government shall be met by the two wings equally or in a ratio to be fixed; indigenous products shall move free of duty between the two wings, and the constitution shall empower the units to establish trade links with foreign countries.*
>
> *East Pakistan shall have a separate militia or paramilitary force.*[2]'

The six-point demand had a consideration for a federal form of the government, based on the 1940 Resolution of Lahore, given by A.K. Fazlul Huq, directly elected by the vote of the national people in a parliamentary system of the government, inclusion of two separate currencies or two reserve banks for the two wings of Pakistan, and a paramilitary force for East Pakistan.

### *The Six-Point Movement and its Subsequent Impact in East Pakistan*

The splendid success of the six-point movement in 1966 had enraged the ruling class of Pakistan. Although Ayub Khan's notorious regime had used various kinds of vicious and punitive measures against the protagonist, fellow organizers, and the supporters of the six-point formula, the six-point effectuated a mass upsurge in 1966 that had seriously impacted and conditioned the subsequent political developments in Pakistan.[3]

The demands put forth in the 6 points reflected the sentiment of the mass people that culminated over the years of Pakistani oppression due to their exploitation of East Pakistan and its people. The six-points, also referred to as the 'Magna Charta' of Bangladesh, served as a catalyst for what eventually resulted in the end of the Ayub Khan regime in 1969. In the following year, as mentioned earlier in this chapter, Awami League decisively won the National Election of Pakistan. The six-points were not simply a ploy to garner political powers, but a bridge that would eventually lead to the emancipation of Bangladesh.

It is commonly agreed that the struggle for self-determination of the Bangladeshis promulgated with the six-point movement. Seeing the immense support behind the six-point movement, as well as Bangabandhu Sheikh Mujibur Rahman's immense popularity, the Pakistani ruling class became aggravated and proceeded to suppress this movement as they would usually do when they deemed a movement as 'secessionist.'

Immediately after the six-point programme had been published, Ayub Khan declared it as 'secessionist' and denounced Bangabandhu Sheikh Mujibur Rahman as the number one enemy of Pakistan. Ayub also threatened to use all the possible forces to suppress this charter of demands. Despite all warnings, Awami League and its leader Bangabandhu Sheikh Mujibur Rahman remained fearless in the face of adversity. Then the leaders of the six-point demand started a three months long mass-contact programme that took him to every corner of Bangladesh. Bangabandhu Sheikh Mujibur Rahman was arrested eight times in the first three months of the six-point movement. By then, he has also become the President of the Awami League.

On 20th March, President Ayub, in a speech, compared the situation with the civil war of the USA. President Ayub also threatened in the same speech to use the 'language of weapons' against the 'separatist' forces, suggesting that the nation would have to face a 'civil war' if such were forced upon him by the 'secessionists.'[4]

When he was incarcerated on 8th May 1966, a general strike was observed all over East Pakistan in support of the six-point programme and for his relief. Police fired at the demonstrators in Tejgaon, Tongi and Narayanganj, killing 13 people and injuring hundreds more.

> *This was followed by large-scale arrests of the leaders and followers of Awami League throughout the country. All these measures taken by the Ayub regime proved counter-productive. 6-point programme became the heartfelt demand of the common masses. Students put forward their 11-point programme which complemented the 6-point charter of demands. Thus, the political situation in East Pakistan became even more volatile.*[5]

## *How the Six-Point Movement Impacted the Liberation Struggle*

The six-point demand left its impact and was felt far and wide. The central government dubbed it as a demand for the separation of the Eastern wing from the rest of the country, and launched a propaganda campaign which called for a strong central government. The government also blamed 'foreign interests' in the agitation led by the six-pointers. After about a year, several East Pakistani civil servants and military officers were arrested on the charge that they had conspired to separate the East wing by violent means in collusion with India. Eventually, the so-called Agartala Conspiracy case was initiated Bangabandhu Sheikh Mujibur Rahman and 31 others for by showing an excuse of their treachery. In 1969 the student-mass movement took place against this conspiracy case. Thus, the six-point movement played as a precursor of the subsequent movements.

We can say that the success of the six-point movement had prompted the arrogant and debased Ayub Khan's dictatorial regime to falsely implicate Bangabandhu Sheikh Mujibur Rahman in the Agartala Conspiracy case. However, an anti-Ayub mass movement in late 1968 and early 1969 led to the withdrawal of this so-called case and unconditional release of Bangabandhu Sheikh Mujibur Rahman.

The eleven-point student program was an expanded version of the Awami League's six-point demand for autonomy. The real strength of the Awami League was, along with its organizational network but the growing popularity of the six-point program for regional autonomy with the 70 million Bengalis in East Pakistan. Even the stringent repressive measures and centralized administration couldn't halt the process. As the champion of the cause of regional autonomy, the future of the Awami League lies in its capacity to sustain and strengthen the movement.

The six-point demand was, considered as the most radical demand for East Pakistani autonomy till now. The six-point movement evoked widespread enthusiasm in East Pakistan. Mass meetings and rallies were held throughout the province by the East Pakistan Awami League. Predictably, the six-point movement broadened the Awami League's base of support in East Pakistan against the west Pakistani hegemony. The movements of 1966 succeeded to give a concrete shape to its longstanding demand for regional autonomy in the form of 'The Six-Point Program,' which subsequently was the harbinger of the emergence of Bangladesh as an independent and sovereign state.[6]

The basic idea of the six-point movement was that East Pakistan is not just a province of Pakistan but it is a geographically separated landmass all together. People of this region have always been deprived of their rights. It deserves a complete autonomous statehood. It must get its economy and defence system too. Though there was nothing specific about the labour-class, peasants, and hard-working poor people of East-Pakistan in these six points but everybody supported it because the dominance of West-Pakistan in every section of the administration was clear. The movement started from the demand for state autonomy and ended as a National Liberation war in **1971**.

## *Campaign for Self Determination*

According to international law, the self-determination narrative of Bangladesh stands as an exception (especially considering this to be the only successful case of secession by force between the WWII and the end of cold war). The praxis of international law of self-determination, as observed by Antonio Cassese, is diverse and full of highly contentious issues. In fact, there is a growing consensus among the States and the jurists about the non-applicability of the right to self-determination in contexts beyond colonial domination. The right (which is frequently referred in modern parlance as a doctrine to legitimize independence of a State) therefore, remains with antagonistic ideals and by the same token, is full of uncertainties. This makes it difficult to exactly predict, or, produce an aspired outcome from any particular self-determination narrative (which may range from autonomy to independence). It is noteworthy that the independence of Bangladesh is a glaring exception to these rules, serves as a great hope to the oppressed peoples of different parts of the world. Through this, the idea of self-determination recognizes the equality of every nation. Further, in all plausible senses, Bangladesh (later followed by Bosnia and Herzegovina, East Timor, South Sudan, and Kosovo) provided completely separate sets of apologetic bases, for any people to claim independence legitimately, even beyond a colonial setup.

Self-determination being a partly legal and partly political norm, can be maneuverer, influenced, or legitimized (even often predominantly) by political or factual events. Hence, political legitimacy (which often plays a key role in establishing a claim for an independent state or conversely delegitimizing an existing state) plays a vital role (if not exhaustively) for any such narrative. It is submitted that the birth of Bangladesh is marked by a number of political and military events (with logically clear and unambiguous political consequences) that significantly and rapidly adds legitimacy to the claims of Bengalis to have an independent state. One such event, which is still internationally unrecognized (and academically under-researched), but provides logical and legal premises for our claims to establish a separate State, is the infamous Operation Searchlight.[7]

***********************************

In the early 1950, regionalist sentiment with respect to constitutional order was made public in deliberations and formal recommendations of the Working Committee of the East Bengal Muslim League, which emphasized that it was 'strongly of the opinion' that although a federal constitution was necessary for Pakistan,

> in setting up the actual federal structure, keeping in consideration the geographical position of East Pakistan, its detachment and distance from other units and also from the federal capital itself has to be seriously considered and provisions made in the constitution to accord maximum autonomy to East Pakistan and to that effect it is essential that a separate list of subjects to be administered by East Pakistan be incorporated in the constitution and the residuary powers should rest in the units.

The committee was further of the emphatic opinion 'that since the railways and navigation system of the eastern wing were separate from those of the west,' communications 'cannot and should not be a central subject.' The committee declared

> that so far as the export and import trade of East Pakistan is concerned adequate provision should be made subject to the least possible control of the center for the administration of this subject by the Government of East Pakistan.

These very same issues were to be at the heart of the political conflict 20 years later.[8]

At that time, the two dominant leaders of the United Front, H. S. Suhrawardy and A. K. Fazlul Huq, were both the members of the Muslim League. Suhrawardy had been the Muslim League premier in Bengal just before independence, and Huq had held the same position nearly 10 years before. Suhrawardy had become active in post-independence politics with his founding of the Awami League in 1953. Huq, who, ironically, had moved the historic Lahore Resolution in 1940, had left the Muslim League the same year and founded the peasant-oriented Krishak Sramik Party, a revival of a party with the same political base that he had started and led during the pre-independence period.

Notable in the campaign were the twenty-one points agreed upon by the partners in the front, which emphasized the necessity of a more broadly distributive public policy and an expanded role for East Bengal in national concerns. The first point, for example, called for Bengali to be declared a national language, and another called for a student's mother tongue to be the language of instruction. Point 19 was the most prophetic:

> East Bengal will get complete autonomy according to the Lahore Resolution. Our defence, currency, and foreign policy will be joint subjects

> with the Centre. Army headquarters will be in West Pakistan and Naval headquarters are to be set up in East Pakistan, so that this wing can become strong enough to safeguard her freedom. The Ansars [constabulary] will be equipped with arms.[9]

***********************************

Fast forward to nearly two decades later, many supporters of the Awami League, along with Bangabandhu Sheikh Mujibur Rahman, were being politically persecuted due to the increasing acceptance of the 6-point movement. Following a character assassination campaign conducted by the Central Government, Mujibur Rahman swiftly responded to the false allegations and threats. At a speech at Paltan Maidan, he iterated, 'No number of naked threats can distract the deprived Bengalis from their demand for provincial autonomy based on their six-point plan.' He also mentioned the six-point movement as the charter of emancipation and freedom at Laldighi Maidan, Chattagram (The Daily Ittefak, 1966, 27 February). Along with top leaders of the Awami League, Bangabandhu Sheikh Mujibur Rahman kept on addressing numerous public meetings in every corner of then East Pakistan. The entirety of the Awami League was geared toward mobilizing and motivating the general masses in favour of self-government and autonomy Bangabandhu Sheikh Mujibur Rahman had not only presented the bold proposal for 'maximum autonomy,' but also bolstered a mass movement (which he led till he was put in jail on 9 May 1966) for mobilizing mass support for the six-point program. He invested all of his energy and resources in disseminating the fundamental message and articulating both the rationale and the justification of 'maximum autonomy' for East Pakistan. Before launching a full-fledged mass movement, the working committee of the Awami League was restructured and reshaped in the historic Council Session of the East Pakistan Awami League that was held on 18–20 March 1966. While Bangabandhu Sheikh Mujibur Rahman and Tajuddin Ahmed were unanimously elected the president and general secretary, respectively, of the newly revamped Awami League, the proposed six-point program was also fully endorsed by the council session.

The entire nation was galvanized throughout February to June 1966. In other words, the six-point program evoked tremendous enthusiasm among the people of East Bengal would be an understatement. Encouraged by overwhelming popular support, Bangabandhu Sheikh Mujibur Rahman launched a vigorous campaign. For about three months from mid-February to mid-May, the urban centres of East Bengal seemed to be in the grip of a 'mass revolution.'

Instead of dealing fairly with the legitimate grievances of the neglected eastern province of Pakistan, the power elite of Pakistan took a deliberate decision to suppress the Bangalis' quest for maximum provincial autonomy through the use of colonial types of repressive methods and procedures. Obviously, Bangabandhu Sheikh Mujibur Rahman became the main target of various virulent forms of harassment, intimidation, and fraudulent cases. The government intensified its policy of repression and persecution against him and his followers. The central government arrested Bangabandhu Sheikh Mujib and his assistants as Tajuddin Ahmed, Khandokar Mustaq Ahmed, Mansoor Ali, Zahur Ahmed Chowdhury, and others under the Defence Act of Pakistan. As a result, Awami League put down a complete general strike in Dacca on 7 June 1966. On that day government force geared the movement by killing 13 participating strikers.[10]

## *Agartola Conspiracy Case*

Agartala Conspiracy Case was framed by the Pakistan Government in 1968, during the Ayub regime against Bangabandhu Sheikh Mujibur Rahman, the chief of Awami League, along with some in-service and ex-service army personnel and high government officials. They were accused of involvement in a conspiracy to secede the East wing from Pakistan with the help of the government of India. The *petitio principii* in the petition was that the conspiracy was concocted between the Indian party and the accused persons at Agartala city of Tripura in India. The case was thus called Agartala Conspiracy Case. However, the Pakistan government was compelled to withdraw the case in the face of a mass movement in East Pakistan.

Since the inception of Pakistan, the people of East Pakistan were deprived of their legitimate rights in all spheres. Consequently, a general resentment against the Pakistani rulers brewed among the people of East Pakistan. The demand for autonomy as placed through the SIX-POINT PROGRAMME of the Awami League chief Bangabandhu Sheikh Mujibur Rahman thus received the spontaneous support of the people of East Pakistan.

The acute disparity in the armed forces led some Bangali army officers and soldiers to be united secretly. Knowing full well that the interest of the Bangalis could never be served under the rulers of West Pakistan, they decided to make East Pakistan independent through an armed revolt. With this end in view, they began to mobilize army personnel secretly. The conspiracy was, however, detected by the intelligence department of the government. Nearly one thousand five hundred Bangalis throughout Pakistan were arrested by the intelligence force.

The Home Department of Pakistan declared through a press-note issued on 6 January 1968 that the government had detected in December 1967 a conspiracy detrimental to the national interest of Pakistan. The press-note disclosed the news of the arrest of 8 persons including 2 CSP officers and alleged that the persons seized were involved in attempting to separate East Pakistan through armed revolt. Through a separate declaration issued on 18 January 1968 the Home Department implicated Bangabandhu Sheikh Mujibur Rahman in the conspiracy. He was then detained in jail along with many others since 9 May 1966. They were released, only to be arrested again under martial law regulations and were taken to Dhaka Cantonment under military custody.

Initially the government decided to court martial the accused, but subsequently in the interest of the proper holding of the general elections of 1970 the government resolved to frame charge only against 35 concerned political personalities and high government officials under civil law. The persons included in the charge-sheet were Bangabandhu Sheikh Mujibur Rahman, Commander Moazzem Hossain, Steward Mujibur Rahman, former LS Sultanuddin Ahmad, LSCDI Nur Mohammad, Ahmed Fazlur Rahman CSP, Flight Sergeant Mahfiz Ullah, Corporal Abdus Samad, former Havildar Dalil Uddin, Ruhul Quddus CSP, Flight Sergeant Md. Fazlul Haq, Bibhuti Bhushan Chowdhury alias Manik Chowdhury, Bidhan Krishna Sen, Subedar Abdur Razzaque, former clerk Mujibur Rahman, former Flight Sergeant Md. Abdur Razzaque, Sergeant Zahurul Haq, AB Khurshid, Khan Mohammad Shamsur Rahman CSP, AKM Shamsul Haque, Havildar Azizul Haq, Mahfuzul Bari, Sergeant Shamsul Haq, Shamsul Alam, Captain Md. Abdul Motaleb, Captain A Shawkat Ali Mian, Captain Khondkar Nazmul Huda, Captain M Nuruzzaman, Sergeant Abdul Jalil, Mahbub Uddin Chowdhury, Lt. M Rahman, former Subedar Tajul Islam, Ali Reza, Captain Khurshid Uddin Ahmed, and Lt. Abdur Rauf.

A special tribunal was formed after an amendment was made in the penal code to that end for the disposal of the case. The hearing of the case started on 19 June 1968 under Sections 121-A and 131. Bangabandhu Sheikh Mujibur Rahman was enrolled as accused No.1. The case was entitled 'State vs Sheikh Mujibur Rahman and others.' The tribunal started proceedings of the case in a highly protected chamber inside Dhaka Cantonment. A charge-sheet consisting of 100 paragraphs against the 35 accused was placed before the tribunal. There were 227 witnesses including 11 approvers. However, 4 approvers were declared hostile by the government.

Thomas William, a British lawyer and a member of the British Parliament, filed a writ petition in Dhaka High Court on behalf of Bangabandhu Sheikh Mujibur Rahman challenging the legality of the formation of the tribunal. He was assisted in conducting legal proceedings in the special tribunal by Abdus Salam Khan, Ataur Rahman Khan, and others. The government lawyers leading the case were the former foreign minister Manzur Quader and Advocate General TH Khan. Justice SA Rahman, the Chairman of the three-member tribunal, was a non-Bangali. The other members MR Khan and Maksumul Hakim were Bangalis. The government was bent on identifying Bangabandhu Sheikh Mujibur Rahman as a separatist and an Indian agent thereby arousing public support against him. But the approvers on the witness box declared that the government had compelled them by threat and persecution to submit false evidence in its favour. Thus, the governmental machination against the accused got exposed.

By this time the Sarbadaliya Chhatra Sangram Parishad supported by Maulana Abdul Hamid Khan Bhasani organized mass movement against the conspiracy of the government and demanded immediate withdrawal of the case and release of all prisoners including Bangabandhu Sheikh Mujibur Rahman. At a point when the streets of Dhaka became a hot bed of turmoil, Sergeant Zahurul Haq, 17th accused in the case, was mercilessly shot to death while in confinement in Dhaka Cantonment. The news of his death led a furious mob to set fire to the State Guest House as well as other buildings. S.A Rahman, Chairman of the tribunal, and

Manzur Quader, chief lawyer on the government side, who were then residing in the guest house, evacuated secretly. Some of the files concerning the case were burnt to ashes. In the face of the mass movement, the Ayub government was ultimately compelled to withdraw the Agartala Conspiracy Case on 22 February 1969. All the accused, Bangabandhu Sheikh Mujibur Rahman, were released unconditionally. On the following day (23 February), a grand public reception was accorded to the accused at Paltan Maidan in Dhaka where Sheikh Mujibur Rahman was vested with the appellation of 'Bangabandhu.'[11]

## Part B

## *Epilogue*

### *The 1972 Constitution*

The Constitution of the People's Republic of Bangladesh is the supreme document of Bangladesh. It was officially adopted on 4th November, 1972 by the Constituent Assembly and implemented on 16th December, 1972.

> *It provides the framework of the Bangladeshi republic with a parliamentary government, fundamental human rights and freedoms, an independent judiciary, democratic local government and a national bureaucracy. The constitution also includes references to Socialism, Islam, Secular democracy and the Bengali language. It commits Bangladesh to "contribute to international peace and co-operation in keeping with the progressive aspirations of mankind.*[12]

### *Background Behind The Adoption of The Original Constitution*

On 10 April 1971, The Provisional Government of Bangladesh, led by Tajuddin Ahmed, issued the first Proclamation of Independence. This document ascertains that 'equality, human dignity, and social justice' will be the fundamental principles upon which the republic will be governed.

After attaining independence through vicious armed struggle, on 23 March 1972, the Awami League government, headed by Bangabandhu Sheikh Mujibur Rahman, declared the 'Constituent Assembly Order.' This Assembly consisted of those who were elected to be members of the national and provincial assembly in the 1970 election. The key function of this assembly was to assemble a draft of a constitution, based upon which the functions of this Assembly were to be exercised.

The first positive step towards framing a constitution was taken on 23 March 1972, with the promulgation of 'Bangladesh Constituent Assembly Order' (P.O. No. 22) providing for a Constituent Assembly. The Assembly was to comprise the members who had been elected from Bangladesh to the then Pakistan National

Assembly and the East Pakistan Provincial Assembly in the elections held in 1970 and I97I. The President would convene or prorogue the session and might dissolve the Assembly. Another Presidential Order provided that, if a member of the Constituent Assembly resigned or was expelled from the political party which nominated him at the election to the Assembly, his seat in the Assembly would become vacant; this provision, obviously intended for ensuring party discipline, had its impact on the constitution-making itself.[13]

The 430-member Constituent Assembly was called into a 2-day session on 10 April 1972. On the first day, it elected the speaker and deputy speaker and adopted its own rules of procedure. On 2 April, a 34-member Constitution Drafting Committee was set up with Dr. Kamal Hossain, Minister of Law and Parliamentary Affairs, as its chairman, and also in- clouding four other top-ranking ministers. All members of the Committee belonged to the ruling Awami League, except Suranjit Sengupta, the lone opposition member from National Awami Party (pro-Moscow). The Committee was to submit its report to the Assembly by 10 June 1972.[14]

The Drafting Committee held 74 meetings and took nearly 300 hours to complete its work. On the basis of a resolution adopted in its first meeting the Committee 'invited from any institution or person interested to send proposals in writing for consideration of the Committee during the preparation of the Draft Constitution for the People's Republic of Bangladesh,' these proposals to reach the secretary of the Committee on or before 15 May, 1972. The invitation was publicized through the press, radio, and television, but only 98 memoranda were received. One reason for the poor response was that there was already a general consensus about the fundamentals of the constitution. Parties and groups had difference only on matters of detail. A general invitation for suggestions was not enough to evoke public interest. The Committee would have done better to issue a questionnaire on different aspects of the constitution. Besides, three weeks' time given for sending proposals was not adequate; opposition parties which were very vocal against the government and had some ideological difference with the ruling party did not send a single proposal to the Committee.[15]

The last meeting of the Committee was held on 2 October, when the text of the Constitution Bill was finally approved. Conclusions were reached in regard to most of the clauses by unanimous decision and in other cases by a decision of a majority of the members present. But on some matters, six members did not agree with the majority view and issued their notes of dissent separately; of these six, five belong to the ruling Awami League and one to the opposition National Awami Party.

It is worthwhile to note the main points of dissent.[16] Two members (Awami League) raised objections to Articles 42 and 47 dealing with the right to private property and the power of the parliament to make laws authorizing compulsory acquisition and nationalization of individual property with or without compensation. They argued that for the purpose of progressive realization of socialism the state should have an absolute right to nationalize any property to any extent with or without compensation, but there should be a guarantee in the constitution that the compulsory acquisition for purposes other than nationalization must be for 'public purposes' and 'on the payment of compensation.' Article 70 was perhaps the most controversial, at both the drafting and the enacting stage. This provided that 'if a person elected as a member of parliament at an election at which he was nominated as a candidate by a political party, either resigns from or is expelled by that party, he shall vacate his seat.' Four members of the Committee, all belonging to the ruling Awami League gave notes of dissent on this. According to them, 'it is against all principles of democracy and violative of the rights of electors'; it would render the members of parliament subservient to the party leadership and would lead to undesirable rivalry and disruption. They particularly opposed the provision for expulsion and one of them suggested that a member of parliament should lose his seat only if he resigned or voted against the decision of his party in the parliament, (the article as finally adopted by the Constituent Assembly did include this modification).

Most objections came from the opposition member of the National Awami Party, who put forward 24 recommendations and termed 14 articles as undemocratic. His most important point was that the draft did not adequately provide for the establishment of socialism. Maximum limits to private property had not been determined in the constitution; nor were there any guarantee that all properties would be brought under state ownership. Provisions for food, clothing, shelter, medical care, education and employment for the citizens had been incorporated in Part II of the constitution (Fundamental Principles of State Policy), but by adding the words, 'shall not be judicially enforceable' (Art. 8), the whole content of Part II had been made nugatory. He suggested that those words should be deleted. He also attacked the chapter on Fundamental Rights as being vague and inadequate, inasmuch as most of the rights had been described as subject to 'reasonable restrictions' to be imposed by law in the name of 'public order,' 'morality or decency,' etc. He recommended an increase of seats of Parliament from 300 to 350 and opposed the reservation of 15 seats in the Parliament for women for 10 years (Art. 65). He also suggested that the term of Parliament be reduced from five years to four.

On 12 October 1972, the Law Minister introduced the Constitution Bill in the Constituent Assembly. The text of the draft constitution was published in all the important dailies of Bangladesh; it had already been distributed among and discussed by the members of the Awami League Parliamentary Party in its meetings on 9 and 10 October. After the publication of the draft various political parties and student organizations expressed their views through the Press; by political philosophy and type of criticism, these organizations may be divided into four groups:

The National Awami Party (pro-Peking, popularly known as NAP-Bhashani, led by Maulana Abdul Hamid Khan Bhashani), the Communist Party of Bangladesh (popularly known as Leninist), the Communist Party of Bangla; the Revolutionary Students Union and the Bangla Students Union.

The Bangladesh Students League (an anti-government faction popularly known as the Rab group); the National Socialist Party (Jatio Samaj-tantrik Dal), and the Labour-Peasant Socialist Party (Shramik-Krishak Samajbadi Dal).

The National Awami Party (pro-Moscow, popularly known as NAP-Muzaffar, led by Professor Muzaffar Ahmed); the Communist Party of Bangladesh (pro-Moscow, led by Moni Singh); and the Bangladesh Students Union.

The Awami League and the Bangladesh Students League (pro-government faction, popularly known as the Siddique Group).[17]

## Reaction to the New Constitution

The parties and organizations in the first group can generally be considered as pro-Peking leftists. They do not believe in parliamentary democracy. They differ from each other on minor details and strategies but their main objective is to bring about socialism through revolutionary means. They attacked the draft constitution most severely, even challenging the right of the Constituent Assembly to frame the constitution. According to Maulana Bhashani, "the present Constituent Assembly was elected under the Legal Framework Order (I970) of General Yahya Khan to frame the Constitution of Pakistan. It got it mandate on the 6-Point Programme of the Awami League (which envisaged maximum regional autonomy of the Provinces within the framework of one united Pakistan); consequently, it had no right to give a constitution to a sovereign Bangladesh." Abul Bashar, General Secretary of the Communist Party of Bangla, also expressed a similar view.[18] They demanded that the constitution be framed by a national convention comprising the representatives of all the political parties and mass-organizations which had participated in the liberation struggle and should be adopted through a referendum.

According to this group, the draft constitution was neither socialist nor democratic. Though some principles of socialism had been incorporated in the Fundamental Principles of State Policy, there was no guarantee of food, clothing, shelter, education, medical care, and employment for the citizens. There was no provision for confiscation of 'foreign imperialistic capital' and 'abolition of feudalism.' Private property had not been totally prohibited, nor its maximum limit fixed. Thus, the constitution would not aid in the transition to socialism. Usual democratic human rights had been denied by providing for so many restrictions to be imposed by law in the name of security, public order, morality, and so on.

The Communist Party of Bangladesh declared that the draft constitution was beyond correction and rejected it, claiming that there were much better guarantees of fundamental rights in the Ayub Constitution of 1962. Maulana Bhashani also declared that his party would not accept the constitution. The Bangla Students Union called upon the 'progressive political parties' to launch a mass-movement against the draft Constitution. The Revolutionary Students Union, which is, in fact, the student front of Bhashani's NAP, held identical views.[19]

In the second group, A. S. M. Abdur Rab, the former leader of Bangladesh Students League (anti-government) and now the Joint Convenor of the newly formed (31 October 1972) National Socialist Party (JSD), remarked that the draft Constitution was 'worthless' but added, 'a bad constitution is better than no constitution.' According to him, it did not reflect he hopes and aspirations of the people. By imposing so many restrictions on the fundamental rights, democracy had been turned into 'controlled democracy.' It did not recognize 'class-conflict' nor was there any provision for removing economic inequality and exploitation; accordingly, the realization of socialism was not possible through this constitution. He also objected that the Prime Minister had been given dictatorial power and the President had been made a 'show-boy.' (It may be noted that Rab does not like to be identified as a Marxist or Maoist, but his slogan is 'scientific socialism' through 'social revolution' and 'class-struggle).'

The Labour-peasant Socialist Party termed the kind of socialism envisaged in the draft as 'socialism of abandoned property' (key industries nationalized by the Bangladesh Government were mostly owned by Pakistani capitalists who left the country on the eve of independence). They objected that the constitution did not provide for the abolition of private property and the ownership of all properties by the state. According to them, if the draft was adopted, the rule of the rising capitalists and bourgeoisie would be strengthened and class exploitation would continue in the name of socialism.[20]

In the third group, the National Awami Party (NAP), led by Muzaffar Ahmed, and the Communist Party of Bangladesh, led by Moni Singh, are generally known as pro-Moscow leftist organizations. They are the followers of the Russian line adopted in their 20th Congress and believe that socialism can be established through a parliamentary road. Though in the opposition, they had been working with some understanding and in cooperation with the ruling Awami League on the basis of certain basic principles. The outlook of the Bangladesh Students Union is more or less the same, since, in fact, it is the student front of the NAP (pro-Moscow).

The Communist Party of Bangladesh did not think that the Constituent Assembly had the sole authority to frame the constitution, but it did not challenge it because the country needed a constitution without further delay. It considered that, the draft constitution was on the whole democratic, though certain provisions were not. It was not a 'socialistic' constitution, but under the present circumstances a socialistic constitution could not be expected from the present Constituent Assembly. In order to make the constitution 'really democratic' and 'socialism-oriented,' the party put forward an 11-Point amendment proposal.[21] The Party leaders also held discussions on the draft with the Awami League leaders, including the Law Minister.

> *The National Awami Party hailed the draft Constitution for its provision for parliamentary government and secularism and inclusion of fundamental rights, but contended that fundamental rights had been infringed by imposing certain restrictions*

> *on them. According to the party, adequate provisions had not been made for the establishment of socialism which was one of the accepted fundamental principles of state policy. There was no Constitutional guarantee of basic necessities of life. The Prime Minister had been given too much power and as a result the smooth progress of parliamentary democracy might be handicapped.*[22]

The party suggested a number of amendments for the improvement of the constitution and demanded their acceptance by the Constituent Assembly. (It may be noted that the NAP was the only opposition party with a single member in the Constituent Assembly).[23]

In the fourth group is the ruling Awami League, a nationalist party which initiated and promoted Bengali nationalism culminating in the liberation movement. It firmly believes in parliamentary democracy and, through it, the progressive realization of a welfare state on the basis of a socialist economy. Naturally it termed the Constitution Bill excellent. According to the League leaders, the constitution had been formulated on the basis of the four accepted fundamental principles of state policy (democracy, socialism, nationalism, and secularism) and was the manifestation of popular hopes and aspirations. It would best serve the purpose of establishing socialism through democracy.

Regarding the authority of the Constituent Assembly, the Political Secretary to the Prime Minister, Tofail Ahmed, said that the Awami League Government was both morally and legally competent to frame the constitution. In the 1970 elections, the people had given an unqualified mandate to the League (it had captured 167 out of 169 National Assembly seats from former East Pakistan and 288 seats out of 300 in the Provincial Assembly). Moreover, the party had spearheaded the liberation struggle by forming the Revolutionary Government and achieved independence with the support of the people. He rejected the idea of holding a national convention to consider the constitution and said that there was no logic in discussing the constitution with those elements who had been totally rejected by the people in the last elections. He declared that the result of the next elections would indicate the continuing support of the people for the Awami League and the constitution framed by it.[24]

## Content of the Constitution

### Preamble

The preamble to the Constitution of Bangladesh is a brief introductory statement that sets out guidelines, which guide the people of the nation, and to present the principles of the constitution, and to indicate the source from which the document derives its authority, and meaning. The hopes and aspirations of the people are described in it. The preamble can be referred to as the preface which highlights the entire constitution. The preamble of the constitution as follows:

> "We, the people of Bangladesh, having proclaimed our Independence on the 26th day of March, 1971 and through [a historic war for national independence], established the independent, sovereign People's Republic of Bangladesh;
>
> Pledging that the high ideals of absolute trust and faith in the Almighty Allah, nationalism, democracy and socialism meaning economic and social justice, which inspired our heroic people to dedicate themselves to, and our brave martyrs to sacrifice their lives in the war for national independence, shall be fundamental principles of the Constitution.
>
> Further pledging that it shall be a fundamental aim of the State to realise through the democratic process to socialist society, free from exploitation-a society in which the rule of law, fundamental human rights and freedom, equality and justice, political, economic and social, will be secured for all citizens;
>
> Affirming that it is our sacred duty to safeguard, protect and defend this Constitution and to maintain its supremacy as the embodiment of the will of the people of Bangladesh so that we may prosper in freedom and may make our full contribution towards international peace and co-operation in keeping with the progressive aspirations of mankind;
>
> In our Constituent Assembly, this eighteenth day of Kartick, 1379 B.S corresponding to the fourth day of November, 1972 A.D., do hereby adopt, enact and give to ourselves this Constitution."

## *Characteristics of the 1972 Constitution*

The constitution is spread over 72 printed pages and contains a preamble, 153 Articles divided into II parts, and 4 appended schedules. It establishes a unitary republic with a parliamentary form of government resembling most the British system. Most of the unwritten conventions of the British constitution, which govern the relations between the Monarch, the Cabinet and the Parliament, have been written into the constitution in unambiguous terms. However, the Head of state is a president elected by the single-chamber Jatio Sangsad (National Parliament) directly elected by citizens of 18 years or above. A major theme of the constitution is the supremacy of the Sangsad, but it is not as supreme as the British Parliament. It must work within the framework of the written constitution, which though amendable by two-thirds majority in the parliament, imposes certain restrictions on its powers by guaranteeing certain fundamental rights (Part III, Articles 26–47) to the citizens.

The framers of the constitution seem to have learned lessons from the bitter experience of Pakistan days and have made clear provisions to keep the President out of the arena of power politics. Except in case of appointment of the Prime Minister, the president must act in accordance with the advice of the Prime Minister (Art. 48:3). The Prime Minister has been given enough powers with respect to the cabinet. He is 'central to its formation, central to its life, and central to its death,' just as in Britain. The Cabinet is collectively responsible to the Parliament (Art. 55:3), but the Prime Minister can advise the President to dissolve the Parliament even if he ceases to retain the support of the majority, and the advice is binding on the President (57:2). The constitution also provides that a member of the Parliament loses his seat if he resigns from or votes against his party in the Parliament (Art. 70). This provision has been deliberately incorporated in the constitution to prevent the members from crossing the floor of the house and thus ensuring the party discipline essential for the success of Parliamentary government. It is alleged that this provision is an infringement on the freedom of members of Parliament, but the same article includes a provision that members who thus lose their seats shall not be de- barred from contesting the by-elections which must be held within 90 days of such vacation (Art. I23:4).

The judicial power has been vested in a Supreme Court in which judges are appointed by the executive and hold office up to the age of 62 years. They are removable only through impeachment by a two-thirds majority of the Parliament. The High Court Division of the Supreme Court is empowered to enforce the fundamental rights by issuing writs of habeas corpus, mandamus, certiorari, and prohibition (Art. 102). The judicial system is marked by one major departure from the past. The constitution empowers the Parliament to provide by law for the establishment of Administrative Tribunals to exercise jurisdiction in respect of matters relating to the terms and conditions of service and the penalties and punishment of the civil servants, and the acquisition, administration, management, or disposal of property vested in or managed by the government (Art. 117).

Unlike the Pakistani practice, the constitution does not make any provision for special protection of the rights of civil servants. They hold office during the pleasure of the President (Art. 134) and may be removed or dismissed or demoted by the appointing authority whose decision is final (Art 135). According to the Law Minister, this is necessary to curb the power of 'bureaucracy' and reorganize the whole service structure in the light of national objective of establishing socialism through democratic means. The most important feature of the constitution is its attempt at a synthesis between democracy and socialism (popularly known as 'Mujibism' in Bangladesh). It provides for the usual democratic rights of the citizens in Part III (Art. 26–47). Right to equality before the law; protection from arbitrary arrest; freedom of movement, freedom of thought and conscience, freedom of religion, freedom of speech, press, association and assembly are also guaranteed. But the exercise of most of the rights is subject to 'reasonable restrictions' imposed by law in the interest of the 'security of the state' or 'public order' or 'public health' or 'morality' or 'decency.' 'No person shall be deprived of life or personal liberty save in accordance with law' (Art. 32). All laws inconsistent with the fundamental rights shall be void to the extent of inconsistency (Art. 26). Thus, the constitution protects citizens against arbitrary and unjust actions of the executive and administrative branches, and also envisages a judiciary with the power of determining whether the laws of parliament imposing restrictions on the rights are 'reasonable.'

The constitution recognizes three kinds of ownership-state-ownership through a nationalized public sector, collective ownership through co-operatives, and private ownership, i.e., ownership by individuals 'within such limits as prescribed by Law' (Art. I3). Every citizen has the right to acquire, hold, or transfer private property, and no property shall be compulsorily acquired, nationalized, or requisitioned save by the authority of law. But such law may authorize nationalization or acquisition with or without compensation, which may not be challenged in any court of law (Art. 42). This provision is perhaps the outcome of the lesson drawn from the difficulties experienced by the Indian government in 1970, in its effort to nationalize banks and abolish the pensions allowed to the former rulers of princely states.

But most of the social and economic measures directed towards the establishment of socialism have found expression in Part II of the constitution dealing with the Fundamental Principles of State Policy. It is stated to be a fundamental responsibility of the state to attain, through planned economic growth, a constant increase of productive forces with a view to securing to its citizens (a) the basic necessities of life, including food, clothing, shelter, education and medical care; (b) the right to guaranteed employment with reasonable wage; (c) the right to reasonable rest, recreation and leisure; and (d) the right to social security (Art. 15). The principle, 'From each according to his ability to each according to his work,' has been recognized (Art. 20). These Fundamental Principles are 'the basis of work of the state and of its citizens' but they are 'not judicially enforceable' (Art. 8). This provision was severely attacked by the opposition parties.

The opposition NAP member in the Assembly said that by keeping the Fundamental Principles out of judicial review the whole objective of establishing socialism had been made meaningless. On the other hand, the Law Minister observed that those who advocated that economic rights be made justiciable, exposed themselves as being non-socialist and unscientific. This could not be the socialist approach to secure economic rights. 'It can only be through planned and purposeful mobilization of all the resources-human and material. Such mobilization can only be effected through the executive and legislative organs of the state.' According to Finance Minister Tajuddin Ahmed, the Parliament democratically elected by a politically conscious people, would determine the priorities on the basis of objective conditions obtaining in the country at a particular phase and would implement the Fundamental Principles in accordance with the wishes of the people.

The constitution is based on the experience gained over the last 25 years and is broadly acceptable to the general populace. Socialism is the cry of the hour and the new constitution may not be an impediment to the progressive realization of socialism through democratic means. But it needs a good start. The first general election under the constitution is scheduled to be held on 7 March 1973. There are indications that the major political parties will participate in the elections and that the constitution will be an election issue. Maulana Bhashani of the pro-Peking NAP, who is also the leader of a proposed combined opposition camp, has declared that his party will contest the ensuing elections and, if elected, will give a new constitution ensuring food, clothing, medicine, shelter and education for all. Awami League leaders also treat the elections as a referendum on the constitution.

## Notes

1 Muntassir Mamun, The Vanquished Generals and the Liberation War of Bangladesh.
2 A.A. Shawon. 7 June 1966: Six Points were Bengalis charter of freedom. 6 June 2020. (https://www.dhakatribune.com/bangladesh/2020/06/06/june-7–1966-six-points-were-bengalis-charter-of-freedom).
3 S.S. Islam. The impacts of the major events of 1966 on the struggle for independence of Bangladesh. 1.11.2016.
4 Full text of President Ayub's speech at the final session of the Pakistan Muslim League (Convention Group) at Dhaka on 20 March 1966; see *The Daily Ittefaq* (Dhaka), 21 March 1966.
5 Ibid.
6 Ibid.
7 M.S. Reza. Operation Searchlight in the national self-determination narrative, 26 March 2019. (https://www.thedailystar.net/law-our-rights/news/operation-searchlight-the-national-self-determination-narrative-1720294?amp).
8 Richard Sisson. *War and Secession*, p. 11.
9 Richard Sisson. *War and Secession*, p. 12.
10 Ibid.
11 Ibid.
12 https://www.docsity.com/en/amendments-of-bangladesh-constitution/5800405/
13 Ibid.
14 F.A. Huq, Constitution-Making in Bangladesh. Pacific Affairs, University of British Columbia.
15 Ibid.
16 Summarized from Report of Constitution Drafting Committee, pp. 5–24.
17 Bangabandhu Sheikh Mujibur Rahman was one of the founders of the Students League and it was all along the student wing of the Awami League. In May I972, it split into two rival factions. The more revolutionary group, led by A. S. M. Abdur Rab, took an anti-government stance, while the other group, led by Nure Alam Siddique, remained with the League. The two groups are virtually two separate organizations under the same name.
18 October 20th, 1972. Maulana Bhasani's Presidential Address to NAP Executive Committee.
19 For the views of this student organization, see the address of its President, Atiqur Rahman Saloo, at the meeting of its National Executive Committee, published in the Dainik Bangla, 24 October 1972.
20 Press-statement of Khan Saifur Rahman, Convenor of the party, published in the Dainik Bangla, October 19, 1972.
21 Proceedings of the press conference of Moni Singh and Abdus Salam, President and General Secretary of the Communist Party of Bangladesh, published in *The Bangladesh Observer*, Dacca, 19 October 1972.
22 Haroon-ar-Rashid Khan, "Problems of Political Development in Bangladesh" (1979). Masters Theses. 3169. https://thekeep.eiu.edu/theses/3169
23 Press statement of Pir Habibur Rahman and Pankaj Bhattacharjee (respectively Vice-President and the General Secretary of the NAP), published in the Dainik Bangla, 17 October 1972.
24 Tofael Ahmed's interview with Eastern News Agency (ENA) published in *The Bangladesh Observer*, 14 October 1972.

# 3

# INCEPTION AND HOPE

## First Amendment—The Outset

The Bangladesh constitution was one of the most acclaimed constitutions when it was originally prepared. With the course of time, various notable amendments were made to it, among which some were necessary for the state and its citizens and some were extensively criticized.

Passed on 15 July 1973, the first amendment was made to the Article 47 of the constitution, which inserted an additional clause, Article 47(3) that allowed punishment and prosecution of war criminals under international law.

The first three constitutional amendments in Bangladesh continue to remain as three important milestones in our political history since those aimed at protecting the sovereignty of the new-born state and consolidating state power by defying anti-liberation forces.

The whole exercise relating to the trial of the war criminals by the Bangabandhu Government was initiated and materialized in accordance with relevant international laws, acts, provisions, conventions and practices, specifically, the Geneva Conventions, Tokyo Tribunal, Nuremberg Tribunal (and Principles); and the London Charter. The first amendment to the Constitution provided the Government with sufficient authority to try the war criminals without facing legal or administrative impediments, since clause (3) of Article 47 barred the accused from the protection of part III of the Constitution (**fundamental rights**). The provisions under Article 47(3) were further strengthened by 47(A). This amendment reflected the Bangabandhu Government's clear commitment to the trial of the war criminals. With the repeal of the International Crimes (Tribunals) Act, 1973 the process of rehabilitation of the collaborators and war criminals in the politics of Bangladesh started. Some of the leading collaborators such as Shah Azizur Rahman and Moulana Mannan became cabinet Ministers of General Ziaur Rahman's Government. The

DOI: 10.4324/9781003363002-3

political parties that collaborated directly with the occupation forces: Jamaat-e-Islami, Muslim League, Nejam-e–Islami, etc. and their subsidiary organizations were rehabilitated simultaneously. 1972 manifested accelerated activities of ultra-leftist groups. These groups and their leaders were sceptical about the Liberation War, independence of Bangladesh and the split of Pakistan. During the Liberation War these radical groups opposed *Mukti Bahini* and confronted Liberation Forces consistently. On the other hand, war time socio-political peculiarities provided them ample scope for acquiring additional military strength. They attacked police stations and small groups of *Mukti Bahini* and captured arms and ammunition which they used against the establishment and ruling party activists after the liberation. Prominent among these groups were Purbo Bangla Sarbohara Party (PBSP) of Siraj Sikder and Purbo Banglar Communist Party led by Abdul Matin and Alauddin Ahmed. The underground radical groups were also supported and sponsored by Mohammd Toaha, Abdul Huq and Shukhendu Dastidar.

After the liberation the Purbo Bangla Sarbohara Party (PBSP) of Siraj Sikder emerged as an organized underground force. Sikder consolidated his position by forming Maoist Unity Group (MUG), which subsequently became a safe shelter for the absconding with arms anti-liberation forces. PBSP started challenging the police in different areas and raided rural police stations and captured weapons. The 'People's War' of Siraj Sikder targeted ruling party workers and leaders in villages in the name of liquidation of the class enemies. Some of the PBSP cadres got involved in murder, robbery, extortion, land grabbing, and abduction for ransom. The activities of ultra-leftist groups instigated unprecedented unrest and lawlessness in the new-born country.

The most important political incident was the formation of the Jatiyo Samajtantrik Dal (JSD) in 1972 by the left leaning leaders of Sramik League, Chhatra League and retired army officials: Sirajul Alam Khan, A.S.M Abdur Rab, Shahjahan Siraj, Major (Retd.) M.A Jaliland and others. From the very beginning JSD aimed at toppling the Mujib Government and with that purpose formed an armed wing of the party known as Gonobahini. Colonel Abu Taher, one of the valiant Sector Commanders of the Liberation War was the de facto commander of the Gonobahini. Although all the founders and leaders of the JSD were freedom fighters and thus, loyal to the people of Bangladesh, the party ultimately became a safe shelter for the anti-liberation forces, who desperately searched for a political and armed platform for conducting their anti-Bangladesh activities. By 1973, the anti-Government activities of JSD had spread drastically all over the country. The local Awami League leaders were killed indiscriminately, the banks were looted, and anti-liberation propaganda reached culminating points.

After independence, one of the political priorities of the Government of the new-born state was to initiate trial of the war criminals. Although 93,000 Pakistani troops and servicemen surrendered to Allied Forces on 16 December, 1971, the 50,000 local collaborators never did. Most of them escaped with their arms and the newly independent state was under the threat of sabotage. The first amendment to the constitution was made by the Bangabandhu's Government to ensure trial of the war criminals.

To state in brief, this amendment was to make way for the prosecution of genocide, crime against humanity and war crimes committed in the liberation war of 1971. This is one of those amendments that were required to defend the main principles of the constitution of Bangladesh. On 20 July 1973, The International Crimes (Tribunals) Act, 1973 came in effect to try Pakistani war criminals. Subsequently, 73 special tribunals were formed, more than 37,000 cases were filed, around 50,000 suspected war criminals were arrested and 752 were punished immediately under this Act.

During the liberation war of 1971, Pakistani occupation army led by General Yahya Khan and his colleagues in collaboration with the anti-liberation forces (Jamat, Muslim League, and other religious political parties) of Bangladesh killed a total of 3 million unarmed Bengalis, molested and raped about 450,000 Bengali women and, on the eve of the independence, murdered hundreds of leading intellectuals to spiritually cripple the nation. A crime far exceeds, in its atrocity and inhumanity, the crimes of Hitler, Melosovitch, the Nazis and the Fascists.[1]

The war criminals of Bangladesh liberation war were not tried for the longest time and they have never apologized for their crimes to the nation for the killing of 50,000 Bengalis in Dhaka on 25 and 26 March, 1971 under the military operation code-named 'operation searchlight' and ruthless massacre of 3 million unarmed Bengalis over nine months of armed occupation by the Pakistani military.

> *They have caused senseless and wanton loots, rapes, arson and killings in Bangladeshi countryside during the course of the "sweeping operations" following the military crackdown. Pre-planned killings of intellectuals and professionals like doctors, engineers, civil servants, students and social workers and burying them in mass graves over 9 months of occupation to spiritually cripple the Bengalis.*
>
> *Rapes and molestation of 450,000 Bengali women by the officers and soldiers of the Pakistani occupation army as a deliberate act of revenge, retaliation and torture. Use of thousands of Bengali women as sex slaves and comfort girls in military camps and bunkers by the members of all ranks of the Pakistani occupation army. Ethnic (Hindu) cleansing. Forced pregnancy of Hindu women and deliberate killing of Hindu males to exterminate Bengali Hindus as a race.*[2]

It was needed to punish the criminals after the war of 1971, the criminals who caused mass genocide and crossed all the extents of brutality during the war. Keeping the post-war socio-political situation of 1972 and 1973 in consideration, this amendment needed to be formed as separate trial of the criminals was not allowed due to the provision of fundamental rights in the constitution. The insertion of the new clause, Article 47(3), in the constitution of the parliament made space for any law to be formed for the trial of the war criminal where the fundamental rights were made inapplicable for those under trial of this law.

Rights such as, right to protection of law, under Article 31 of the constitution was made inapplicable for them along with the right to protection against trial under *expost facto* law under Article 35(1) of the constitution of Bangladesh so that they cannot escape from getting punished by law. To make the stand strong, their right to a speedy and public trial by an independent and partial tribunal under Article 35(3) was barred too. Lastly, their right to enforce fundamental rights under Article 44 was also taken away.

A crime tribunal was thus formed namely The International Crimes Tribunal (Bangladesh) which is a domestic war crimes tribunal in Bangladesh set up in 2009 to investigate and prosecute suspects for the genocide committed in 1971 by the Pakistan Army and their local collaborators, Razakars, Al-Badr and Al-Shams during the Bangladesh Liberation War.

> *the International Crimes Tribunal was re-established in 2010 in order to hold the perpetrators of war crimes, crimes against humanity and genocide, during the liberation war of Bangladesh in 1971 accountable. An War Crimes Fact-Finding Committee was tasked to investigate and find evidence for the 1971 war crimes and identified 1, 600 suspects in a report submitted in 2008. In 2009, the government amended the International Crimes (Tribunals) Act, 1973 (ACT NO. XIX OF 1973) to pave way for a tribunal, which was finally set up on 25 March 2010. On 22/3/2012 the government established another tribunal namely International Crimes Tribunal-2, under the same jurisdiction mentioned in section 3 of the International Crimes (Tribunals) Act (1973). However, the main perpetrators of the war crimes, the Pakistan soldiers, remained out of bounds of the courts. The first indictment was issued in 2010 and by 2012, nine leaders of Jamaat-e-Islami, and two of the Bangladesh Nationalist Party, had been indicted as suspects in war crimes. The testimonies provided by the witnesses, and the documents submitted by the Prosecution and the Defense, remains as an important collection of memories of the 1971 genocide. During 2011 – 2018, 30 judgments were issued under International Crimes Tribunal-1, and 11 judgments have been issued under the International Crimes Tribunal-2.*[3]

At that time, among the Bangladeshis a sum of population volunteered to help the Pakistani militants, commonly known as the 'Razakars.' The Wall Street Journal then published an article mentioning,

> *To help control of Bengali population, the army has been setting up a network of peace committees superimposed upon the normal civil administration, which the army cannot fully rely upon. Peace committee members are drawn from … .. Beharis and from the Muslim Leagues and Jamat-e-Islami. The peace committees serve as the agent of army, informing on civil administration as well as on general populace. They are also in charge of confiscating and redistribution of shops and lands from Hindu and pro-independence Bengalis. The peace committee also recruits Razakars … … many of them are common criminals who have thrown their lots with the (Pakistan) army.*[4]

The term Razakar is originally derived from an Arabic word meaning volunteer. In the context of Islamic history, Razakars were volunteers to defend or support Islam. But in Bangladeshi context, Razakar means traitors or collaborators of the Pakistan army who helped them, in our liberation war in 1971, in identifying and killing millions of Bangalees involved in or even supporting the liberation war. The Razakars were mainly the members of the Muslim league, Jamat-e-Islam and other Islamic groups and factions.[5] Jamaat leaders collaborated with them [Pakistan army] not only to advance their ideals of Pakistan as an Islamic state, but also to wreak vengeance on people they were at enmity with. The New York Times has mentioned that, '*Razakars … … should be especially helpful as members of rural communities, who can identify guerrillas (freedom fighters)",' an army officer (Pakistan) said … The government says it has already recruited more than 22,000 Razakars of a planned force of 35,000.'*[6]

> "*The former leader of Jamaat-e-Islami, Bangladesh's largest Islamist party, was sentenced to 90 years in jail for crimes against humanity on 15 July 2013. Azam is alleged to have created and led pro-Pakistan militias which carried out numerous murders and rapes during the 9-month war. Described by his party colleagues as a writer and Islamic thinker, Azam was strongly opposed to Bangladesh's independence from Pakistan, arguing at the time that it would divide the Muslim community. He also cautioned that an independent Bangladesh would come under the political and economic influence of neighbouring India.*[7]
>
> *Nizami, who led Jamaat-e-Islami, was hanged in Dhaka's prison early on 11 May after refusing to seek mercy from Bangladesh's president. He was sentenced to death for war crimes in October 2014. The Supreme Court rejected his final appeal on 5 May 2016.*[8]
>
> *Mir Quasem Ali was accused of involvement in a "reign of terror" in the city of Chittagong. He was found guilty of eight of the 14 charges he faced. The tycoon, 63, was hanged at a high-security prison outside Dhaka.*[9]
>
> *Delwar Hossain Sayeedi, a prolific speaker and a well-known leader of the Jamaat-e-Islami, the 72-year-old former MP had his death sentence overturned on appeal and is now serving life in jail.He was found guilty in February 2013 of charges including murder, torture and rape.*[10]
>
> *Ali Ahsan Mohammad Mujahid, 64, was the secretary-general of Jamaat-e-Islami and an influential figure within the party. He was executed in November 2015 after being sentenced to death in July 2013—a decision that was upheld in June 2015 when the Supreme Court rejected his appeal.*[11]
>
> *A former minister, Salahuddin Quader Chowdhury was a BNP MP and the most senior leader from the party to be sentenced for crimes against humanity. He was executed in November 2015 after the Supreme Court rejected his appeal in June 2015.*[12]
>
> *Muhammad Kamruzzaman, the assistant secretary-general of Jamaat-e-Islami was found guilty in May 2013 of masterminding what the prosecution described as one of the bloodiest single episodes in the independence war. The Supreme Court later*

*upheld his death sentence on appeal and he was hanged in April 2015. The war crimes tribunal heard that he played a prominent role alongside Pakistani troops in the "slaughter" of at least 120 unarmed farmers in the remote northern village of Sohagpur which subsequently became known as the "village of widows".*[13]

*Abdul Kader Mullah, assistant secretary general of the Jamaat-e-Islami party since 2010 and a former executive editor of The Daily Sangram, was found guilty on five of six counts of crimes against humanity and war crimes on 5 February 2013.He was sentenced to death in September of that year after a failed appeal and hanged in December. Mullah, who denied all the charges, was convicted of killing 344 civilians as well as rape and other crimes. Many of the atrocities for which he was convicted took place in Dhaka's Mirpur area, earning him the name "Butcher of Mirpur"".*[14]

Dr. Kamal Hossain, who was the Chairman of the Constitution Drafting Committee in the Constituent Assembly of Bangladesh, has mentioned that, *'It was of immense necessity that, this amendment was made for the people of this state who have sacrificed so much for their motherland, it was the socio-political need of that time.'* Dr. Modud Ahmed, has also mentioned in this regard that, *'It was only fair to apply this amendment to provide adequate justice to this nation and its people.'*

This amendment was not only necessary to protect the principles of the constitution of Bangladesh but also to make sure that justice was well served. It was to set an example for the new generation of a country which has earned its independence by making sacrifices no other nation ever has. Needless to mention that after the establishment of this amendment, the International Criminal (Tribunal) Act for the trial of 195 prisoners of war was passed in the Parliament within a week.

Unfortunately, as mentioned by MD Abdul Halim in his book, 'Constitution, Constitutional Law and politics: Bangladesh Perspective,' this initiative of the government regarding this amendment to try the war criminals ended in a failure due to tricks played by Bhutto.

*"Some claim that the Razakars did not even exist—apparently, they were conjured up by the Awami League for political benefit. That the Razakars were officially created by the Pakistani military and trained and paid by the government of Pakistan should not be forgotten—and will become an important element in any future genocide trial. The history of 1971 and the Bangladesh Genocide is under attack from revisionists and genocide deniers. The victims of this attack will be the younger generation of Bangladeshis unless we make an attempt to preserve that history."*[15]

*The failure to deal with the crimes committed during the 1971 war in a comprehensive and transparent manner and to specifically acknowledge the many victims of the war has left many people resentful and this constitutes a problematic legacy. To this day, there is a culture of impunity for serious human rights violations. This impunity is now entrenched, as manifested in the disrespect for the rule of law and the separation of powers, the enactment of repressive laws and the abuse of the state apparatus for the achievement of party political and personal goals. In this context, the status and affiliation of the perpetrator(s) and victim(s) often seem to be more important than the fact of the crime of torture itself. Added to this, there are various shortcomings in the legal and institutional framework that inhibit accountability and effective recourse for torture survivors and relatives of torture victims to courts or other bodies. The failure of successive governments to set up an independent human rights body is particularly glaring in this context.*[16]

## Second Amendment—Necessity Knows No Laws

Exercising the extreme power of preventive detention, though it is considered as a contradiction to the basic rights of individual liberty by allowing executive dispensation, is justified to some extent as a necessary administrative practice during the dire instances of external aggression, war, civil unrest or subversion in order to prevent the perceived threats to the state. Exercising the power of preventive detention is originally prohibited in the constitution of Bangladesh, unlike that of India and Pakistan, under any circumstances. However, the constitution amendment, made on 22 September 1973, empowered the Parliament to sanction the laws regarding preventive detention without specifying safeguards required to mitigate the malevolent aspects of such laws. To elaborate, the Amendment of 1973 neither clarifies the time frame of the detention of an individual nor limits the power of preventive detention only to the mentioned cases of emergency.

The Second amendment of Bangladesh constitution was a blessing to some and a destructive blow to others. The two main significant features of the original constitution of Bangladesh were—firstly, its absence of provisions for preventive detention and secondly, the absence of provisions for emergency cases and suspension of fundamental rights although, in less than nine months, the second amendment of the constitution was passed. This Act resulted in the (i) amendment of Articles 26, 63, 72 and 142 of the constitution; (ii) substitution of Article 33 and (iii) the insertion of a new part, that is, IXA in the constitution. Provisions were made through this amendment for the suspension of some fundamental rights of citizens in an emergency. The increasing political and social unrest instigated by the anti-liberation forces with the support of ultra-leftists compelled the Government to undertake preventive measures. One of those was the provision of declaring the state of emergency via the second amendment to the constitution. This amendment of 22 September 1973 sanctioned provisions for the declaration of emergency and curtailment and suspension of certain fundamental rights of the citizens during emergency. Article 141A elaborates provisions for proclamation of emergency by the President if he is 'satisfied that a grave emergency exists in which the security or economic life of Bangladesh, or any part thereof, is threatened by war or external aggression or internal disturbance.' The amendment pronounced that a proclamation of emergency 'shall cease to operate at the expiration of hundred and 20 days' unless before the expiration it is approved by the Parliament.

Preventive detention, the most debatable issue in the field of law in Bangladesh, means detention of an individual without trial or declaration from the court, rather on suspicion of the executive body. From the dawn of civilization, the practice of violating human rights prevailed which now has emerged as a culture around the world through the introduction of preventive detention, specifically in third world countries including Bangladesh. This custom is very common in all the ensuing government parties of Bangladesh to continue their rule and, at the same time, suppress the movement of the opposition party. As a result, camouflaging the preventive detention law, the administrative authority exerts unaccountable power to arrest and detain anyone they wish.

There was no trace of provision of emergency or any preventive detention in the original constitution of Bangladesh. The resolution was praiseworthy and resourceful for the growth of living democracy. But within a span of nine months, in the 2nd amendment, preventive detention and provisions of emergency were introduced in the constitution. *Dr. Kamal Hossain has mentioned in his interview with us that he believes as for the time being, it was necessary to have been amended. He also mentioned that the constitution would have to be amended from time to time for the greater good of the country and its people. Barrister Modud Ahmed also agrees with the statement as drastic decisions are to be made deciding on the on-going situation of the country.*

The provision for declaration of emergency happens to be an essential component of the Constitutions of almost all the countries of the world, including those with high democracy and governance indicators: USA, UK, Australia, etc. For example, during 1976–2001, the Presidents of the United States declared 32 national emergencies for different purposes. Interestingly, the constitution of Bangladesh initially did not have any such provision. As mentioned above, at the backdrop of emerging opposition from the radicals, both legal and underground, and with the deterioration of the law-and-order situation, the second constitutional amendment was enacted which aimed at inserting relevant provisions to tackle the emerging difficulties. Later these provisions were indiscriminately used by the military regimes to consolidate their power and suppress democratic movements. Another priority of independent Bangladesh was to resolve its age-old territorial disputes with India. The Radcliffe Mission's (1947) hastily created demarcation lines between India and Pakistan, particularly between India and East Bengal on the East and India and Punjab on the West, went through densely populated and established settlements and resulted in creation of 192 enclaves in India and Pakistan: 119 inside India were claimed by East Pakistan and 75 inside East Pakistan claimed by India. The fate of more than 50,000 inhabitants of these enclaves depended on the political solution of the problem. During the initial 23 years, India and Pakistan took only one initiative in 1952 to resolve this problem, when Jawaharlal Nehru and Firoze Khan Noon agreed to exchange the enclaves. Ultimately the initiative was proven futile due mainly to the lack of political will from both sides. The subsequent Governments of Pakistan, especially those of Iskandar Mirja, Ayub Khan and Yahya Khan, opted for confrontational politics with India aimed at instigating anti-Indian sentiment among the people of

Pakistan and thereby diverting the attention of the people from internal chaos, corruption and mismanagement. After the liberation, the Bangabandhu Sheikh Mujibur Rahman's Government undertook practical measures to resolve territorial disputes with India and with that purpose made the 3rd amendment to the constitution.

Laws authorizing the detention of a person without trial were considered necessary by the British Indian Government to suppress subversive political activities of the people in the subcontinent but after achieving independence, the Governments of India and Pakistan continued these laws. The framers of the Constitutions of both India and Pakistan, however, created certain limitations of the powers of the legislature as well as the executive in their attempt to detain a person without trial. In Bangladesh, these limitations have been provided in the Constitution by amending Article 33. Clauses (4), (5) and (6) which have been inserted by this Amendment, contain these limitations. Before examining the nature of the Constitutional protection of the restrictive laws, the origin of such laws may be considered.

Article 33 as originally adopted did not leave any scope for preventive detention. Preventive detention, though an evil deed, is a necessity for State security and the Constitution (Second Amendment) Act, 1973 the old Article 33 was replaced by the present one providing that the above rights will not be available in the case of persons arrested or detained under any law providing for preventive detention. Preventive detention has three distinguishing features—(i) it is detention and not imprisonment, (ii) it curtails the liberty of a person by executive order without any preceding trial or inquiry and (iii) its object is preventive and not punitive.

Under Article 32 a law providing for preventive detention must both substantively and procedurally be free from arbitrariness and unreasonableness and must not be vague or disproportionate to the mischief sought to be remedied. In order to protect the individuals from arbitrary or high-handed arrest and detention by the executive, clauses (4) and (5) of Article 33 provide two important safeguards—(i) approval by the Advisory Board and (ii) communication of the grounds of detention. Both these safeguards are to be observed by the detaining authority. It is immaterial whether the constitutional safeguards are incorporated in the law as even if not so incorporated, it would be deemed to be incorporated in the law as superimposed by the Constitution.[17]

If we look back to the history and think of reasons why these provisions were not added in the first place, we come to know that, during colonialism of the British and in the history of the constitution of Pakistan, arbitrary exercising of the preventive detention law and emergency was a bitter experience. As a result of this experience, the AL learnt of such provisions, which contradicts the idea of nurturing living democracy. In Bangladesh, a large number of political workers and leaders are detained without trial through preventive detention under the Special Powers Act, 1974 known as a 'Black Law.' But the picture of detention without trial is not the same in western countries where this preventive detention also exists. It has to be kept in mind that to maintain the colonial state, the British government used this law under the government of India Act, 1935 as necessary weapons to crush the opposition and perpetuate their rule.[18] Because of enacting this law, jeopardy took place and hundreds and thousands of Indians and their leaders had to suffer imprisonment without trial for an indefinite period. It has to be kept in mind that in Bangladesh, we do not have a fixed maximum period of detention not in our constitution or in the Special Powers Act, 1974. This is also a negative aspect of Preventive detention. In Pakistan, the period of Preventive detention is eight (8) months in a year and in India, it is maximum two years. Golam Mohammed and Iskander Mirza, the two Governor Generals of Pakistan, continued to rule using the power of emergency and crushed the existing political parties. Ayub Khan imposed an emergency in 1965 and continued to rule until he was forced to leave power in 1969. During this period of extended emergency, suppressed and forced to leave power. Moreover, a huge number of citizens were imprisoned for years without trial. This experience made the AL declare a commitment since the emergence of the United Front in 1954 to remove both these back laws and any prevailing scope that might enable anyone to retard the process of democracy.

> *In Bangladesh the original constitution, there was no provision introducing preventive detention. But the 4th amendment by "The Special Powers Act 1974" (9th February) enacted the Preventive Detention Act which was an anti-people black law still continuing. In Bangladesh without trial 6 months detention can be conferred to the detainee. This is a bad process because nowhere in the world such a long period is not found anywhere. In India, this time is 3 months (Article 22 of Indian Constitution.) and in Pakistan the initial period of detention is 3 months.*

*Even though it is universally perceived that preventive detention is a serious invasion of personal liberty and an abnormal measure of curtailing personal liberty of an individual, even in the past, many countries contained or enacted preventive detention law either in war or in peace time. Preventive detention in case of an emergency of war is well recognized because national security and interest are more important than the personal liberty of citizens. Personal liberty depends upon the safe security of the state.*[19] *Considering the justification for preventive detention Lord Atkinson in R v. Halliday observed, 'Where preventive justice is put in force some suffering and inconvenience may be caused to the suspected person.' This is inevitable. But the sufferings are inflicted for something much more important than his liberty or convenience, namely for securing the public safety and the defense of the realm. Similar view was also exposed by Lord Alfred Denning.*[20] *He said that if there are traitors in our midst, we cannot afford to until we catch them in the act of blowing up our bridges or giving our military secrets to the enemy. We cannot run the risk of leaving them at large. We must detain them on suspicion (Bhuiyan, Md. J. H., 2004). All international and regional documents of human rights recognize and make provision for derogation of rights in case of emergency and national crisis.*[21] In recent times, the necessity of having such provision in time of peace has been felt to prevent anti-social and subversive elements from imperilling the existence and welfare of states. The ruling government justifies the practice of preventive detention with the excuses that without this law, the country cannot be administered and this law is a must to run the government and to suppress terrorism and that it is essential to control anti-social activities. One of the former general secretary of Bangladesh Awami League has said,

> The Special Powers Act was introduced to combat looting of police station, setting fire on jute godowns, slogan Muslim Bengal, Noxalite activities and above all to combat the nefarious tendency to destroy the sovereignty of the state (Sufian, Md. A. A., 2008).

Though there are 90 justifications behind the practice of preventive detention in war time but in times of peace, preventive detention is not at all known in all democratic countries, especially in developed countries. The greatest constitutional expertise of India has explained one of the reasons of incorporation of preventive detention in India as

> there may be many parties and persons who may not be patient enough to follow constitutional methods but are impatient in reaching their objective and for that purpose they resort to unconstitutional methods, and then there may be a large number of people who have to be detained by the executive. In such a situation, would it be possible for the executive to prepare the cases only do all that necessary to satisfy the elaborate legal procedure prescribed.

Hence the virtual necessity of the law of preventive detention in certain situations can hardly be overestimated.[22]

> *Government may exercise preventive detention only in case of grave emergency and the government cannot violate one's fundamental rights which are prescribed in Bangladesh constitution. Though preventive detention is a tool of the constitution for social needs, but now it is working for others purpose behind its legal or theoretical purpose. The excessive use of laws of preventive detention, affects the liberty of the individual and as well as dangerous for a big community. The law-abiding person should not forget that this law is for the protection of society and state and not for oppression to the people who are in different communities or thoughts. The philosophy lying behind preventive detention is the safety of the community at large, but may create an atmosphere which affects the community in general and liberty of the person in particular. The government should remember that in an organized society it exists for the welfare of the people. The power of detention is available no doubt, but it should be used only in exceptional circumstances. So, in order to show respect and follow the constitution, exercise the Practice of true democracy every government should give its attention to establish the fundamental human right of the citizens but not to violate their rights. Government should remember that in an organized society preventive detention exists for the welfare of people but not to encroach their basic human rights.*[23]

## Third Amendment—Consensus and Harmony

Boundary disputes (whether relating to land or maritime boundaries) between neighbouring countries are complex processes under international law and national law. Bangladesh and India have been peacefully coexisting as a neighbouring country for the last five decades. No major border conflict has been seen over the last five decades except illegal border killings for illegal trespassing. Bangladeshi leaders, from Bangabandhu Sheikh Mujibur Rahman to Lt. General Ziaur Rahman, always had a friendly sentiment over their neighbouring country India and they never failed to emphasize the maintenance of friendly ties with India. Indian leaders also did the same and had always expressed similar sentiments. Bangladeshi leaders had shown their gratitude to India for their intervention in the Liberation war of 1971 and for the political, economic and military aid during that time. In 1947, the partition of Bengal done by the British was a poor and insensitive process in terms of border divisions, and it left a disorganized and cluttered demarcated international boundary between India and (then-East Pakistan) Bangladesh. Both nations have contested and denied possession of some villages on both sides of the de facto border. This demarcated process left the residents of those villages hanging in terms of their nationality and fundamental rights. For the last six decades, residents have been trespassing and crossing the border to be with their family or to conduct farming and business. Many people died because of illegal trespassing, and these people simply did not have any fault as their nationality and their land kept on hanging between two countries.

Bangladesh and India share a 4,096-kilometre-long (2,545 mi) international border, the fifth-longest land border in the world, including 262 km (163 mi) in Assam, 856 km (532 mi) in Tripura, 318 km (198 mi) in Mizoram, 443 km (275 mi) in Meghalaya, and 2,217 km (1,378 mi) in West Bengal. It was important to identify these areas precisely in order to exchange enclaves between two countries. The total transfer of 111 enclaves, adding up to 17,160.63 acres, from India to Bangladesh was done. Conversely, India received 51 enclaves, adding up to 7,110.02 acres, which were in Bangladesh.[24] Prior to this historic agreement, the 2011 Protocol signed between Manmohan Singh, the president of India, and Sheikh Hasina, Prime Minister of Bangladesh, agreed to maintain the status quo in addressing the issue of adverse possessions of land, whereby India will receive 2,777.038 acres of land[25] from Bangladesh and in turn transfer 2,267.682 acres of land to Bangladesh.[26] The 2011 Protocol was made in an accord with the state governments of Assam, Meghalaya, Tripura and West Bengal.

The enclaves are small pieces of Bangladesh completely bounded by India, and vice versa, and are concentrated along the Lalmonirhat/Cooch Behar border. As per official counts, there are 51 Bangladeshi enclaves inside India and 111 Indian enclaves inside Bangladesh. Though the Chhitmahals date from Mughal times, the particular complications for those living within them began with Partition and became acute in 1952, with the implementation of a passport/visa system between the two countries.[27] Residents were previously crossing the border to conduct their daily life such as going to the market or to cultivate their land or simply even meet their family who lives on the other side or the border. However, small conflicts started to take place in the border areas and because of the two countries' declining relationship, the 1953 tension started to arise. Regulation and control between borders became formal when the parliamentary proposal was passed to secure the border. Ansars from East Pakistan and Bangiya Jatiya Rakshi Bahini from East Bengal India started to be in charge to regulate the border. This gradual formalization created an asymmetrical relationship of rights and order in the enclave areas. As India and Pakistan were divided into two nations based on religious differences, stress between the East Pakistan border and India border caused small clashes. For example, Dahagram's population consisted of both Hindu and Muslims. When the movement between borders started to become more legally strict, Muslims living in Dahagram started to move less in the other areas where Hindus were the majority. This implied separation meant that Hindus living in Dahagram were the citizens of India and Muslims Living in Dahagram were the citizens of East Pakistan. Muslims Living in Dahagram wanted to be part of a Muslim country to gain the rights of a citizen of East Pakistan. The clash started to take place when there was a dispute between the land of the Hindu and the land of the Muslim. This separation was not made by any state rather it was more of an ideological difference that led to the religious separation of the population of Dahagram by themselves.

Even after the separation of British India, Pakistan and India could not come up with a solution to divide enclaves that were an old issue since the Mughal period. The end of the Monarch system and the beginning of the Republic system left a significant gap between the pre-existing territorial boundaries. Also, the British government played a very insensitive role while partitioning the country, later many issues along with enclaves' issues aroused from the mismanagement of the British Government. Before 1947, Chitmahals were discontinuous land to Mughal incursion. They were known as the Kingdom of Kooch (cooch) Behar in the late 17th century. Areas in the frontier between Kooch and Mughal, lands such as Boda, Patgram and Purbhag, were in the control of powerful chieftains, and Mughals were unable to take back the power. An official treaty was signed between Mughal and the king of Kooch Behar in 1713. The enclaves came into existence after the treaty was signed. According to this treaty, both parties were allowed to own pieces of land they controlled at the time of the treaty even though they were surrounded by enemy territory.

These lands were officially part of the state of Kooch Behar and enclaves within the Mughal Empire. During British colonialism, many of these enclaves were spread along the border of Rangpur. Both British administration and Kooch Behar, as a sovereign state, were in the rule of these enclaves. This territorial ambiguity between a sovereign state and the British administration led to massive confusion. And this confusion did not lead anywhere even though both the parties tried to solve it several times. Nearly two hundred Chitmahals became state enclaves because it was surrounded by another sovereign state namely Cooch Behar.

After the partition, later in 1949, the kingdom of Cooch Behar merged with India. Before 20th August 1949, Cooch Behar was a Princely State ruled by the Kings of Cooch Behar. After 1949, Dahagram was the largest shared border area situated on the banks of the Tista River. Nearly 170 meters of Dahagram became the official border between India and East Pakistan.

In 1958, both the countries felt it necessary to reach an agreement. The then Prime Minister of India, Jawaharlal Nehru and Feroze Khan Noon, Prime Minister of Pakistan, reached an agreement on this issue. This agreement provided, among other things, for 'Exchange of enclaves on the basis of enclaves for enclaves without any consideration of territorial loss or gain' (9th Amendment of Constitution act, 1960, Article I and Part I of First Schedule). As a result of this agreement, Dahagram and Angorpota became part of Indian Territory. This agreement, *inter alia*, provided for the transfer of 1 1.29 sq. kms of southern half of Berubari to Pakistan as per the interpretation of Radcliffe award. Along with the political tension between India and Pakistan, Dahagram became the place for political stress between Hindus and Muslims for sharing their crops and market. Hostility towards its residents grew and Indian border security camps were established near Dahagram. This camp area is known as 'Tin Bigha' in present days. In present days, these residents of these areas are crossing the Indian Border to brand their cow. Border Security Force (BSF of India) lists people's names who want to cross the border to go to the market or to cultivate their land who live on the other side of the border. Residents were frequently arrested for crossing the border without enlisting their names officially daily. Many of the residents were confined in the Indian jail for crossing the border illegally and many were killed by the border security of both East Pakistan and India.

After 1971, India proposed to Bangladesh that India might continue to retain the southern half of South Berubari Union No. 12 and the adjacent enclaves and, in exchange, Dahagram and Angorpota may be retained by Bangladesh. As part of the package, a strip of land would be leased in perpetuity by India to Bangladesh by giving her access to Dahagram and Angorpota in order to enable her to exercise sovereignty on these two enclaves.[28] Later on, this was carefully accepted by the Land Boundary Agreement 1974. Though Bangladesh amended its constitution to comply with the bilateral treaty to handover and take over territories, India could not do the same. India amended its constitution after four decades on 1st August 2015.

Following the independence of Bangladesh, India and Bangladesh signed the 1974 Land Boundary Agreement ('1974 LBA') to resolve territory issues. On 16 May 1974, this agreement was signed by Former Prime Minister of India, Indira Gandhi, and Father of the nation and Prime Minister, Bangabandhu Sheikh Mujibur Rahman, to settle for the exchange of enclaves and the surrender of adverse possessions. According to the agreement, Bangladesh agreed to transfer South Berubari Union amounting to 2.64 square miles (approximately) to India and get back Dahagram, Angarpota, Lathitila, and Pathuria forest from India in return. It is said that Bangladesh only wanted free access to these areas. These areas are a part of Bangladesh but Indian central authority put a bar on Bangladeshi citizens to enter these areas. The government of Bangladesh passed the third amendment to the Constitution of Bangladesh in compliance with the treaty obligation and to make the handover absolute. Third amendment made some changes in article two to take over the sovereignty in order to give the promised border territory to India under the Land Boundary Agreement 1974.

The East Pakistan period was full of territorial uncertainty and periodic violence. It is important to note that the people in the Indian subcontinent before British colonialism and partition were living peacefully despite their religious or cultural background. When the British divided Bengal into two-part followed by the religious majority and handed over one part to Pakistan and another part to India, people started to differentiate themselves not only by their religious background but also by different political histories such as the partition of Bengal in 1905 and the Calcutta Riot in 1946. These events, along with their religious beliefs, shaped their sentiments and political views. During the Liberation War of Bangladesh in 1971, a climate of cooperation emerged between Bangladesh and India as the Indian Military intervened on humanitarian ground. During this period, residents were crossing the border without hesitation. India opened its border for refugees during the war. This relaxing tension came to an end with the 1974 Indira-Mujib pact which is also known as the Land Agreement act 1974.

## *Land Boundary Agreement 1974 and Its Development*

During the Liberation war, the border between India and Bangladesh was temporarily erased. Two countries decided to address the border and enclaves' issues that were linked to the animosity between India and Pakistan. India and Bangladesh were in a friendly relationship even before the liberation of Bangladesh. The idea of the separation of Bangladesh from Pakistan was highly supported by India. The Indira-Mujib pact was made to resolve the unsolved demarcated lines in the border and also to exchange enclaves with the exception of Dahagram and Berubari Union. The pact proposed to cede the disputed area of Berubari to India in exchange for the leasing of the 'Tin Bigha' Corridor to Bangladesh into perpetuity. The pact made Dahagram into an important place of territorial tension and political dispute between Bangladesh and India. The Mujib Government was criticized for being unable to address Farakka Barage and the issue of water sharing of Ganges River. Different political parties of India and Bangladesh disagreed with the pact and criticized that India is handing over their motherland for the sake of friendship which was not acceptable by different parliament members of India. A constitutional amendment needed to be done to handover the Berubari Union to India. Third amendment to the constitution of the People's Republic of Bangladesh made the exchange possible. The leasing of 'Tin Bigha' was legally problematic because of India's unchanged constitution and mainly the political disagreement.

Article 2 and article 3 of the Treaty of Land Boundary Agreement mention land settlement between India and Bangladesh. Article 2 sub section (i) mentions the

Muhuri River (Belonia) sector and this article includes that, the two Governments should raise embankments on their respective sides with a view to stabilizing the river in its present course as stipulated in the 1974 Agreement. The Parties agree to fencing on 'zero line' in this area.[29]

## *The Third Amendment*

**Brief Account:** This was enacted on 28 November 1974 by bringing in changes in Article 2 of the constitution with a view to giving effect to an agreement between Bangladesh and India in respect of exchange of certain enclaves and fixation of boundary lines between India and Bangladesh.

| SL No. | The Constitution (Third Amendment) Act 1974 |
|---|---|
| Original Article | **The territory of the Republic.**<br>The territory of the Republic shall comprise:<br>The territories which immediately before the proclamation of independence on the 26th day of March, 1971 constituted East Pakistan; **and**<br>such other territories as may become included in Bangladesh. |
| Amended Article | Section 3 of the Constitution (Third Amendment) Act 1974 substituted in article 2 clause (a) the words '[and the territories referred to as included territories in the Constitution (Third Amendment) Act, 1974, but excluding the territories referred to as excluded territories in that Act; and]' in place of the semicolon and word '; and.' |

While Bangladesh handed over the South Berubari to India immediately after the Third Amendment to the Constitution, no measure was taken by the Indian Parliament with regard to the transfer of a corridor to Bangladesh for the passage of the Dahagram and Angarpota people. India has taken no action to hand over the forests of Lathitila and Pathuria to Bangladesh. It is argued that by Third Amendment Bangladesh did give 2.64 square miles territory to India but got nothing in return. Scholars uphold that the Awami League government did hand over the South Berubari to India in order to express its gratitude to India for what India had done for the Awami League during the liberation war and after.[30]

## *Aftermath of the Amendment*

A constitutional amendment is required to exchange enclaves and to enact the transfer of territories which are adversely possessed from one state to another. Though Bangladesh has already ratified this agreement through Third Amendment in 1974, India has not taken any step-in order to legitimize the agreement even after five decades of signing the agreement. In compliance with the bilateral treaty between Bangladesh and India, India needed to amend its constitution for the one hundredth time. On 7th May 2015, the Constitution One Hundredth Amendment Act 2015 was passed in the Parliament of India, approved by the President of India on 28th May, 2015, and ratified on 6th June, 2015 to deal with three cardinal issues, namely, the un-demarcated segments, the exchange of enclaves, and adverse possessions that permanently resolved the decade-old border disputes. There was a distinction between the Radcliffe line (Thana Boda) written text and the interpretation of the 1974 Land Boundary Agreement. The lack of clarification created tensions and distressed people's lives in these areas and made them subject to a situation of social unrest. Population living in that area has suffered for decades and their status of nationality and land possession kept on hanging to be solved by two countries. Along with the amendment, a clear identification of the places and line was required as well and this identification became clear in the new signed protocol in 2011 where both countries' prime ministers agreed and signed on it.

In 2015 finally, the suffering of thousands of people came to an end. A long-waited issue between the two countries got solved by swapping their enclaves.[31]

## Fourth Amendment—Revolutionize

> The 4th Amendment Act was passed on 25 January, 1975 by an Awami League led government under the leadership of the father of the nation Sheikh Mujibur Rahman. Through this act, major changes were brought into the constitution by this amendment. The parliamentary form of government was replaced by a presidential form of government. A one-party system in place of a multi-party system was introduced; the powers of the Jatiya Sangsad were curtailed; the Judiciary was deprived of much of its independence; the Supreme Court was deprived of its jurisdiction over the protection and enforcement of fundamental rights. This Act (i) amended articles 11, 66, 67, 72, 74, 76, 80, 88, 95, 98, 109, 116, 117, 119, 122, 123, 141A, 147, and 148 of the constitution; (ii) substituted Articles 44, 70, 102, 115, and 124 of the constitution; (iii) amended part III of the constitution out of existence; (iv) altered the Third and Fourth Schedule; (v) extended the term of the first Jatiya Sangsad; (vi) made special provisions relating to the office of the president and its incumbent; (vii) inserted a new part, i.e., part VIA in the constitution and (viii) inserted articles 73A and 116A in the constitution.

At that time, this amendment to the newly promulgated Constitution was made, the young nation was undergoing a time of political upheaval. Although, the ruling party Awami League won by a significant margin in the election held in the previous year (1973), they were facing vehement opposition. A leftist element emerged mostly within the youth population of the country that idealized the concept of an armed revolution and believed that it was the only way to diminish the hegemony of the Awami League and also to implement the ideology of their choice—scientific socialism.[32]

The then Prime Minister Bangabandhu Sheikh Mujibur Rahman initiated this significant amendment to the Constitution with the approval of the national assembly with the intention introduced the presidential form of government in Bangladesh. Though the Fourth Amendment was controversial at that time, it was mainly undertaken for a number of reasons. The amendment was brought because Bangabandhu Sheikh Mujibur Rahman, the father of the nation, envisioned, prior to the amendment, building national unity by bringing all the mainstream political parties together and also by dissolving his own party Awami League to form the Bangladesh Krishak Sramik League or BAKSAL for the interest of the nation. Bangabandhu formed BAKSAL in the election of March 7, 1973.

This radical reformation of the political system was termed as the 'Second Revolution' and consequently the purposes and effects of launching BAKSAL were numerous. Bangabandhu wanted to bring a radical change in the economic system of Bangladesh in order to build a prosperous nation in accordance with the four main principals of the Constitution. Also, establishing non-communal and non-discriminatory social system with justice and equality was one of the many reasons. Apart from that, development in agricultural production, decentralization of government and good governance to reduce public sufferings worked as key motivators for the initiatives. Moreover, the deterioration of law and order and other criminal activities such as killings of freedom fighters needed such measures. The effects of these were seen on different levels of national life. Law and order were restored significantly. Additionally, price hike stopped sharply. Above all, quality of life increased in general because of the 'Second Revolution.'

However, of all the amendments, the 4th one was certainly the most debatable one. This particular amendment held the most devastating step in the growth of Constitutionalism in Bangladesh. It had altered and consequently demolished the essential features and core of the Constitution.

## Background

Following independence, the people of Bangladesh were presented a constitution that, to a large extent, reflected the aspirations and desires of the people that they harboured and nurtured for nearly two decades since the partition of the Indian Subcontinent. However, only three years after coming to life, AL government which had adopted the Constitution, due to then current situation had to transformed it to such an extent that by the 4th Amendment, it had been changed its original self. From the surface it appeared that the liberal overtone of the Constitution that had once been applauded for its modernistic views and democratic ideals, was somehow changed into a restrictive one.

Due to extreme political instability, emergency state was announced all over the country on the 28th of December, 1974, thus dismissing fundamental rights promised in the Constitution. It was declared on behalf of the then government that some dissenters who opposed the independence and the rise of Bangladesh as an autonomous state, were plotting activities that were subversive to the state. It was seen that an active conspiracy was joined by the people who were unable to attain power within a constitutional frame. Furthermore, it was declared that alliances of those people were eradicating the state laws and were being engaged in affairs that continuously created obstacles in the way of the state to attain highly needed political stability as well as a systematic progress in its economy as planned by the then Prime Minister Bangabandhu Sheikh Mujibur Rahman. Therefore, in response to the political trauma the declaration of emergency was done to stabilize the degrading condition of the economy.

Consequently, after 27 days of the proclamation of the emergency, on the 25th of January, 1975, the Constitution of Bangladesh went through the most remarkable and extreme change, which was the infamous Fourth Amendment Bill.

## The Major Ideas of the Amendment

Following are the most important changes introduced in the Constitution by the Fourth Amendment including their consequences and impact on Constitutionalism in Bangladesh—

## Introducing the Presidential System

The idea of the separation of power is a core component of the Presidential System. Unlike absolute separation of power, the separation must be balanced in the separation of power. In order to maintain this balance, checks and balances are to be structured so that it can retrain any organ of the government body from growing dictatorial and arbitrary. But the Presidential System that was established by the 4th Amendment was formed without consider any of the two crucial principles. In the actual Presidential System, ministers cannot be a parliament member as per the law of separation of power. However, the 4th Amendment provided the President with the power to appoint Ministers from inside or outside the Parliament [Art. 58(3)]. However, it has been argued that, this was done to accommodate leaders from outside the then current government party for a greater national political unity.

The second most essential element under this Amendment is that the President should be elected by the people in a direct election (Art. 48). So, the then new President was to be elected in a direct election under the Amendment. Bangabandhu Sheikh Mujibur Rahman was made the President by operation law, inserting a special provision in the Fourth Schedule. Following is the provision:

> (b) *Bangabandhu* Sheikh Mujibur Rahman, Father of the Nation, shall become, and enter upon the office of the President of Bangladesh and shall, as from such commencement *hold office as President of Bangladesh as if elected to that office under the Constitution as amended by this Act,*

Thirdly, it was essential to hold a new general election as the whole system was changed. But like the life of the President the life of the parliament was also given an auto-extension by operation of law. By the operation law, the life of the Parliament was extended automatically like that of the President. In the 4th Schedule, a special provision was made which reads:

> *Notwithstanding anything contained in the constitution, the parliament functioning immediately before the commencement of this. Act shall unless sooner dissolved by the President, stand dissolves in the expiration of the period of five years from such commencement.*

Thus, the lives of both, the President and the Parliament, were extended in a completely extra-ordinary manner.

## Amendment Made to Provisions to Remove or Impeach the President

Under the 4th Amendment, the number of votes required to impeach and remove of the President on the ground of physical or mental incapacity in both the cases of initiation of motion and passing the resolution was increased to two-thirds and three-fourths respectively which were previously done simply by a majority and two thirds (Art. 53 & 54). To make an amendment to the constitution, two-third of the majority was required whereas previously an impeachment or removal required three-fourth of the majority. It is to be mentioned here that in Pakistan Constitution of 1962 made by Ayub Khan, such a stringent procedure for the impeachment was introduced. The provision there was that to impeach the President, a resolution was needed to be moved by written notice of at least one-third of the total members and to be passed by not less than the three-fourth of the majority. Moreover, it was provided that if less than half of the total members of the National Assembly voted in support of the resolution, all the members opposing the resolution, will cease to be the members of the assembly. This was criticized by saying that, a stringent provision like that is usually made in a dictatorial system so that no one dares to raise any voice to remove or impeach the President.

> *Currently, this provision concerning the President as introduced by the 4th amendment is no longer in force. The 12th Amendment has reintroduced the provisions of the original Constitution of 1972.*[33]

## Limitation of the Legislature Power

The legislature was given the status of the supreme and sovereign law-making body in the original Constitution. It was the source of law and authority and the fountain of power sanctioned by the people. Though the President and his ministers are not responsible to the Parliament in a presidential system, the Parliament still holds strong checks and balances on the cabinet through relevant functional committees of the Parliament.

It is customary in every system that when a Bill is passed in the Parliament, it cannot be transformed into an enforceable law unless it is stated by the President or the head of the state. However, if the president is given the power of using absolute veto, a Bill opposed by the president cannot be passed or come into force. In democratic countries, for this specific reason, the veto power of the President is allowed either in a limited form (as in the USA under Art. 1 Sec. 7 of the US Constitution) or is completely abolished (as in the UK it is absolutely abolished by convention) so that the President cannot undertake any autocratic action.

In the original Constitution, it was provided that the President should assent to a Bill, within 15 days of the Bill being presented to him. He could also return the Bill to the Parliament to be reconsidered without giving assent. If the President failed to do so, the Bill would be considered to have duly assented by him on the expiration of the time period of 15 days. So, the original constitution of Bangladesh armed the President with suspense veto as opposed to absolute veto which was similar to the US Constitution.

Provision regarding veto that was introduced by the 4th Amendment is not in force. The provision of absolute veto eradicated deleted in 1978.

The interval between the two sessions of the Parliament was of 60 days in the original constitution. But the Second Amendment extended this period to 120 days and by the 4th Amendment, the provision was modified to the following: *'there shall be at least two sessions of parliament in every year'* (Art. 72).

This provision is not in force and that of the original Constitution has been revived.

Thirdly, according to the Article 70 of the original Constitution, a seat of a member of the Parliament needed to be vacated for two reasons—(i) if the person resigned from the party which had nominated him as a candidate; or (ii) if he voted against that party in the Parliament. In the 4th Amendment, an explanation to the meaning of 'voting in the parliament against the party' was inserted providing that even remaining absent from the Parliament session or abstaining oneself from voting ignoring the instruction of the party would be considered as voting against the party.

Fourthly, Article 76, under the original constitution, provided that the Parliament will appoint definite standing committees at the very first meeting of each session. This provision was removed in the 4th amendment. It decreased the importance of the Parliament even more because the Parliament was no more bound to appoint committees at the beginning, it now had the choice to pass away most of its time period without framing standing committees. These undemocratic provisions are still in existence.

## *Intervention in the Judiciary*

There was provision for 18 fundamental rights in the original Constitution of Bangladesh and the High Court Division of the Supreme Court was given the power to enforce these rights. Article 44 ensured the right to relocate the High Court Division of the Supreme Court and these rights could be enforced by this court under the authority of Article 102.

In the Constitution, those rights which were enumerated as fundamental rights was turned into a mere show then and it was nothing as the name suggests. As their enforcement now mostly depended on the implementation of an ordinary law, they were essentially transformed into ordinary rights although they were still termed as fundamental rights.[34]

Another issue regarding the nature and constitution of the Constitutional court or tribunal arose as it was not mentioned in the amended Constitution. Also, there were other issues like who would chair that court or tribunal and what would be their qualification etc. Thus, the body which was responsible to enforce the fundamental rights was not a constitutional body rather it was a forum to be formed by an ordinary law and like the department of Ombudsman, the Parliament was not constitutionally bound to construct and implement this forum immediately.

Article 102(1) was removed so that the High Court Division might not be able to raise any question or issue any direction or order regarding fundamental rights. Therefore, many suggests that as the sinister-looking aim was to strip away all fundamental rights from the jurisdiction of the Supreme Court, it is very much clear that the Constitutional court or tribunal stipulated in Article 44 of the Amendment would never remain an impartial body.

The abovementioned rights as mentioned in the Constitution were technically rendered barren. In almost all legal systems where there is constitutional supremacy, the Supreme Court is considered as the protector of constitutional rights. The role of a sentinel on the *qui vive* for fundamental rights which is the traditional jurisdiction of the Supreme Court was snapped away. Dismissing the jurisdiction of the Supreme Court to enforce constitutional rights is an unprecedented action in the history of the sub-continent.

This provision was removed and the democratic provision that was present in the original Constitution was restored by President Sayem on the 28th of May, 1978 by the 2nd Proclamation (Seventh Amendment) Order.

## *Appointment of Chief Justice and Intervention of the Judiciary*

It was provided in the original Constitution regarding the appointment procedure that the Chief Justice will be appointed by the President and the other judges will be appointed after consultation with the Chief Justice (Article 95). However, the provision of 'consultation with the Chief Justice' was withdrawn in the 4th Amendment. An unchecked nomination of judges like that by the executive is unrecognized in most democratic countries. To do so, an objective assessment by the Chief Justice or consultation with the Judiciary is a must so that men of acute intellect, high legal knowledge, integrity, and independence of judgment from among the lawyers can be taken to ensure two important things, independence and impartiality of the judiciary and development of the standard of the judicial review. But the 4th Amendment ignored resulting in making the higher judiciary completely subservient to the executive.

These undemocratic provisions are still in existence.

## Tenure

To maintain the independence of the judiciary, security of tenure is the most important condition. If the judges feel at risk while discharging impartial judgement, the independence of the judiciary cannot be retained. According to the provision in the original Constitution, a judge could not be abolished unless the Parliament passed a resolution approved by a majority of at least two-thirds of the total members of the Parliament on the ground of proven misbehaviour or incapacity [Art. 96(2)]. Therefore, the original Constitution had made provisions for absolute security of tenure and the judges were totally independent in discharging their duties. The provision of impeachment was deleted in the 4th Amendment and the amendment provided that the President was now empowered to remove a judge including even the Chief Justice simply issuing an order on the ground of misbehaviour (Art. 96). Now there was no need to provide any proof on the part of the President against the incapacity or misbehaviour, President's subjective intention became the ultimate power to remove a judge. Therefore, the President became both, the authority to appoint and remove the judges.

President Justice Sayem, on the 28th of May 1976, removed this provision and restored the provision of the original Constitution by issuing a proclamation. Later, President General Zia, on 22nd April, 1977, introduced the provision of Supreme Judicial Council. This provision is still in existence and it is a healthy provision regarding the security of tenure of judges.[35]

## Subordinate Courts

Regarding the appointments in the subordinate courts, it was provided in the original Constitution that—

Appointment of the district judges would be done by the recommendation of the Supreme Court.

Other judicial officers along with the Magistrates who exercise judicial functions would be appointed by the President after consultation with the Public Service Commission and the Supreme Court (Art. 115)

Again, it was provided that the control, including the power of promotion, posting and grant of leave, and discipline of the judges and the magistrates in the lower courts would be vested in the Supreme Court (Art. 116). Thus, the appointment process and security of tenure in subordinate judiciary, both were moderately democratic and healthy.

But the 4th Amendment made both the elements executive dependent in Article 115 and the amended to the effect that 'appointments of persons to offices in the judicial service or as Magistrates exercising judicial functions shall be made by the President in accordance with the rules made by him in that behalf.' Similarly, amendment with Article 16 was done to the effect that 'the control including the power of posting, promotion and grant of leave and discipline of people employed in the judicial service and Magistrates exercising judicial functions shall vest in the President.'

It is obvious from the above discussion that the whole judiciary now was under the total grip of the President. He now had the sole power to appoint and terminate the judges. "The whole judiciary which traditionally held a special position in every Constitution of the sub-continent as a basic organ for the functioning of rule of law was now made completely subservient to the executive." "The Amendment had reconstructed the entire institutional context of the judiciary which played crucial role in keeping a balance between the extremes of the executives and their victims and between law and its application for a long time. "The Amendment demolished the sanctity of the service as well as the institution of the judiciary itself. In the words of Justice Abdur Rahman Chowdhury", "if the government has the power to select judges suitable for itself, that will simply destroy the idea of the judicial system which is the last hope for the general people to rely upon against any unconstitutional law or arbitrary execution. We can conclude from our experience that while it is a need to inject justice into politics, it is completely a disaster to inject politics into justice. Once the Judiciary becomes subservient to the executive and to the governing party's ideology, any amount of enumeration of fundamental rights in the constitution will not be available to the citizens because the court of Justice would then be converted into the court of the government. The proverb—'If the salt has lost its savour wherewith shall it be salted' fits in this context. It can be understood in the light of the changes in the judiciary that it is totally illusory to say that everyone employed in the judicial services and all the Magistrates will be independent while exercising their judicial functions (Art. 116A)".

Regarding the control and discipline of the subordinate judges, the provisions introduced by the 4th Amendment were removed and instead another provision, 'in consultation with the Supreme Court,' which was provided by the original Constitution was resumed in 1978 by the Second Proclamation. It is needless to mention here that the provisions regarding adequate remuneration and privileges as indicated in Article 147(2) were kept unchanged.

### *Introduction of the One-Party Political System*

The provision for a single national party in the state was comparatively the most important and most bewildering aspect of the 4th Amendment. For this purpose, a new part **VI A** with a new article 117A was inserted in the Constitution.

According to this new arrangement, the formation of the National Party depended on the subjective satisfaction of the President.

In order to give full effect, it was provided that, to any of the fundamental principles of state policy as it was set out in part II of the Constitution, the President was vested with the power to—

> *Direct that there shall be only one political-party in the state. Once the President made an order for one party under Article 117A—*

i. *Necessary actions would be taken by the President to form the National Party and all the other political parties of the state would be dissolved.*
ii. *Everything ranging from the programme, nomenclature, membership organisation, finance, function and description of the National Party would be determined by the order of the President.*
iii. *After the formation of the National Party, every of the Parliament must join the party within a fixed time determined by the President.If they did not join, their seat would be considered as vacnt and they would not be considered as a member of Parliament*
iv. *If the National Party did not nominate a person as a candidate, s/he would not be qualified for election as a member of Parliament or as President.*
v. *Anyone, who is in the service of the Republic, will be qualified to get the membership of the National Party.*

Some features, which were looking cynical, began to emerge with the arrangement of incorporating the one-party system.[36]

1. The fundamental principles of state policy was made directly linked to the agenda of forming one National Party in the country. Though it remained the subjective satisfaction of the President to declare one National Party by abolishing all existing parties in the country, there was a condition that he had to justify the declaration of one party by stating that formation of one party was essential to give effect to any of the fundamental principles of state policy
2. All civil and military bureaucrats were now given the right to participate in politics given the fact that they worked for the cause of the nation.
3. By operation of the law, members were liable to lose their membership given the fact that they did not join the National Party even if they are directly elected by the people. Therefore, one man namely the President was vested with the power to demolish and trample people's aspiration and mandate.
4. The National Party could not completely be called a political party. As it retained an integral position as part of the Constitution, it served the purpose of the Constitution. Its declaration and organization were supposed to be publish through extra-ordinary gazette notification, therein, making it a part of the government.

### *The Spirit of Liberal Democracy in Bangladesh was Undermined in the 4th Amendment*

The emergence of the concept of political liberalism or liberal democracy can be traced back to the aftermath of the French Revolution and the American Declaration of Independence in 1776. The declaration of Rights of Man and Citizens in 1789 where it was said that the formation of the government must be followed by consent of the governed and the civil and political rights of the people must be preserved. These two things are the prerequisite of practicing Liberal democracy.

### *Final Thoughts on 4th Amendment*

The story of Bakshal and 4th Amendment covers a huge space to discuss the political context of our national history. As discussed above there are many criticism and misconceptions about this. From any ongoing political discussion, it has been historically overlooked that through 4th constitutional amendment, Bangabandhu Sheikh Mujibur Rahman merged most of the then political parties of the country with it for a greater political unity. Apart from the strong presidential government system, the newly introduced system has to be moved towards a more multifaceted reason. One of the notable features of this system was administrative decentralization. The country was divided into 61 districts for reconstruction. The head of each district was one governor each. They were appointed on July 16, 1975. Of the 61 governors, 33 were Members of Parliament, 13 were government servants, one was a military officer, and the remaining 14 were well known as individuals for various positive activities.

Justice M. Enayetur Rahim, Hon'ble Justice of the Appellate Division of the Supreme Court of Bangladesh has wrote in an article published in Daily Bangladesh Pratidin on 22 January, 2021 about the last day of the parliament life of the father of the nation Bangabandhu Sheikh Mujibur Rahman on January 25, 1975.[37] In his article he mentioned on that day, Bangabandhu as the Prime Minister and the Leader of Parliament changed the rule of the country by passing the Fourth Amendment Bill of the Constitution in the National Assembly. He very rightly mentioned in his article that the Bangladesh Kisan Shramik Awami League (Bakshal) was formed in an effort to create national unity for the economic liberation of the country. As per his article, Bangabandhu said in his last speech in Parliament about his move,

> *Effort is new, today I want to say—this is second revolution. This revolution means smiling at the faces of the sad people. This means that torture-injustice has to be stopped. Mr. Speaker, today we have to amend some parts of the Constitution. When the Constitution was passed, I said that this Constitution would be changed or amended if necessary, to establish an unexploited society for the economic liberation of the people of this country. Today, the new system that we are going to make in*

*Amended to the Constitution is also democracy. Democracy of the exploited. People will have the right to vote here. Here we want to do socialism. Here we want to have a democracy of the exploited. The seeds of communalism will never come to the soil of Bengal, I will not allow.*

Regarding the democracy of the exploited, Bangabandhu also said,

*One day I have said in this House that we want the democracy of the exploited. Those who loot money in the dark of the night, who are very wealthy people who get money to buy votes from abroad, are not democracy of the exploited. It's not about today -it's been a long time since we had to change our rule today. We have to build a society without exploitation. We are committed to this.*

Explaining what the democracy of the exploited is, Bangabandhu said,

*People have an idea and we have seen before that democracy works to protection capitalists in countries where democracy is seen and to protect the exploiters there. Democracy is used. We do not believe in that democracy. We want the democracy of the exploited and the democracy of the exploited to mean that the provision that are made in the rules of democracy in my country so that the poor people of this country get protection—there is no provision for those exploiters to get protection. That is why there is a difference between our democracy and others.*

From the point of self-realization about the fourth amendment to the Constitution, Bangabandhu further said in Parliament,

*I have not amended this Constitution in less sorrow, Mr. Speaker. Let no one think that those who have fought all their lives have taken away the right to vote of the people. If the people have asked for it, it is System here. In that, the members of parliament will be elected by the people. Whoever is president must also be elected by the people's vote. People have the right to vote.*

Most importantly, as explained in Mr. Justice Rahim's article that Bangabandhu called for national unity for the overall liberation of the people of the country as Bangabandhu said,

*I will therefore tell the people from the House, Mr. Speaker, through you, to all the people irrespective of party affiliation, who love the country, love four principle-nationalism, democracy, socialism and secularism -come and work. The door is open. I call upon all who believe in this. Let all those who believe in this way come and work and protect the country. Save the country, save people, remove the sufferings of the people. And overthrow the corrupt, the bribe-takers, the smugglers. Today we who are here, who are the representatives of the people, who have come here through the votes of the people, our duty is; irrespective of caste, religion, party affiliation, wherever the*

> *people of Bengal are from, today we will promise to start a new life. We will start a new revolution. So today we have to create a new life. And the stimulus must be created. People have to mobilize.*

Bangabandhu concluded his speech in Parliament by saying that,

> *Today you have amended the Constitution and made me president. I had no less power. You gave me all the power as Prime Minister. I won't sit in this seat again -it's no less sad for me. Don't be with you in this House -it's no less sad for me.*

Bangabandhu called upon all concerned and said,

> *If all of you come together with a new soul and a new mind and take god forward and criticize yourself, correct yourself, purify yourself and if Inshallah moves forward, they will do what you say to the people in Bengal. Inshallah, we shall be the successful.*

Therefore, from the above analysis and words of Bangabandhu during the time of making 4th amendment bill, despite having a lot of stereo type criticism, the intention of 4th amendment was mainly to give a new perspective to the then Bangladesh. Furthermore, this amendment was also a response to the then political reality and also making the constitution to people friendly in a sense to give the constitution a homegrown feeling rather an ideal and utopian constitution borrowed from developed country context.

## Notes

1 Collaborators and War Criminals, Bangladesh Genocide Archive.
2 Ibid.
3 Ibid.
4 *The Wall Street Journal*, 27 July 1971.
5 Collaborators and War Criminals, Bangladesh Genocide Archive.
6 *New York Times*, 30 July 1971.
7 Bangladesh war crimes trial: Key accused https://www.bbc.com/news/world-asia-20970123
8 https://www.bbc.com/news/world-asia-20970123
9 https://www.bbc.com/news/world-asia-20970123
10 https://www.bbc.com/news/world-asia-20970123
11 https://www.bbc.com/news/world-asia-20970123
12 https://www.bbc.com/news/world-asia-20970123
13 https://www.bbc.com/news/world-asia-20970123
14 https://www.bbc.com/news/world-asia-20970123
15 http://www.genocidebangladesh.org/collaborators-and-war-criminals/?cv=1
16 Ibid.
17 Preventive Detention, Lawyers and Jurists.
18 Md. Abdul Halim, Constitution, Constitutional Law and Politics: Bangladesh Perspective.
19 Preventive Detention and Violation of Human Rights: Bangladesh Perspective, Md. Nazir Ahmed.

20 Ibid.
21 Ibid.
22 Ibid.
23 Preventive Detention, Violation of Individual Human Rights: An Overview from Bangladesh Perspective.
24 Protocol to the Agreement between the Government of the Republic of India and the Government of the People's Republic of Bangladesh Concerning the Demarcation of the Land Boundary Between India and Bangladesh and Related Matters (adopted 16 May 1974, entered into force 6 June 2015) annex 1,2.
25 Ibid, annex 3.
26 Ibid, annex 4.
27 *The Daily Star Forum*, Volume 2, Issue 9, October 2007.
28 Subhashis Sen. ""Tin Bigha"—Where the People Live their Daily Life Is Complicated." *Proceedings of the Indian History Congress* 73 (2012): 1321–1328. <http://www.jstor.org/stable/44156333.> Accessed 27 July, 2020.
29 Protocol to the Agreement between the Government of the Republic of India and the Government of the People's Republic of Bangladesh Concerning the Demarcation of the Land Boundary between India and Bangladesh and Related Matters (adopted 16 May 1974, entered into force 6 June 2015) art 2.
30 *Prothom Alo*, 12 October 2011.
31 *BBC India*, 31 July 2015.
32 A. Ahmed (1998). Theory & Practice of Bangladesh Constitution. HA Publisher. Constitution, B. (1972). Ministry of Law and Parliamentary Affairs. Government of People's Republic of Bangladesh.
33 12th Amendment to the Constitution of the People's Republic of Bangladesh.
34 Ibid.
35 Ibid.
36 Constitution, B. (1972). Ministry of Law and Parliamentary Affairs. Government of People's Republic of Bangladesh.
37 The last day of Bangabandhu's parliamentary life https://www.bd-pratidin.com/amp/editorial/2021/01/22/610465?fbclid=IwAR2VDLAxlG7_EqZR9rmo6Fy-MHqGjGgyVEOsfhD2a_lIRtVX7HNQKlxAU7A visited on 19 July 2021.

# 4

# AGE OF THE MILITARY JUNTA (1975–1989)

## Fifth Amendment—Clean Slate

The father of the nation Bangabandhu Sheikh Mujibur Rahman the then President, along with his family members, was brutally killed on 15th August 1975 in a military coup led by a group of rogue army officers. It initiated first martial law regime in Bangladesh that remained in power till 6th April 1979. The Constitution was not abrogated though martial law was declared on 15 August 1975. It was made subordinate though it was the supreme law 'which allowed no means of martial law.' Proclamation and orders of various sorts made changes in the Constitution. All these changes to the Constitution were illegal from constitutional point of view as it was not allowed by the Constitution to make such amendments.

In 1979, the second parliamentary election was held where two-thirds majority was secured by the political party of General Zia who was the martial law administrator. On 1st April, the first session of the parliament was assembled and a constitutional Amendment Act (5th Amendment) was passed on 6th April to legalized every change made and everything that was done by the martial law government from the period between 15th August, 1975 and 9th April, 1979. The 4th Schedule to the Constitution was also amended by the Act that added a new paragraph 18 thereto which provisioned, inter alia, that all amendments, omissions, modifications, additions and substitutions brought in the constitution during the time frame of the 15th August, 1975 to the 9th April, 1979 by any Proclamation or Order of Proclamation of the Martial Law. It made sure that the authorities were made validly and they were confirmed and ratified and would not be subject to any question before any tribunal or court or authority under any circumstances. According to the wish of the Martial Law government, several amendments of the constitution were done by various Proclamation Orders and

DOI: 10.4324/9781003363002-4

four major Martial Law Proclamation. Constitution came to be a different one after the adoption of the 5th Amendment Act. However, it was not completely an uprooted one as it was initiated by the 4th Amendment.

## *Changes Made by the 5th Amendment*

The Proclamations (Amendment) Order 1977 and the Second Proclamation (15th Amendment) Order 1978 replaced many of the paragraphs in the Preamble and in various provisions of the original Constitution. These proclamations made changes in the first and second paragraph of the Preamble and in Articles 6, 8, 9, 10, 12, 25, 38, 42, and 142 of the Constitution. These changes were, subsequently, ratified under paragraph 3A and 18 to the fourth schedule by the enactment of the 5th Amendment. Among other things, the following important changes were made in the Constitution with the 5th Amendment.

## *Preamble*

The words, commas, and brackets 'BISMILLAH-AR-RAHMAN-AR-RAHIM' (In the name of Allah, the Beneficent, the Merciful) were inserted before the word 'PREAMBLE' by the above-mentioned order. In the first paragraph of the Preamble in the original Constitution, the words ***'a historic war for national independence'*** were substituted for the original words ***'a historic struggle for national liberation.'*** In the second paragraph of the Preamble in the original constitution, the words **'high ideals of absolute trust and faith in the Almighty Allah, nationalism, democracy and socialism meaning economic and social justice'** were substituted for the words **'high ideals of nationalism, socialism, democracy and secularism.'** Thus, one of the fundamental bases of our nationhood 'Secularism' was omitted from the Preamble and the meaning of 'Socialism' was also altered.

## *Article 6*

In the original Constitution, Article-6 contained the following words, '***Citizenship of Bangladesh shall be determined and regulated by law; Citizens of Bangladesh shall be known as Bangalees.***'

But the amended version of this Article was divided into two clauses-

1. ***The citizenship of Bangladesh shall be determined and regulated by law.***
2. ***The citizens of Bangladesh shall be known as Bangladeshies.***

Thus, the concept of 'Bangalee Nationalism' was transformed into 'Bangladeshi Nationalism.'

## *Article 8*

Like the second paragraph of the Preamble, the principle of absolute trust and faith in the Almighty Allah, nationalism, democracy and socialism meaning economic and social justice were incorporated in the Article-8 which were substituted for the original words '***the principle of nationalism, socialism, democracy and secularism***.'

## *Article 9*

Article 9 of the original Constitution, which dealt with the basis of Bangalee Nationalism, was repealed completely by the 5th Amendment and the substituted Article was in respect of local government which had no nexus with Bangalee Nationalism. Moreover, the provision of local government was already incorporated in the Article 59 and 60.

## *Article 10*

In Article 10 of the original Constitution, the words '***step shall be taken to ensure participation of women in all spheres of national life***' were substituted for the original words '**A socialist economic system shall be established with a view to ensuring the attainment of a just and egalitarian society, free from exploitation of men by men**.' This amended provision provides for participation of women in national life but this is already well provided for in Article 28, as such, this was unnecessary and this substituted provision has no nexus with the original provision which spelt out establishment of a Socialistic economic system and exploitation free society for Bangladesh.

## *Article 12*

Article 12 of the original Constitution contained the principle of Secularism in the following words,

> ***The principle of secularism shall be realized by the elimination of***
>
> a. ***Communalism in all its forms;***
> b. ***the granting by the state of political status in favor of any religion;***
> c. ***the abuse of religion for political purposes;***
> d. ***any discrimination against, or persecution of, persons practicing a particular religion.***

But this Article was totally deleted by the enactment of the 5th Amendment and thereby sought to change the secular character of the Republic of Bangladesh.

### *Article 25*

In the original Constitution, clause-2 of Article 25 was absent. But by the impugned Amendment clause-2 was inserted in the following words-

> ***The state shall endeavor to consolidate, preserve and strengthen fraternal relation among Muslim Countries based on Islamic Solidarity.***

This clause-2 is redundant. The original Article 25 itself provides for promotion of International peace, security, solidarity amongst all the nations including, of course, Muslim Countries in accordance with the charter of the United Nations.

### *Article 38*

The proviso of the Article 38 of the original Constitution had been omitted by the 5th Amendment contained that

> ***provided that No person shall have the right to form or be a member or otherwise taken part in the activities of any communal or other association or union which in the name or on the basis of any religion has for its object, or pursues, a political purpose.***

This proviso was meant to protect the secular character of the Republic of Bangladesh. But it was omitted to change the secular character.

### *Article 42*

Article 42 of the original Constitution dealt with the provisions of acquisition, nationalization, and requisition. But according to original Article, the acquisition or requisition can be made with or without compensation while the amended version of the Article stated that acquisition, nationalization or requisition can be made only with compensation. Furthermore, **a new paragraph being paragraph 3A was added to the fourth schedule of the Constitution in order to validate all actions taken thereon since August 15, 1975 till revocation of the proclamation and the withdrawal of the Martial Law.**

### *Article 142*

In the Article 142 of the original Constitution, clauses 1A, 1B, and 1C were inserted by the Second Proclamation Order, 1978 which provided a special procedure to be followed to amend the Preamble and provisions of Articles 8, 48, 56, 80, 90A when passed in the parliament and presented to the president for assent. '***The president shall within the period of 7 days after the bill is presented to him, caused to be referred to a referendum the question whether the bill should or***

***should not be assented to***,' and the referendum should be conducted by the election commission and if the majority of total votes cast are in favour of the bill, the president shall be deemed to have assent to the bill.

By amending the constitution within four years after the 15 August 1975, the fundamental principles of state policy were altered, destroyed the secular character of the constitution and allowed politics based on religion and provided political right to anti-liberation forces including Jamaat-e-Islami and war criminals that resulted in an alarming growth of political parties and organizations based on religion in Bangladesh since then.

Despite having these criticism, number of people would argue about the 5th Constitutional Amendment that, it opened the door of constitutionalism and liberal democracy by restoring multi-party democratic system as it was adopted in the original Constitution and by abolishing a dictatorial one-party system which was a permanent block to constitutionalism. By reverting Article 44 of the Constitution to its original form of 1972, all fundamental rights were enforced and given a full life though these rights remained nothing but meaningless versions of the Constitution before the reversion. Furthermore, the absolute veto power of the President, the undemocratic provisions which were introduced by the 4th Amendment, were abolished. Thus, in the matters of law making to be particular, the check and balance of democracy between the President and the parliament was restored.[1]

In regards to the composition of the parliament, the number of seats which were reserved for women was extended to 30 from 15. The period, for this provision to remain in force, was increased from 10 to 15 years. General Zia's Government managed to secure two-thirds majority in the parliament because of this provision. On the other hand, the spirit of representative government in Bangladesh was undermined by this provision, for these seats which were reserved for the women members in the parliament actually works as a balance of power but the ruling party of the parliament uses them as tools to meet their undemocratic political aims.

This Amendment introduced a new Article 145A regarding international treaties. It was mentioned that all international treaties must be submitted to the President who should cause them to be presented before parliament. However, there was a significant sub-clause that stated, 'no such treaty should be so laid if the President would consider it to be against the national interest.' This proviso armed the President with dictatorial power to make decisions regarding international treaties ignoring the consent of the Parliament as the power of the Parliament, in matters of international treaties, has been virtually curtailed by it, for it actually. In a true presidential system, the President is not vested with the power to make any treaty without the consent of the Parliament as it exists in the USA.

This Amendment paved the way to a new Article 92A and the parliament's power over the financial matter was curtailed and the President was empowered to draw money from the Consolidated Fund and to expend it without the approval of the Parliament. In a true presidential system like that of the USA, without the permission of the Congress, the US president has no power to expend even a penny from the public purse. 'This curtailment of the power of the legislature in matters of finance was, therefore, a serious setback in the evolution of constitutionalism and democracy in Bangladesh.'

'*Bismillahir Rahmanir Rahim,*' religious words of Islam, was included at the very beginning of the Constitution i.e., above the preamble. This was done mainly with a political end. It was a trick played constitutionally by General Zia to gain blind support from the majority of the people who are politically unconscious but very religious in their sentiments In the same manner, 'secularism,' one of four major fundamental principles of state policy, was omitted and principles of absolute trust and faith in the Almighty Allah were asserted in the place of 'secularism.' This was also done to achieve same effect like that of the former.

In the preamble the words, 'historic war for national independence' were asserted by replacing the word words 'historic struggle for national independence.' Thus, the spirit of the struggle against 24 years long Pakistani exploitation and colonialism, the role of cultural workers, intellectuals, teachers, students, professional groups and that of the common people along with the growth and role of political parties were ignored, undermined and concealed. The contribution of the army in 1971 liberation war brought into focus though the war was fought by the common people in most cases.[2]

## *Nature of the Governmental System after the 5th Amendment*

The above discussion makes it clear that the relations among different government institutions brought up by 4th amendment were modified by the 5th Amendment. However, it neither made the system democratic which could materialize constitutionalism nor it changed the basic structure of the constitution as it was introduced by the 4th Amendment. Also, it cannot be expected particularly from a military government who rises to the power in an illegitimate way. The modified governmental system after the 5th Amendment was neither a parliamentary system as it is practiced in the UK nor it was a presidential system as it is practiced in the USA. In addition to that, it was nothing like the presidential system like that of the France where the Prime Minister along with the cabinet members is collectively responsible to the Parliament.

The power of the President after the 5th Amendment was higher than the presidency power allowed by the French Constitution. The presidency was designed in such a way that it automatically allows all the devices to administer his dictatorship making it an all-powerful and one of a kind presidential system. Rather this model of presidency resembled that of Ayub Khan of Pakistan. The president was directly elected by the people for a period of five years and practiced executive authority. There was no limit to the number of terms in office. Impeachment procedure brought up by 4th Amendment was very complex and extremely difficult. Therefore, it was almost impossible to take away his office.

> *The amendment also did not reveal any of the extraordinary constitutional devices like emergency, ordinance making, preventive detention etc, through which the president was capable of exercising almost dictatorial power. The President was also the chief legislative initiator though his power to address and power of dissolution of parliament. Also, the power of the parliament was kept restricted in many important cases. General Zia's system was, therefore, neither a fully democratic responsible government; nor was it a one-party dictatorship as introduced by Mujib. It was a multi-party president system with a mix of democratic and autocratic features.*[3]

The year 1979 began with preparation for general elections to elect a Parliament that would work within a system of government in which the President would be an elective and omnipotent chief executive. The long-awaited parliamentary elections came on 18 February 1979. The parliamentary elections, originally scheduled for February 1977 had been postponed in the wake of the serious Ganges waters dispute with India, pressures on the border, a deteriorating law and order situation within the country and alleged indiscipline in the army.

However, with the easing of the law-and-order situation and the pressure on the border following Indira Gandhi's fall in March 1977, General Ziaur Rahman took over as President in April 1977 from Justice Sayem. With a massive victory (98.88%/confidence vote) in the 1977 referendum (30 May) and of the 3 June 1978 presidential election (76.63% of the votes) legitimized General Zia's capture of power, and the Farakka Agreement (November 1977) with India, the political situation appeared to be stabilized substantially. As a result, in November 1978, General Zia announced that parliamentary elections would be held on 27 January with the promise that the parliament would be sovereign, equipped with powers to enact and amend laws, and to approve the budget and agreements entered into with foreign countries. He also promised that the parliament would be able to amend the constitution, impeach or remove the president, and that the martial law would be with- drawn within a week of the new parliament's first meeting.

The opposition political parties reacted strongly to the government's election announcement. After a series of dialogues, 12 of the political parties decided to boycott the elections unless their five point demands-namely—withdrawal of martial law and restoration of fundamental rights, restoration of parliamentary democracy through repealing the Fourth Amendment, unconditional release of all political prisoners, General Zia's retirement from the army if he continued in politics, and restoration of press freedom-were not met.[4]

Supported and encouraged by the pro-election stand of some rightist and leftist political groups, President General Zia, through a series of 'concessions,' long 'parleys' with the opposition leaders, and deferring elections (in two installments) to 18 February, finally got the opposition to participate in the election. The result of the election was as discussed next.

**Election Results:** Of the total of 2125 candidates, 1709 belonging to 30 political parties and 416 independents contested 300 seats. None of the major parties could put up candidates for all 300 seats. There were three notable aspects of the elections. First, the formation of electoral alliances by the smaller parties: an extreme rightest alliance; the ideologically heterogeneous 'Bangladesh Gono Front'; and a leftist-centrist combine. Second, the nominations given by both the Awami League (Malek) and General Zia's Bangladesh National Party (BNP) consisted of a good number of retired army personnel to contest the elections. Third, since of clear-cut political issues-the BNP campaigned for Bangladeshi nationalism, a production-oriented democracy, a presidential form of government with a 'sovereign' Parliament whereas the AL (Malek) campaigned for the implementation of the programs of Mujib's 'second revolution,' the restoration of the 1972 constitution (prior to the 4th Amendment). Also, the leftists campaigned for the democracy of the people and the rightists campaigned for parliamentary democracy and social justice based on Islam.

In the elections, the BNP bagged 207 seats followed by 39 seats for the AL (Malek) and 20 seats for the rightist alliance. The remaining seats were won by the smaller parties and 16 independent candidates. The election eliminated a large number of little-known parties that had been hastily formed before the election while a number of political stalwarts also failed to win seats. All the ministers, in General Zia's cabinet, who contested were returned with convincing majorities. Inevitably, there were allegations of poll-rigging which was strongly denied by General Zia and his new government. The BNP's number of seats in the parliament was further swelled as 11 of the 16 independents joined the BNP before the first sitting of the Parliament, and as the BNP bagged all 30 'reserved' women's seats and won 4 by-elections.

The first session (27 April) was marked by altercations, walkouts, warnings from the chair, and frequent points of order, but it did accomplish some important tasks. The controversial 5th amendment to the constitution, validating all proclamations and martial law orders since 15 August 1975, was passed. It eventually paved the way to the withdrawal of martial law on 6 April 1979.[5]

Political leaders of different groups persistently tried to utilize the session in order to project their ideologies and programs. Veteran Muslim Leaguer Khan A. Sabur called for the designation of Bangladesh as an 'Islamic Rpublic,' with Islam as its political ideology. Mohammad Toaha tried to rationalize the role of his party during the 1971 Liberation War. The JSD leader Shahjahan Siraj and his party members repeatedly demanded the release of JSD political prisoners. Ataur Rahman Khan and Rashed Khan Menon confined their speeches mainly to the criticisms of the economic policy of the government. The second session (i.e., the first budget session of the second parliament) sat for 41 days from 21 May to 30 June. Unlike the first session, the budget session, even though marked by an unfortunate manhandling of a member of the lobby, sharp debates on the Rajshahi University campus incidents, the Farakka issue, the food crisis, and spiralling prices, was noted for better cooperation among the opposition groups in the Parliament.

On 31 May, all the opposition groups staged the first combined walkout as a mark of protest against the Deputy Speaker's 'indecorous' remark about the privileges of the opposition members. Furthermore, after a joint meeting of the opposition groups, they provided a joint statement condemning the remark and decided to boycott the sessions of Parliament when it is chaired by the Deputy Speaker. On the Farakka Agreement of 5 November 1977, Deputy Prime Minister Maudud Ahmed argued that the five-year 1977 agreement was an improvement upon the temporary India-Bangladesh Arrangement of 1975. But Shahjahan Siraj termed the Farakka issue as a political squeeze by India on Bangladesh. On one particular point, during the Farakka debate, both, the government party and opposition members were equally vocal in their total opposition to India's proposal for a canal through Bangladesh connecting the Brahmaputra with the Ganges.[6]

The 5th Amendment retained, intact, the provisions of the 4th Amendment with regard to the formation and position of the council of ministers. Moreover, it provided that certain parts of the constitution could be amended only through a referendum that, in the opposition's view, was tantamount to the Constitution of the People's Republic of Bangladesh. In a BBC interview in early 1979, General Zia said that a no-confidence vote by the Parliament would not remove the prime minister.

Above all, the provisions of the 5th amendment validating all proclamations and martial law orders (making some of them part of the constitution) since August 1975 and General Zia's induction of a good number of army personnel into top positions in many government and autonomous organizations led the opposition to characterize General Zia's system as 'martial democracy.' Two important steps, Civil and Army Bureaucracy in 1979, were taken by the government to reform the administration.

In March, the Senior Policy Pool, comprising 625 posts with the rank of Secretary, Additional Secretary, Joint Secretary, and Deputy Secretary, was instituted. In November, the government finally approved the new 14-cadre administrative setup of the Bangladesh Civil Service. All posts in administration and specialized service were now included in Bangladesh Civil Service. A special feature of the new system is that it would allow all 'civil servants' from all cadres to reach, through talent and efficiency, the top-most position within the Senior Service Pool, thereby eliminating the dominance of one cadre in administration.

However, the former officers of the Civil Service of Pakistan and of East Pakistan seem to be unhappy with both steps, as they see their privileged elitist position threatened. Moreover, they apprehended the induction of a large number of army personnel into the administration through the Senior Policy Pool system. Bureaucrats are already critical about the large number of army officers in top positions in mills, corporations, and government offices, and allege that most of these 'in- ducted' people lack administrative efficiency and are 'arrogant.'

The involvement of army officers in administration, however, is symptomatic of the general involvement of the military in politics since the 1975 coup that resulted in the death of Bangabandhu Sheikh Mujibur Rahman. Almost all the major parties in Bangladesh today include soldiers-turned-politicians. Over a dozen retired military officers are in parliament and General Zia's present cabinet contains six retired army personnel. The continued involvement of the army in Bangladesh politics on terms similar to those in Pakistan seems to be assured for quite some time.

General Zia called for a change in the social system through a new politics (i.e., peaceful revolution) to ensure consolidation of national independence, doubling of food production, and the exploitation of minerals, manpower, and other resources to ensure food, clothing, and education for all. He warned that if the 'Revolution' did not take place through peaceful and democratic means through parliament, it was bound to be a 'bloody' one. However, what was noted was the lack of specifics on the method with which to achieve the 'Revolution.' Rather, General Zia's repeated emphasis on landholding and land reforms caused uneasiness and tension in the BNP. The party became sharply divided on these issues and on the call for 'Revolution.'[7]

To some people, the effect of the stability purported to be upheld in the society. To some people, the move smacked of Bangabandhu Sheikh Mujib's 'Second Revolution'; to some it aimed at side-tracking the main issues of the country; to some it appeared to be a clever move by General Zia to expropriate the radical slogans of the ultra-leftists. Partly to oblige pressure from within the party and, perhaps, to allay the fears of investors, General Zia tended to modify his stand on 'Revolution' by the middle of November.

Ultimately General Zia's 'Revolution' was reduced to the excavation of canals and eradication of illiteracy, to be achieved in two phases-the first beginning in December and the second in February 1980. According to a top-level source, no bill on land re-form was likely to be placed before the Parliament during its January 1980 session. Drastic land reforms would adversely affect all MPs, whatever their party affiliations and General Zia appear poised to give them time to think it over. General Zia's 'Revolution' at the moment seemed to be another broader and more vigorous version of the 'Grow More Food' program or 'Green Revolution' of earlier governments, benefitting the large peasants more than the small farmers (or the landless people who constituted a substantial element of the population). Political factionalism, grouping, and regrouping the opposition were very common and the Bengalis are notoriously noted for over-politicization and squabbles among themselves.

They indulge enthusiastically in hair-splitting arguments and paradoxically often fall apart (or disunite) in their efforts to unite. Partly because of this and partly because of the subcontinental heritage of political factionalism, politics of Bangladesh in 1979 (as in 1978) saw intra-party schisms, new political grouping, and regrouping, with a new political party coming up every two or three months. The three electoral alliances formed to fight the parliamentary elections disintegrated soon after the elections. The Jatiyo Janata Party experienced a formal breakup in December 1978 because of differences of opinion between the party convenor General M. A. G. Osmany and a few influential members of the convening committee, particularly the (224 ASIAN SURVEY, Vol. XX, No. 2, February 1980) general secretary Ferdaus

Ahmed Qureshi. The NAP (Mozaffar) experienced two splits in less than a year. The CPB was reportedly facing a similar problem with widening differences between the party chairman Moni Singh and the party secretary Mohammad Farhad. The JSD faced a leadership crisis, with its leadership outside of jail allegedly in 'conclusion' with the General Zia government and at variance with the leaders in jail. The intra-group fighting of the JSD came out into the open when the cultural secretary Harunor Rashid was expelled from the party in August for his 'anti-social' and anti-party activities. Even after the exit of the anti-Baksal elements headed by Mizanur Rahman Chowdhury in August 1978, the AL (Malek) remained riddled with intra-party feuds. It was alleged that serious differences existed within the party among powerful factions led by Johra Tajuddin, Mohiuddin Ahmed, Abdur Razzak, Abdul Malek Ukil, Tofael, Korban Ali, and Asaduzzaman, and the Awami League may face yet another split after the next council meeting in March-April 1980. The AL (M) split after the next council meeting in March-April 1980. The AL's (M) problem is that t is being opposed both by the ruling BNP and the opposition parties, except for the pro-Moscow CPB and NAP (M). Although the Awami Leaguers sometimes feel baffled at the all-out attack against them, it perhaps also helps them to pacify restive groups within.

A border ground rules agreement was initiated by Bangladesh and India in July 1978 and a draft for an agreement on marking the boundary along the Naaf River with Myanmar was also finalized in early December 1979. The bitter Dacca-New Delhi relationship, following Bangabandhu Sheikh Mujib's assassination in 1975, began to improve with Indira Gandhi's fall in 1977. General Zia's visit to India in late 1977 and the signing of the Ganges Waters Agreement that year bored sign of that. The visit by Indian Prime Minister Morarji Desai, accompanied by Foreign Minister Vajpayee, to Dhaka in April 1979 was a further breakthrough in the renewal of neighbourly relations between the two countries. During Desai's visit, Dhaka and New Delhi agreed to set up committees, in addition to the high-powered Joint Rivers Commission, to work out a formula to prevent erosion along the Kushiara River and to share the waters of the Khowai and Teesta rivers. Deputy Premier Moudud Ahmed disclosed in May that0 the Commission had decided to set up a joint committee that would consider Dhaka's proposal to include Nepal in talks in order to find out ways to control the water supply in the Ganges, particularly in the lean period. During Desai's visit, through negotiations, India agreed to import more items from Bangladesh, including jute, timber, paper, naphtha, rayon, newsprint, pulses, and specialized textiles.

## *5th Amendment, Judicial Intervention and Politics*

In the 2000, the owner of the Moon Cinema Hall filed a writ petition under Article 102 of the Constitution being Writ Petition No. 6016 of 2000 claiming that the declaration of Moon Cinema Hall as an abandoned property was unlawful and sought a direction upon the government to hand over the physical possession of the premises known as Moon Cinema Hall at 11, Wiseghat, Dhaka to their original owners. In that writ petition, the petitioners challenged the constitutionality of the Fifth Amendment Act by which various proclamations of the Martial Law were condoned by Parliament in 6 April 1979. By a Judgment and Order dated 29th August 2005, a division bench of the High Court Division of the Supreme Court of Bangladesh comprised by Mr. Justice A.B.M. Khairul Haque And Mr. Justice A.T.M. Fazle Kabir declared the Fifth Amendment to the Constitution unlawful and directed the Government to hand over the physical possession of Moon Cinema Hall to its original owners.

Further, the High Court made the following 22-point[8] observations in its historical verdict that declared the fifth amendment to the constitution illegal:

1. Constitution of Bangladesh is the embodiment of the will of the people of the Republic of Bangladesh.
2. Constitution is the supreme law and all other laws and actions must confirm to it.
3. Any law or action made in violation of the constitution is void.
4. All functionaries of the republic owe its existence to the Constitution.
5. The legislature, the executive and the judiciary are the three pillars of the republic, created by the constitution, as such, are bound by its provisions.
6. Likewise, the defence services, the civil services, and all other services of the republic owe its existence to the constitution and must obey its commands.
7. Proclamation of emergency can only be made by the president of the republic on the advice of the prime minister, in case of imminent danger to the security of the republic.
8. No person can declare martial law; if anybody does, he will be liable for high treason against the republic.
9. Constitution stipulates a democratic republic, run by the elected representatives of the people of Bangladesh but any attempt by any person or group of persons, how high so ever, to usurp an elected government, shall render them liable for high treason.
10. The taking over of powers of the Government of People's Republic of Bangladesh with effect from the morning of 15 August 1975 by Khandaker Mustaque Ahmed, an usurper, placing Bangladesh under martial law and his assumption of the office of the president of Bangladesh on 20 August 1975, were in clear violation of the constitution, as such, illegal, without lawful authority and without jurisdiction, consequently all his subsequent actions as the president of Bangladesh were illegitimate and void.
11. The making over of the office of president of Bangladesh, in favour of Justice Abu Sadaat Mohammad Sayem, on 6 November 1975, was beyond the ambit of the constitution.
12. The taking over of the office of president of Bangladesh and his such entering in the said office on 6 November 1975, by Justice Abu Sadaat Mohammad Sayem and his assumption of the chief martial law administrator and appointment of the deputy chief martial law administrators and the

proclamation of 8 November 1975, were all in violation of the constitution, as such, all his subsequent functions and actions as such president and or the chief martial law administrator were illegitimate.

13. The handing over of the office of martial law administrator to Major General Ziaur Rahman BU, PSC, by the aforesaid Abu Sadaat Mohammad Sayem by the Third Proclamation on 29 November 1976, enabling the said Major General Ziaur Rahman to exercise all the powers of the chief martial law administrator being beyond the ambit of the constitution, was illegal, without lawful authority and without jurisdiction. Consequently, all his subsequent functions and actions as such (chief martial law administrator were illegitimate.
14. The nomination of Major General Ziaur Rahman, BU, to become the president of Bangladesh by Abu Sadaat Mohammad Sayem, the nominated president of Bangladesh, on 21 April 1977, and also the handing over of the office of president to him, being beyond the ambit of the constitution, was illegal, without lawful authority and without jurisdiction.
15. The assumption of office of the president of Bangladesh by Major General Ziaur Rahman, BU, on 21 April 1977, on nomination being beyond the ambit of the constitution was illegal, without any lawful authority. Consequently, all his subsequent functions and actions as such president of Bangladesh, without lawful authority and without Jurisdiction.
16. Since addition of Paragraph 3A to the fourth schedule to the constitution by the Proclamations (Amendment) Order 1977 (Proclamations Order No. 1 of 1977) dated 23 April 1977, and as amended by the Second Proclamation Order No. IV of 1978, was made by a usurper and a nominated president, the Paragraph 3A to the fourth schedule is illegal, void … in the eye of law.
17. The Referendum Order, 1977 (Martial Law Order No 1 of 1977) published on 1 May 1977, unknown to the constitution, being made only to ascertain the confidence of the people of Bangladesh in one person, namely, Major General Ziaur Rahman, BU.
18. Since Paragraph 18 to the fourth schedule (Transitional Provisions) of the constitution precluded judicial review defying and undermining the supremacy of the constitution, this provision is unconstitutional being beyond the power of parliament under Article 142 of the constitution.
19. MLRs including the MLR VII of 1977 are also illegal.
20. Violation of the constitution is a grave legal wrong and remains so for all time to come. It cannot be legitimized and shall remain illegitimate forever, however, on the necessity of the state only, such a legal wrong can be condoned in certain circumstances, invoking the doctrine of Salus Populiest suprema lex.
21. Condonation of certain acts and provisions has been made as stated above but such condonations are made not because those are legal but only in the interest of the republic, those shall remain illegitimate forever.
22. Condonations of provisions were made, among others, in respect of provisions, deleting the different provisions of Fourth Amendment. Condonation of provisions were also made in respect of the words 'Bismillah-hir-Rahmanir

> Rahim' but the provision deleting the original four fundamental principles of the republic as enshrined in the original constitution was not condoned

This judgment delivered by the High Court Division is well acceptance from everyone in Bangladesh as this judgment is the pure projection and reflection of people's rudimentary aspiration that they will no longer be in any subjugation or in the hands of the usurpers within an independent State. As General Ziaur Rahman, founder of the BNP, who amended the constitutions frequently by martial law proclamations and orders and destroyed some basic structures of the country's supreme law and it is the BNP that got majority in the second parliament in 1979 and passed the constitution's fifth amendment act ratifying and validating all actions and orders of the martial law regime led by General Ziaur Rahman, Khandaker Mushtaque Ahmed, and Justice Sayem.a Judge. Therefore, immediately after 5th Amandment Judgment by High Court, when BNP was in power, on the same day in Chamber of the Supreme Court stayed the operation of the judgment of the High Court upon an appeal filed by the Government. The present Government headed by Awami League came to power in January 2009 and the present government has decided not to continue the appeal any more, the Appellate Division has allowed filing of petition for leave to petition by the then Secretary General of BNP Khandker Delwar Hossain and other two interveners. Decision has been taken by the current government to discontinue the appeal and the Appellate Division, therefore, allowed petitions for leave to be filed by Khandker Delwar Hossain and other two interveners. The Appellate Division in February 2010 upheld the watershed verdict scrapping the constitution's fifth amendment that ratified and validated all actions, orders of the martial law regime in between 15 August 1975 and 9 April 1979.

> *The Appellate Division has upheld the High Court judgment, but will add some modifications and observations of its own. Following is what the HC said in its 2005 verdict.*[9]

Bangladesh is a Sovereign Democratic Republic, governed by the Government of laws and not of men.

The Constitution of Bangladesh being the embodiment of the will of the Sovereign People of the Republic of Bangladesh, is the supreme law and all other laws, actions and proceedings, must conform to it and any law or action or proceeding, in whatever form and manner, if made in violation of the Constitution, is *void and non est.*

The Legislature, the Executive and the Judiciary are the three pillars of the Republic, created by the Constitution, as such, are bound by its provisions. The Legislature makes the law, the Executive runs the government in accordance with law and the Judiciary ensures the enforcement of the provisions of the Constitution.

All Functionaries of the Republic and all services of the Republic, namely, Civil Service, Defence Services and all other services, owe its existence to the Constitution and must obey its edicts.

State of emergency can only be declared by the President of the Republic on the advice of the Prime Minister, in case of imminent danger to the security or economic life of the Republic.

The Constitution stipulates a democratic Republic, run by the elected representatives of the people of Bangladesh but any attempt by any person or group of persons, how high so ever, to usurp an elected government, shall render themselves liable for high treason.

A proclamation can only be issued to declare an existing law under the Constitution, but not for promulgating a new law or offence or for any other purpose.

There is no such law in Bangladesh as Martial Law and no such authority as Martial Law Authority, as such, if any person declares Martial Law, he will be liable for high treason against the Republic. Obedience to superior orders is itself no defence.

The taking over of the powers of the Government of the People's Republic of Bangladesh with effect from the morning of 15th August 1975, by Khandaker Mushtaque Ahmed, an usurper, placing Bangladesh under Martial Law and his assumption of the office of the President of Bangladesh, were in clear violation of the Constitution, as such, illegal, without lawful authority and without jurisdiction.

The nomination of Mr Justice Abusadat Mohammad Sayem, as the President of Bangladesh, on 6 November 1975, and his taking over of the office of President of Bangladesh and his assumption of the powers of the Chief Martial Law Administrator and his appointment of the Deputy Chief Martial Law Administrators by the Proclamation issued on 8 November 1975, were all in violation of the Constitution.

The handing over of the office of Martial Law Administrator to Major General Ziaur Rahman BU, PSC, by the aforesaid Justice Abusadat Mohammad Sayem, by the Third Proclamation issued on 29 November 1976, enabling the said Major General Ziaur Rahman, to exercise all the powers of the Chief Martial Law Administrator, was beyond the ambit of the Constitution.

The nomination of Major General Ziaur Rahman, BU to become the President of Bangladesh by Justice Abusadat Mohammad Sayem, the assumption of office of the President of Bangladesh by Major General Ziaur Rahman, BU, were without lawful authority and without jurisdiction.

The Referendum Order, 1977 (Martial Law Order No 1 of 1977), published in Bangladesh Gazette on 1st May, 1977, is unknown to the Constitution, being made only to ascertain the confidence of the people of Bangladesh in one person, namely, Major General Ziaur Rahman, BU.

All Proclamations, Martial Law Regulations and Martial Law Orders made during the period from 15 August 1975 to 9 April 1979, were illegal, void and *non est* because:

Those were made by persons without lawful authority, as such, without jurisdiction.

The constitution was made subordinate and subservient to those Proclamations, Martial Law Regulations and Martial Law Orders.

Those provisions disgraced the Constitution which is the embodiment of the will of the people of Bangladesh, as such, disgraced the people of Bangladesh also.

From 15 August 1975 to 7 April 1979, Bangladesh was ruled not by the representatives of the people but by the usurpers and dictators, as such, during the said period the people and their country, the Republic of Bangladesh, lost its sovereign republic character and was under the subjugation of the dictators.

From November 1975 to March 1979, Bangladesh was without any Parliament and was ruled by the dictators, as such, lost its democratic character for the said period.

The Proclamations etc., destroyed the basic character of the Constitution, such as, change of the secular character, negation of Bangalee nationalism, negation of Rule of law, ouster of the jurisdiction of Court, denial of those constitute seditious offence.

Paragraph 3A was illegal, firstly because it sought to validate the Proclamations, MLRs and MLOs which were illegal, and secondly, Paragraph 3A, made by the Proclamation Orders, as such, itself was void.

The Parliament may enact any law but subject to the Constitution. The Constitution (Fifth Amendment) Act, 1979 is ultra vires, because:

> Firstly, Section 2 of the Constitution (Fifth Amendment) Act, 1979, enacted Paragraph 18, for its insertion in the Fourth Schedule to the Constitution, in order to ratify, confirm and validate the Proclamations, MLRs and MLOs etc. during the period from August 15, 1975 to April 9, 1979. Since those Proclamations, MLRs, MLOs etc., were illegal and void, there were nothing for the Parliament to ratify, confirm and validate.
>
> Secondly, the Proclamations etc, being illegal and constituting offence, its ratification, confirmation and validation, by the Parliament were against common right and reason.
>
> Thirdly, the Constitution was made subordinate and subservient to the Proclamations etc.
>
> Fourthly, those Proclamations etc. destroyed its basic features.
>
> Fifthly, ratification, confirmation and validation do not come within the ambit of 'amendment' in Article 142 of the Constitution.
>
> Sixthly, lack of long title which is a mandatory condition for amendment, made the amendment void.
>
> Seventhly, The Fifth Amendment was made for a collateral purpose which constituted a fraud upon the People of Bangladesh and its Constitution.

The Fourth Schedule as envisaged under Article 150 is meant for transitional and temporary provisions, since Paragraph 3A and 18, were neither transitional nor temporary, the insertion of those paragraphs in the Fourth Schedule are beyond the ambit of Article 150 of the Constitution.

The turmoil or crisis in the country is no excuse for any violation of the Constitution or its deviation on any pretext. Such turmoil or crisis must be faced and quelled within the ambit of the Constitution and the laws made thereunder, by the concerned authorities, established under the law for such purpose.

Violation of the Constitution is a grave legal wrong and remains so for all time to come. It cannot be legitimised and shall remain illegitimate forever, however, on the necessity of the State only, such legal wrongs can be condoned in certain circumstances, invoking the maxims, Id quod Alias Non-Est Licitum, Necessitas Licitum Facit, salus populi est suprema lex, and salus republicate est suprema lex.

As such, all acts and things done and actions and proceedings taken during the period from 15 August 1975 to 9 April 1979, are condoned as past and closed transactions, but such condonations are made not because those are legal but only in the interest of the republic in order to avoid chaos and confusion in the society, although distantly apprehended, however, those remain illegitimate and void forever.

Condonations of provisions were made, among others, in respect of provisions, deleting the various provisions of the Fourth Amendment but no condonation of the provisions was allowed in respect of omission of any provision enshrined in the original Constitution. The Preamble, Article 6, 8, 9, 10, 12, 25, 38 and 142 remain as it was in the original Constitution. No condonation is allowed in respect of change of any of these provisions of the Constitution. Besides, Article 95, as amended by the Second Proclamation Order No IV of 1976, is declared valid and retained.

## *We further Declare*

i. The Constitution (Fifth Amendment) Act, 1979 (Act 1 of 1979) is declared illegal and void ab initio, subject to condonations of the provisions and actions taken thereon as mentioned above.
ii. The 'ratification and confirmation' of The Abandoned Properties (Supplementary Provisions) Regulation, 1977 (Martial Law Regulation No VII of 1977) and Proclamations (Amendment) Order, 1977 (Proclamation Order No 1 of 1977) with regard to insertion of Paragraph 3A to Fourth Schedule of the Constitution by Paragraph 18 of the Fourth Schedule of the Constitution added by the Constitution (Fifth Amendment) Act, 1979 (Act 1 of 1979), is declared to have been made without lawful authority and is of no legal effect.

We further direct the respondents to handover the physical possession Hall at 11, Wiseghat, Dhaka, in favour of the Petitioners, within 60 (Sixty) days from the date of receipt of the copy of this Judgment and Order.

In the result, the Rule is made absolute but without any order as to costs.

The Constitution of Bangladesh the symbol of the will of the Republic of Bangladesh. It is the supreme law of the land and all other laws, actions, proceedings must conform to it and any law or action or proceeding, in whatever form and manner, if made in violation of the Constitution, is void as per Article 7 that prevails Constitutional Supremacy. Therefore, under no circumstances, a parliament cannot legislate in any manner that actually infringes the supremacy of the Constitution as per Article 7 of our Constitution. It also cannot ratify, confirm or validate any act which is unconstitutional and which has destroyed the basic feature of the Constitution. However, the Martial Law Proclamation is in itself against the nature of the Constitution and when through this Proclamation any change is made in the constitution it puts double illegality. Therefore, a parliament cannot ratify such acts, it is not within their authority.

Most of the modern constitution has dynamic features to grow steadily over time in response to the demands of socio-political- economic life of the society and therefore, making changes in the constitution may be the demand of time. However, that changes cannot be done without the mandate of the Constitution. 5th Amendment was mainly politically motivated only to accommodate military regime headed by General Zia and his government. This amendment neither represent people's will nor constitutional mandate as a supreme law of the land.

The spirit and goals of the liberation war and the freedom struggle were wound up by issuing military decrees by General Zia. Later, the Fifth Amendment to the Constitution in the National Assembly sought to give constitutional and legal validity to that stratocracy and that was amount to fraud with the constitution, the people who own the state and the country as a whole.

It has been sadly observed that for a long time, the country's highest Courts and Judges have not been able to get out of the 'influence' and 'darkness' of that military rule and military decrees. In addition, the then Chief Justice of the country, Mr. Justice Abu Sadat Mohammad Sayem, failed to keep his oath and took over the post of the Chief Martial Law Administrator and President, questioning and tarnishing the image of the Supreme Court and Judges. However, on August 29, 2005, the High Court Division comprising with Mr. Justice ABM Khairul Haque and Mr. Justice ATM Fazle Kabir formed the *Bangladesh Italian Marble Works Ltd v. Government of Bangladesh.* In the case, the politically controversial Fifth Amendment to the Constitution, i.e., all military declarations, regulations and orders (from 15 August 1975 to 9 April 1979) were issued or enacted, declaring some provisions and actions to be illegal, ineffective, and non-existent.

Although thus case was influenced by the then BNP government at the time it was declared unconstitutional by the High Court Division. The then BNP Government had stayed the High Court's verdict by filing appeal and obtaining stay at the Appellate Division of the Supreme Court of Bangladesh mainly the patrons and conspirators tried to hinder the trial of Bangabandhu killing case. It is the shameful fact that for 21 years from 1975 to 1996, the course of justice was obstructed by the infamous indemnity ordinance protecting the assassins. The ordinance, decreed by the usurper regime of Khondokar Moshtaq in

September 1975, was incorporated in the constitution through the **Fifth Amendment** by the General Ziaur Rahman regime in 1979. This is such an extraordinary incident in the history of modern nation state where there has been there was deliberate closing of all avenues to justice. Until the Awami League government led by Sheikh Hasina repealed the black law in 1996 and brought Bangabandhu's assassins to trial. In November 1998, Bangabandhu's assassins were condemned to death. The processes unfortunately were not taken to a logical judicial conclusion. The delays, the frequent instances of judges feeling embarrassed to hear the appeals of the convicted and the clear, pathetic indifference of the BNP-Jamaat alliance government toward pursuing the case were to lead to a stalemate. Despite exhortations to reconstitute the bench by placing new judges there, the then government kept looking the other way.[10] However, in 2009 when Awami League again came to power finally the wheels of justice have rolled and finally Father of the Nation Bangabandhu Sheikh Mujibur Rahman killing cases' justice has been done. Subsequently the 5th Amendment to the constitution has been declared incantational by the Apex Court of the country. The Supreme Court of the country has not only set free from stigmatized the judiciary with that historic verdict in the Fifth Amendment case, but also tried to repay the blood debt of Father of the Nation Bangabandhu Sheikh Mujibur Rahman and millions of martyrs in the freedom struggle and liberation war.

## Sixth Amendment—Setting of a New Stage

In an unsuccessful army coup, President Zia was killed on 30 May 1981. Justice Abdus Sattar, the then Vice-President, took the role of Acting President of Bangladesh upon his death. According to Article 123 of the Constitution, any presidential vacancy caused by accidental death was to be filled within 180 days of the event by an election. In the election, BNP nominated acting President Sattar as a presidential candidate. However, regarding the process of Sattar's nomination, a constitutional problem arose because the Constitution prohibited any candidate who holds an office of Profit while contesting the election.

Article 50 states, Vice-President could be appointed by the President. Any person qualified for election as a member of parliament Under Article 66 (dd), a person would be disqualified to contest in an election though he might be qualified to be a member of the Parliament 'of parliament if he was holding an office of profit in the service of the Republic other than an office which is declared bylaw not to disqualify-such holders.'[11] However, there was no law which stated that the office of Vice-President did not count as an office of profit. On the other hand, under Article 66(2A), positions like—that of the Prime Minister, Deputy Prime Minister, Minister, Minister of State and Deputy Minister to hold an office of profit. It was, therefore, evident that the office of the -Vice-President counted as an office of profit and Sattar was debarred by this Sattar from contesting in the election.[12]

On 1 July 1981 a Bill namely the Sixth (Constitution Amendment) Bill was raised in the Parliament House to solve this problem. On 8th July, Sattar was eligible to contest in the election without withholding his position as the Bill was passed This Amendment created amendment of Articles 51 and 60 which exclude, inter alia, the office of President, Vice-President and Acting President free from being considered as an office of profit. Therefore, this amendment was launched to face a real situation.

## *The Constitution (Sixth Amendment) Act, 1981, Hereinafter Referred as Sixth Amendment Act*

**Brief Account:** The Sixth Amendment Act was enacted with a view to amending Articles 51 and 66 of the 1981 constitution.

| | |
|---|---|
| Actual Article | 51. President's immunity.<br>(1) Without prejudice to the provisions of article 52, the President shall not be answerable in any court for anything done or omitted by him in the exercise or purported exercise of the functions of this office, but this clause shall not prejudice the right of any person to take proceedings against the Government.<br>(2) During his term of office, no criminal proceedings whatsoever shall be instituted or continued against the President in, and no process for his arrest or imprisonment shall issue from, any court. |
| Amended Article | Following clauses were inserted by Section 2 of the Constitution (Sixth Amendment) Act, 1981:<br>'(4) If a Vice-President is elected as President, he shall be deemed to have vacated his office on the date on which he enters upon the office of President.<br>(5) If a President or a Vice-President is elected as a member of Parliament, he shall not be qualified to be such member until he ceases to hold office as President or Vice-President.<br>(6) If a member of Parliament is elected as President or appointed as Vice-President, he shall be deemed to have vacated his seat in Parliament on the date on which he enters upon his office as President or Vice-President.' |
| Actual Article | Article 66: (2A) For the purposes of this article a person shall not be deemed to hold an office of profit in the service of the Republic by reason only that he is a President, Prime Minister, Minister, Minister of State or Deputy Minister. |
| Amended Article | The words and commas 'he is a President, Prime Minister, Minister, Minister of State or Deputy Minister' were substituted for the words 'he is a Prime Minister' by section 3 of the Sixth Amendment Act 1981, thus stood as follows:<br>"Article 66: (2A) For the purposes of this article a person shall not be deemed to hold an office of profit in the service of the Republic by reason only that he is a Prime Minister."[13] |

Any constitutional amendment lies at the heart of constitutional theory and practice. Constitutionalism implies that the fundamental rules for the effective exercise of state power and the protection of individual human rights should be stable and predictable, and not subject to easy change. This is crucial to the legitimacy of the constitutional system. Furthermore, it is also necessary that any amendment in the constitution must be done in order to improve democratic governance or adjust to political, economic, and social transformations for the society as a whole. However, it appears that the 6th amendment to Bangladesh Constitution was mainly to accommodate one person or to make someone president of the country rather any significance changes for the society as a whole.

## Seventh Amendment—Resurgence of The Military Supremacy

The second military rule started after the death of the former president General Ziaur Rahman on 24 March 1982. General Hossain Mohammad Ershad took the power from Justice Abdur Sattar and continued the rule for four years. On 11th November 1986, he did the Seventh Amendment of the Constitution through passing the constitution Seventh Amendment Act 1986. In the fourth schedule, a new paragraph 19 was added where all other Proclamations, Proclamation Orders, Chief Martial Law Administrator's Orders, Martial Law Regulations, Martial Law Orders, Martial Law Instructions, Ordinances and all other laws made during the period between the 24th March 1982 and 11th November 1986 declared valid. Also, it would not be called in question in or before any court, tribunal or authority on any ground whatsoever. This amendment had not made major changes but with this validity it amended Article 96 where the age of the Supreme Court judges was increased from 62 to 65 years.[14] This amendment gave the validity of all actions of military regime from 1982 to 1986.

### *Factors Determining the Seventh Amendment*

The Chief of the Army Hossain Mohammad Ershad took the power through a bloodless coup on 24 March 1982 and started military rule for the second time in Bangladesh after General Zia. He suspended the Constitution and dissolved the Parliament. He continued the military rule more than four years. Within this time, he realized in future, if there is another government comes then the situation would not like this. His ruling time would be questioned. That is the major reason he decided to give validity to his regime through the constitution amendment. Also, he had an example of his predecessor General Ziaur Rahman who did the same thing and gained a huge popularity through forming a political party. Hossain Mohammad Ershad need not be changed much because the structure given by General Ziaur Rahman regime left in a way which helped him continuation of power through very limited controlled democracy in this country.[15]

At the time of passing the seventh amendment, it needed two third majority of the parliament but the people of the opposition parties oppose in various forms of actions in that time. As a result, they boycotted the parliament session. The President Hossain Mohammad Ershad understood the situation and for passing the seventh amendment he made hostage of the parliament. He threatened the oppositions by saying that if the parliament did not give validity to the actions of military regime then again, the martial law would continue for unspecified period.[16]

## *Validity of The Regime in The View of Kelsenian or Doctrine of Necessity*

It is said that many people try to see the validity of the Seventh Amendment through the doctrine of necessity or Kelsenian Theory. These are referring to a situation when the action taken by the military would be valid if the total order is efficacious and necessary at the time. There are many examples in the world when the doctrine of necessity is applied. Pakistan is known for military rule and it is an exemplary of giving legalization based on this doctrine. In Pakistan, once Ayub Khan got the power through a military coup from the president of that time Iskandar Mirza, the court gave validation to that regime under the doctrine of necessity. It is said in the case State v. DOSSO that

> If the revolution is victorious in the sense that the persons assuming power under the change can successfully require the inhabitants of the country to conform to the new regime, then the revolution itself becomes a law creating fact because thereafter its own legality is judged not in reference to the annulled constitution but by reference to its own success.[17]

In this view, the military rule of Ershad could be considered legal and there is no wrong to give validation through the constitution. The constitution gave just recognition to the validity of the action but the questions arose why the amendment did not discuss about the doctrine of necessity or Kelsenian theory and was the country really in a serious situation where the military intervention was necessary?[18]

The military took the power by saying that the economy of the country was in a very bad situation, corruption spread in the all levels, administrations are ineffective, law and order are not working. All of these situations were existing in the country where the stability of people's life and peace was in danger. So, it was necessary for them to take control of the government to bring back the stability of the country. In reality, the situation got normal and the military need not use any arm power to make the situation better. The whole condition became so normal that the military did not have the necessity to stay any more. Also, the power should have been transferred to the elected representatives of the people. It can be said, upon considering the situation, that the doctrine of necessity did not go with the military rule of Ershad regime. For the fear of future problems and greed of power, it passed the Seventh Amendment.[19]

## Economic Expectation after the Amendment

There were several expectations from Ershad regime. After legalization of all the conducts of the military regime, it was clear that he wanted to stay in the power for an extended period. Also, he got support from a great number of people by that time. There were many expectations considering the problems of the nation and also the Seventh Amendment showed sign to the ordinary people that Ershad would stay in the power, therefore, people were expecting many things from him. At that time, the economic crisis was a big problem and for that, there were many donors like World Bank and IMF who came forward. They gave many corrective measures like currency devaluation, anti-inflationary policy for reducing the growth of money supply and spending while increasing revenues. Also, it suggested to trade liberalization and privatization by eliminating public sectors. In the fiscal year of 1985–1986, total 83.56 billion money was distributed to some limited private entrepreneurs for investment and among this 56% of money came from bank credit for investment but unfortunately about 20 billion remained unpaid of this loan. The Shilpa Kala Bank was left with 6.7-billion-dollar loan due to private industrialization. The amount was approximately 98% of the total unpaid loan of the bank till June 1986. The living cost and unemployment rate increased because of trade deficit, poor economic growth and inflation of the economy.[20] By 1990 to 1991, the living cost came to, on average, 1600 taka which was more than the previous decades. On the other side, in 1986, the public fixed industrial asset came into 40% which was 85% in 1981.[21]

The government was dependent on foreign aid. The whole development part of the budget was fully dependent on foreign aid in 1990–1991. In the other sectors, resources were frustrating and declining where the administration and military expenses were uncheckable. It was surprising that the defence expense was the highest amount comprising of 16.25 billion of the budgets of 1990–1991. In this situation, the government could not succeed to keep the promise to the aid institutions which had been given in 1985 that the loan recovery rate would improve to 50%. The economic situation would not be like this if the aid was distributed or used in proper sectors. It had been seen that the government gave priority of giving loans to those people who were political allies and close to the government. The reasons, for giving less priority to the economically important sectors, were more political. The government needed to make military, bureaucracy, and other pro- government institutions happy.[22]

At this situation, the lending institutions were not willing to continue their activities in this country and as a result, the economy of Bangladesh fell into a crisis. The economy of Ershad regime benefitted only some particular group of people but the ordinary people who were majority in numbers remained victims.

The 7th amendment was challenged at the High Court Division of the Supreme Court o9f Bangladesh and was declared unconstitutional in ***Siddique Ahmed vs Bangladesh*** **(65 DLR AD 2013)** by the Appellate Division.

## *Factors That Determined The Case*

In 1984, a person named Abu Taher was murdered and Mr. Siddique Ahmed, who was also the petitioner of this writ, was arrested. Later on, two other persons, along with him, were charged with section 302 of the penal code in the murder case. The case was transferred to the special martial law court No -3, Zone –c, Cantonment Bazar, Chittagong. The case was renamed as martial law case and the trial proceeded against them in absentia which means that the accused was not present in the court at the time of their trial and the court continues the proceeding with his absence. The court found them as convicts in absentia, declared their imprisonment for lifetime and fined one thousand Taka for each of them.[23] On a review, the conviction was affirmed and the Chief Martial Law Administrator confirmed the sentence in 1986. Then, after a long period, the petitioner of the writ was arrested in 2006. After that, the police sent him to the Court of the Metropolitan Magistrate, Chittagong. The Magistrate sent him to jail and forwarded the relevant records to the Court of Sessions. The Session Judge issued the warrant of conviction against Mr. Siddique. Being aggrieved, he filed a writ petition by challenging the conviction and the vires of the constitution as it legalizes the proclamation of martial law, rules, regulation, and other proclamations through the Seventh Amendment Act 1986.

In this case the petitioner argued that as the Constitution is the supreme Law of Bangladesh, the impugned Martial Law had got no place in our jurisprudence. Therefore, all the proclamations, rules, orders, and notifications promulgated under the Martial Law Proclamation were void ab initio and thus, all the Martial law courts were not legal and all the proceedings before those courts and tribunals were *coram non judice.* Subsequently all the verdicts pronounced by those courts and tribunals were *non est* in the eye of Law. Mr. M. Aminul Islam as an intervener of this case submitted that *Principle of Condonation* would be unnecessary and dangerous in this case. Mr. Rafiqul Haque as an *amicus curie* submitted that the condonation of the past and closed transactions should not be absolute rather it should be proportional to the necessity according to the doctrine of necessity.

The Hono'ble Court had declared that the Section 03 of the Constitution Seventh Amendment Act, 1986 is void. The Trial and Conviction of the Appellant writ petitioner by the Special Martial Law Court is declared illegal and void. The case was ordered to continue from the stage it was transferred from the court of sessions. This decision hjas been taken on the following grounds:

> The Constitution cannot be violated on any excuse and its violation is the gravest of all the offences and remains illegal for all time to come;

> Under Article 150 the temporary provisions only for the period from the date of declaration of independence on 26th March, 1971 to 16th December, 1972 are set out in the Fourth Schedule. No other provision can be inserted after the time. Therefore, Paragraph 19 which has illegally added in the Fourth Schedule is declared void and *non est*;
>
> If a valid amendment is made in the Constitution it may find its place in the Constitution but must not be included in the Fourth Schedule;
>
> The proclamation of Martial Law is not only in clear violation but also in destruction of the Constitution. Therefore, it is absolutely illegal and *void ab initio*;
>
> The Constitution covenants a democratic People's Republic of Bangladesh to be governed by a sovereign people through elected Representatives. Thus, any person who declares Martial Law and ousts an elected Government or attempts to do so he and his associates would be liable for high treason against the Republic of Bangladesh;
>
> Usual past acts and conducts are condoned on the maxim *Salus Populi Est Suprema Lex*. *Salus populi* gets supreme *lex* but not the usurpers and violators of the Constitution. Therefore, no *condonation* is allowed for Martial Law proclamations;

High Court Division may exercise its extraordinary powers under Article 102 of our Constitution if equally efficacious remedy is not available but bail is not available in certiorari.

## *Adoption of Political Ideology in the Judgment*

The Chief Justice A.B.M Khairul Haque has written both the judgments of Seventh Amendment and the Fifth Amendment case. In this judgment, Justice Khairul Haque relied on his Fifth Amendment case judgment and referred to it in many paragraphs. Questions were thrown at a historically important and controversial amendment of a constitution which has a big impact on future and also has influence to develop constitutional jurisprudence. If this case was like other ordinary cases then the impartiality of the judgment might not arise any question but here the scenario is different.[24] In the judgment, it said that this country got a good constitution in 1972 and then it went to the matter of killing Bangabandhu Sheikh Mujibur Rahman. Here the noticeable thing that it had not talked about was the misrules and controversial things happened before the time of Bangabandhu's death. As it discussed the political things of that period, so it should have also considered other things as well.[25] The political biasness again can be smelled when we saw a writ petition was pending at that time in the HCD division which challenged the legality of the second amendment but the amendment gave recognition of validation by this judgment.[26]

The judgment transferred the burden of responsibility from democratic to military leadership. It cannot be denied that it was the failure of democratic leadership to frame the country in a constructive way and that is the reason the military people got the courage to take over the power and inserted illegal ways of ruling in the constitution.[27] As we know that Mr. Khairul Haque was the author of Fifth, Seventh, Thirteen Amendment and declaration of independence judgment, so naturally the neutrality and the role of politics in the judiciary could easily be understood. It has been seen that he was elevated to the Appellate Division where there were other senior judges and also the same thing happened at the time of his appointment as Chief Justice. Even after his retirement, he was serving the law commission which made people bound to think the political influence over the judgment.[28] However, all these judgments were very important and relevant with the constitutionalism of ours country.[29]

In the judgment, two things were specially discussed namely the doctrine of condonation and the doctrine of past and closed transactions. The judgment invoked confusion and contradictory opinion about the condonation and past closed transactions. It is said that from 24 March 1982 to 11 November 1986, all other proclamations and proclamation orders, chief martial law administrator's orders, martial law regulations, martial law orders, martial law instructions, ordinances along with the proclamation and other subsequent acts are illegal or *void ab intio*. Then again it is said that the same thing along with the term are condoned but these are condoned provisionally. It means that the judgment allows the door open for people to challenge the transaction that happened during that time. Again, it is self-contradictory because it condones all day-to-day functions, orders, and other things but creates confusion by saying that 'there shall be no condonation with regard to ordinances passed during the regime.' The confusion and self-contradictory nature of the judgment remain and if the void and illegal part of the judgment is considered about that regime then all the activities in the state are illegal from the time of military government of year 1982 after passing the judgment.[30] The national budgets, state functions, international agreement, judge's power, collection of income tax, special security force for the protection of the President and Prime Minister became illegal as they were not condoned.[31] The government has also given importance to this part of confusion when we saw that it adopted a new law to give validation or retro prospective effect to the actions taken at that period for the interest of the people. The Parliament passed Act No. 7 of 2013 which said, in section 4, that all scheduled Ordinances, other ordinary laws and ordinances amended by any such ordinances promulgated before this amendment or happened between 24th March 1982 and 11th November 1986 shall remain effective in such a way as if they have been enacted by the parliament itself.[32] This again throws a question that whether the Parliament is capable to do such thing by following the constitution and the judgment or not. It is because, in Article 93(2), the constitution did not permit patronage to the ordinances in the same way as the previous Military rulers did.[33] This legal vacuum would not arise if the court cleared this on its judgment and the government would not have fallen under this embarrassing situation. The court cannot deny this negligence and again come under a responsibility to declare this act illegal as it goes against the operative part of the judgment and as well as Article 93(2) of the constitution.[34]

The court should have dealt with the matter which has been taken before the court. In this writ petition, the issue was whether paragraph 19 added by Seventh Amendment should be declared legal or illegal. It is an accepted principle that a court cannot deal with an issue which has not come before it. It is also against the principle of natural justice because the non-issue matter does not get chance to oppose defence. It is not clear that how the contents of paragraphs 21 and 22 of the 4th Schedule have been deleted illegally without issuing rule on the validity of these paragraphs and also through a question that is whether the Supreme Court itself is the creator of the Constitution or has any power or authority to declare any part of the Constitution unconstitutional on the basis of Suo moto.

As much as we say that the judiciary is independent and free to make its own decisions, in reality, politics has significant influence over the judiciary. At the time of Ershad rule, the existing judges were not able to declare that period illegal, rather than that they had accepted it as such, the government, their politics and agendas always have a huge impact on the judgments of the courts.

## Eight Amendment—Islamization of the Constitution

H.M. Ershad, Former President of Bangladesh, had been an unpredictable political leader throughout his political career. However, he has immensely contributed in amending the Constitution of Bangladesh especially in the 8th amendment. Also, he has utilized his political prudence on the politics and governance of the country for near a decade. Therefore, his military regime and his activities brought massive changes to the country in different spheres. On the other hand, his period has been criticized by the critics. In a similar vein, he dictated the course of politics often. Hence, he is known as a dictator.

On a different note, he has subsidized in political, administrative, judicial and economic changes of Bangladesh.

### *Political Background in Ershad's Regime*

Ershad's government was a military dictatorship govt. However, he wanted to move it to a civilian government with the collaboration of the political opposition at that time. When he was in power, his program called for local elections at the union and sub-district levels, followed by presidential and parliamentary elections. Initially, he banned the political activities. However, he made the ban stress-free on political activities in January 1984. After that he again called for dialogue with opposition parties. The major opposition associations refused to cooperate while martial law remained in effect. Despite of the political non-cooperation, the government had held the elections for union and municipal councils between December 1983 and February 1984. At that time, a rising crescendo of violence and civil disobedience was noticeable. As a result, Ershad did reimpose harsh martial law restrictions in March 1985 and had arrested the main opposition leaders such as Hasina, Khaleda Zia, and others. In November 1983, a government-sponsored party, Jana Dal (People's Party) was created.

## Political Settlement/Condition

These growth episodes need to be politically divided into two broader phases: the dictatorial/quasi-dictatorial rule of General Ershad (1983–90); and the vulnerable democratic transition period (1991–2010), characterized by illiberalism and zero-sum elite conflicts, consequently showing little signs of the democratic process being consolidated.[35] The first phase again can be divided into two distinct political stages: military dictatorship/vulnerable authoritarianism (1983–6); and dominant party rule (1986–90). The first stage undid the relative democratic progress that citizens enjoyed under the later stage of the BNP regime, but this form of political governance (constrained pluralism under dominant party rule) was largely restored in the second political stage.[36]

## Administrative Changes

While Ershad was in power, he shaped many changes in the country's political character and governance. A significant modification has been made in the administrative structure of the country with the introduction of the *Upazila* system, which among other things attempted to allow a bottom-up approach to development planning rather than a top-down one. The system was strongly opposed by the BNP.

## Decentralize Local Administration

Most of the times in his political career, he had been criticized by the critics. However, due to his contribution in the local government system, he came to be fondly known as 'Pallibandhu' by his admirers. It is noteworthy to mention that in 1984, Ershad introduced *Upazila* system in the country in order to decentralize local administration at grassroots level. He extended the national highway system and increased number of districts to 64.

## Socio Background and State religion

By analysing the history, it has been observed that to gain popularity and to stay in power, Ershad used religion as a tramp card! Most of the citizens of our country are Muslims. Therefore, he thought that it could not be a better idea making the state religion Islam. Hence, General Ershad amended the Constitution and inserted Islam as the state religion. In this regard, Ershad tried to reflect the choice and views of Muslim majority in Bangladesh by revising the situation through Islamization. Gradually, the amendment divided the countrymen into majority and minority. Hence, it can be said that it was one of the reasons that destroyed the communal harmony in the country.

## *Appeasing the Anti-Liberation Forces*

It is assumed that he did this to appease the anti-liberation forces and particularly to ensure their support for his autocratic and unconstitutional government.

On top of that, the scholars argue that Ershad played on the sentiments of the majority and made Islam the state religion. Interestingly, it is observed that none of the two ruling parties have changed that status since 1991. Therefore, the principle of secularism might be contradictory in this age too!

## *Judicial Background*

*'In the 8th amendment, the legislative body made changes in **Article 100 of Bangladesh constitution decentralizing the judiciary by setting up six permanent benches of the High Court Division outside Dhaka**. However, that amendment was challenged by Mr Anwar Hussain, vide a Writ petition'*[37] *which eventually reached to the appellate division of Bangladesh Supreme Court and finally, the court recognized article 100 of the Bangladesh Constitution is unconstitutional. It was impossible because it was contradictory with the Basic Structure.'*

## *Law Zones*

While Ershad was a chief martial law administrator, he separated the country into five martial law zones; each zone was headed by a senior army officer. At that time, there were 24 special and summary martial law courts which directly involved the military in local administration. Although the civilian court system was about to function but the violations of martial law ordinances were handled by these extra-constitutional martial law tribunals. It is noted that the active-duty military officers had been given immunity through meeting in secret sessions to try cases of violations. However, those convicted of political crimes had no right of appeal, and defendants were tried in absentia. Martial law had been an obstacle against the jurisdiction of the Supreme Court regarding the protection of fundamental rights, and criticism of martial law was punishable by up to seven years' imprisonment. He stimulated compulsorily to end corruption and reorganize the government. So, many politicians, including six former cabinet ministers, had been sent to jail on charges of corruption.

## *The Role in Making Local Administration Organized*

During his tenure, the local administration was unorganized. Therefore, he determined to organize the local administration. In a similar fashion, he appointed the Committee for Administrative Reorganization/Reforms, which introduced comprehensive changes in local administration. The Land Reforms Ordinance of 1984 approved the important rights to tenants for the first time in the history of Bangladesh.

## *The Reasons of Introducing Upazila System in 1984*

Some quarters tend to give credit to Ershad for introducing the *Upazila* system (1984) in the country and thereby promoting the process of decentralization.[38] But it must be mentioned that he did not introduce the system for the benefit of the country, but rather, he wanted to create a political support base for himself and his party at the *Upazila* level with newly elected chairmen who were mostly from the Jatiyo Party which he headed.[39] Through this created political support base, Ershad wanted to perpetuate his autocratic rule for many more years.[40]

## *Economic Policy/Condition on Ershad's Period*

> *During his tenure the overall structure of the Bangladesh economy has experienced a significant transformation over the past four decades. Liberalization of trade during the 1980s and 1990s, and associated economic reforms, led to large growth in import penetration and export orientation in Bangladesh.*[41] *The import penetration ratio (the ratio of import to GDP) was only about 12% during the early 1970s, and has increased to more than 30% in recent years.*[42] *Extensive export promotion measures and favorable market access in the European Union and USA have helped Bangladesh's exports rise remarkably during the past forty years.*[43] *The export orientation ratio (the ratio of exports to GDP) rose significantly, from only 6.5% in the early 1970s to more than 23% in recent years.*[44]

## *Deals Environment/Business Condition*

> *During the regime of Ershad, which largely overlapped with the second growth phase (1983–96), closed but ordered deals can be observed to cover a diverse set of economic activities—granting of licenses and permits for export and import, and large construction projects, but not necessarily setting up of industries.*[45] *A milestone initiative in the modernization of the economy—the establishment of the first telecommunications (mobile phone) business in the private sector—was done through a closed deal, owned by a senior member of Ershad's cabinet, which continued to function as a monopolist under his rule.*[46]

## *Ershad's Economic System*

> *It was Ershad who created the culture of private gain as patronage came to dominate the political and economic system.*[47] *Under Ershad, state power was used to accumulate private wealth, including his own. Ershad centralized power in his own hands, personally reviewed a large number of files, and Ershad's Presidential*

*Secretariat in the words of one observer 'sounded like a brokerage house with calls requesting the status of a contract, an import license, or a bank loan.'*[48]

## A Blueprint by the Oppositions regarding Step down of Ershad

In June 1987, a bill on 'District Council Amendment' has been passed. As a result, public protests arranged by the opposition alliances started against the five-party alliance in Dhaka on 23 June. Ershad's immediate resignation and new elections under a caretaker government was demanded by the opposition parties. On 24 July, Bangladesh observed the longest general strike in its history, a stirke of 54 hours led by the Workers-Employees United Council (Sramik Karmachari Oikkiya Parishad). The strike ended after 11 people were brutally killed and 700 more were injured in street violence between security forces and demonstrators. In October, another lengthy strike was organized by the Workers-Employees United Council, which lasted for 48 hours before ending on 21 October.

## Hasina-Khaleda Cooperation

On 28 October, Sheikh Hasina and Begum Khaleda Zia, the leaders of the then opposition parties, met that signalled a coalition between the two-leading oppositions. To coordinate the moves of the opposition, a liaison committee of the eight, seven, and five-party alliances was formed. Known as the Siege of Dhaka, the 'final showdown,' was arranged between 10 and 12 November, when the opposition parties brought thousands of supporters into the streets. However, the regime was well prepared for such kind of occurrences. Therefore, it lead to the detention of Shaikh Hasina, Khaleda Zia, and other leaders. Moreover, the regime sent thousands of security personnel in urban areas to control any protest or demonstrations.

## State Emergency Declared by Ershad

In order to a return to normal state of affair throughout the country, Ershad was compelled to declare a state of emergency, with familiar restrictions on civil rights, on 27 November. Though the tactics of the opposition parties had shaken the government to an extent, civil disobedience and but street violence proved unable to dislodge Ershad's regime.

## Dissolvent of Parliament

The Parliament was dissolved by Ershad on December 6, 1987. According to the Constitution, a new election was required to be arranged by him within 90 days. The elections of the union councils and the municipal officials in Dhaka, Chittagong, Khulna, and Rajshahi were also scheduled in early 1988. Therefore, these elections were occasions where the political oppositions had the chance to create public agitation.

## *Stepping down of Ershad*

In the early January, five smaller parties joined the opposition coalition, which then implemented a two-day long general strike on 20 and 21 January 1990. Another general strike occurred on 6 February 1990, coinciding with the last date for filing nominations for the municipal elections. On 13 and 14 February 1990 following the union council elections, the opposition held another general strike. None of these actions prevented the government from implementing its election plans, but they kept the nation in a state of constant protest; the opposition may have hoped that Ershad's supporters in the military would eventually view him as a political liability and force him to resign. Following a nationwide mass movement, Ershad was finally forced to step down on December 6, 1990. He was arrested in 1991 and was later released on bail in January 1997.

## *The Present Condition of Jatiyo Party*

Jatiya Party (JaPa) has again decided to join the government of Awami League-led Grand Alliance. JaPa secured 22 seats in the 11th general election held on December 30, after joining the Grand Alliance right before the polls. The current acting chairperson of party is GM Quader. On 3 January 2019, the party announced its decision to join the Bangladesh Awami League-led Grand Alliance after having been in opposition for the previous parliamentary term.

## *Review of the Eighth Amendment Case- Anwar Hussain V Bangladesh*

The case of Anwar Hussain Chowdhury vs. Bangladesh, commonly known as the 8th amendment case, is an important judgment in the constitutional history of independent Bangladesh. In June 1988, article 100 of the Constitution was amended by the Parliament incorporating the provision for six permanent Benches of High Court for Chittagong, Sylhet, Cumilla, Jashore, Rangpur and Barishal.

This is the first decision whereby the Supreme Court of Bangladesh overruled an amendment to the constitution by the parliament. In this case, the Supreme Court of Bangladesh in a 1989 famous decision case recognized the basic structure doctrine or the idea of 'unconstitutional constitutional amendment' ruling that parliament lacks authority to amend the Constitution in a system that would abolish its basic structure. The case which judicial review is shown in sub-article 5 of article 100 is inconsistent with articles 44 and 114. However, Mohammad Moin Uddin and Rakiba Nabi, who said that

> While judicial review itself is a debated phenomenon in democratic countries, its use in constitutional amendments adds further complexity to the debate.

In 1988 the Bangladesh Parliament had amended article 100[49] of the constitution. The ruling party incorporated the provision for setting six permanent benches of a High Court for 6 different districts outside Dhaka in Sylhet, Rangpur, Barisal, Chittagong, Jessore, and Comilla. However, during the 8th Amendment, the parliament lead by Hussain Muhammad Ershad said that one division is not enough as it only in capital city Dhaka. There should be permanent benches outside of Dhaka also in other six divisions. Hence, Anwar Hossain Chowdhury challenges that 8th Amendment as viewing inconsistent of the constitutional article 102[50] because the fundamental principle cannot be changed by a political majority.

## *Why This Decision was Contradictory with The Constitution*

Very naturally, the parliament has the amending power of the constitution. However, this power does not extend to that which can change the basic structure of the constitution. This case is in relation to changing six benches of High Court division outside of the Dhaka, which is contradictory to the Constitution of Bangladesh. The main argument of the judgment was that since the Constitution stands on certain fundamental principles which are its structural pillars, hence, the Parliament cannot utilize its amending power for their benefits. It is noteworthy to mention that if these pillars are dismissed or damaged then the whole constitutional structure (basic structures are: Sovereignty belongs to the people, Supremacy of the Constitution, Democracy, Republican government, Independence of Judiciary, Unitary state, Separation of powers and Fundamental rights) will fall apart. Hence, the constitution cannot change the basic structures by its amending nature.

## *The Judicial Aspects and This Landmark Case*

In Appellate Division, the Amendment in Article 100 was challenged on the question whether the amendment altered the basic structure of the Constitution; 3 learned Judges found the High Court Division (HCD) with plenary judicial power over the entire Republic is a basic structure of the Constitution and the amendment having destroyed the plenary judicial power of the HCD altered the basic structure of the Constitution and is, therefore, ultra vires. Besides, this amended (Article 100) is inconsistent with Art 44, 94. 101 & 102 also reduced Art 108, 109, 110 &111 of the constitution.

According to B.H. Chowdhury, 'the power to frame a Constitution is a prime power, where a power to amend a rigid constitution is a derivative power derived from the constitution.' Yet, there is no limitation of amending power, except in Article 142. However, Justice Shahabuddin rightly commented that 'As to, the implied limitation on the amending power which is inherent in the word 'amendment' of art 142.'

In a similar fashion, in the case of Golak Nath vs. the state of Punjab case, it has been decided that the Parliament has no power to amend the fundamental right to take away any of them. Importantly, the basic structure is not amendable like human rights law when Dr. Kamal Hossen remarked that

> ***Basic structures of the Constitution mean structural pillars on which the Constitution rests and that if these structural pillars are demolished the entire constitutional framework will crumble.***[51]

## *The Comments of The Justices*

> *The Appellate Division consisting of four Judges declared the impugned amendment as void and ultra vires by majority of 3: 1. In this case, for the first time in Bangladesh, the Appellate Division has declared an amendment passed by the Parliament as void and imposed limitation on its amending power.*[52]
>
> *In deciding the constitutionality of the amendment, the Appellate Division followed the doctrine of basic structure of the Constitution, a judicial principle that some certain features of the Constitution cannot be altered or destroyed even by the two-third majority of the Parliament as the Constitution stands on these features.*[53] *The impugned amendment was declared as void and ultra vires as it destroyed some of those features. But the Appellate Division could not reach a unanimous decision as to which features of the Constitution are basic, which are not.*[54] *Shahabuddin Ahmed, J. has specified 6 features as the structural pillars of the Constitution, which cannot be amended by the Parliament.*[55] *While Badrul Haider Chowdhury, J. observed that the number of the basic features of the Constitution, which are not amendable, is 21.*[56]
>
> *M.H. Rahman, J, in deciding the constitutionality of the amendment, stressed on the preamble. He regarded it as an entrenched provision that cannot be amended by the Parliament alone.*[57] *He held: "if any provision can be called the 'pole star' of the Constitution then it is the Preamble and the impugned amendment is to be examined in the light of the preamble".*[58] *He further held: 'one of the fundamental aims of our society is to secure the rule of law for all citizens and in furtherance of that aim Part VI and other provisions were incorporated in the Constitution.*[59]

However, A.T. M. Afzal J., the only Judge among the four, has given a dissenting judgment rejecting the concept of basic structures and opined that the impugned amendment has not destroyed the High Court Division and therefore, it was not to be ultra vires on any of the grounds urged.[60]

## Political Background on This Case

In the Judiciary, for the first time in clear conflict with the Parliament, creation of six permanent benches of the High Court Division outside capital by amending Article 100 of the constitution was a burning issue. However, on 16.02.2017

Mahmudul Islam Memorial Lectures Organizing Committee organized their first lecture at the auditorium of Asiatic Society Bangladesh where chairman of the Constitution Drafting Committee Dr. Kamal Hossain was present as a key note speaker. He made some important comments there. On the basis of his sayings that day, when Ershad's government got the power and declared martial law proclamations, he was worried about the enemies of 'martial law proclamations.' And the most powerful enemy of 'Martial Law Proclamation' is the Supreme Court consisting of both lawyers and judges.[61] Therefore, he detained almost all the senior lawyers of the bar holding important positions in the Bar Council. Making the lawyers afraid, Ershad's government tried to 'decapitate' the Bench of the Supreme Court in the guise of 'Decentralization' so that he doesn't need to worry about the people from legal profession.[62]

Moreover, Dr. Kamal argued that a court becomes something with the passage of the time. It gradually develops and after the so called 'decentralization' of the High Court Division of the Supreme Court into 6 parts, all of these 6 courts had no history and no base.[63] There were not enough resources for the courts. The judges had to live in completely unhealthy environments. Dr. Kamal even told in an interview with the researcher about the Sylhet court where the court did not have even the constitution and he had to give his copy of the constitution to the judges.[64]

In light of above discussion, it can be said that, by the 8th Amendment case judgment the doctrine of basic structure of the constitution has been introduced Bangladesh. Independence of Judiciary, Democracy, Unitary Character of the Government have been declared basic structures of the constitution.

## Notes

1 Ibid.
2 Ibid.
3 http://culaw.blogspot.com/2017/11/constitutional-discussion.html?cv=1
4 C. H. Crothers, & A. Azad (2012). "Bangladesh: An Umpired Democracy." *Journal of Social and Development Sciences*, 3(6), 203–213.
5 Ibid
6 S. S. Islam (1987). "Bangladesh in 1986: Entering a New Phase." *Asian Survey*, 27(2), 163–172.
7 M. M. Khan, & M. S. Islam (2014). "Democracy and Good Governance in Bangladesh: Are They Compatible?" *Millennial Asia*, 5(1), 23–40.
8 http://www.clcbd.org/content/39.html
9 https://www.thedailystar.net/news-detail-124643
10 https://www.thedailystar.net/news-detail-114757
11 Moyeen Firozee, "Constitution Amendment Process: Proper Approach", *The Daily Star*, Dhaka, 9 July 2011.
12 Amendments to the Constitution of Bangladesh 1973–2011: Background, Politics and Impact by Salma Akhter.
13 Ibid.
14 Salma Akter. "Amendments to the constitution of Bangladesh 1973–2011: Background, politics and impacts." PhD, University of Dhaka, 2016, p. 1, 44 & 127.
15 Ibid 70.

16 M. Rafiqul Islam (1995). "The Seventh Amendment to the Constitution of Bangladesh: A Constitutional Appraisal."*The Political Quarterly* 58, no. 3, p. 312.
17 Ibid 313.
18 Ibid 315.
19 Ibid 321.
20 Bhuian Monoar Kabir (1995). "Politico-Economic Limitations and the Fall of the Military-Authoritarian Government in Bangladesh." *Armed Forces & Society* 21, no. 4, pp. 554, 561–562.
21 Ibid.
22 Ibid 562–564.
23 Siddique Ahmed v. Government of Bangladesh and Others [2011] 30 DLR (AD).
24 Abdul Halim, "The 7th Amendment Judgment by the Appellate Division: Judicial Politics or Judicial Activism." *The Counsel Journal*, p. 19, 27.
25 Ibid 35.
26 ibid 34.
27 ibid 39.
28 Ibid.
29 Ibid 44.
30 Ibid 66.
31 Ibid 67.
32 Ibid 71.
33 Ibid 61.
34 Ibid 10.
35 Lant Pritchett, Kunal Sen, and Eric Werker, *Deals and Development: The Political Dynamics of Growth Episodes* (Oxford Scholarship Online: December 2017).
36 Ibid.
37 *Anwar Hossain V Bangladesh* [1989].
38 Dr. Akhter Hussain, *General Ershad and Bangladesh* **(The Daily Sun, 2019).**
39 Ibid.
40 Ibid.
41 Lant Princhett, Kunal Sen and Eric Werker, *Deals and Development, The Political Dynamics of Economic Growth.*
42 Ibid.
43 Ibid.
44 Ibid.
45 Ibid.
46 Ibid.
47 Ibid.
48 Ibid.
49 Before 1989, the article 100 of the Bangladesh constitution said that the permanent seat of the Supreme Court shall be in the capital city Dhaka, but sessions of the high court division may be held at such other place or places as the chief justice may, with approval of the president, from time to time. Nevertheless, parliament wanted to pass a bill that the permanent Supreme Court will be in six divisions outside of the Dhaka.
50 Article 102 said regarding fundamental rights that the High Court Division on the application of any person aggrieved, may give such directions or orders to any person or authority, including any person performing any function in connection with the affairs of the Republic, as may be appropriate for the enforcement of any of the fundamental rights conferred by Part III of this Constitution.
51 J. Basunia (n.d.). On Bangladesh Constitutional 8th Amendment Case. (26 09, 2019).
52 4 Ibid.
53 5 Ibid.
54 Ibid.
55 Ibid.

56 Ibid.
57 Ibid.
58 Ibid.
59 Ibid.
60 Ibid.
61 Ibid.
62 Ibid.
63 Ibid.
64 Ibid.

# 5

# UNDER THE ILLUSION OF REPRESENTATIVE DEMOCRACY

## Ninth Amendment—Insurgent of Democracy

After the passage of the Eighth Amendment to the constitution, Awami League and BNP, two major political parties started mudslinging towards each other. It slowed down opposition movement. Government for a while was able to rule the country quite peacefully. At this time, government took some initiatives to make the constitution more democratic.

Ninth Amendment of Bangladesh constitution was made at the time when neither the opposition nor the people had any say in the making and unmaking of government and legislation. The opposition was vocal and demanded for holding free and fair election under a neutral government. On the other hand, government, ignoring the people's demand, endeavoured to portray the image of the government as democratic government committed to welfare of the people. With the aim of making reign of government more democratic and accountable, the government inserted the Ninth Amendment restricting the term of president to two and making provision for direct election for Vice-President. Though this amendment would have to be commenced on 1 March 1991, its application happened prematurely on 6 December 1990, but the return of parliamentary form of government negated the application of Ninth Amendment. The whims of the regime if not matched with the people or peoples' desire if not incorporated in the business of the government constitution and constitutional amendment both would fall apart like the ninth amendment of Bangladesh Constitution. Regime should stop proceeding along with such type of deeds where the say of the people as a whole is inevitable.

This Amendment amended Articles 49, 50, 51, 53, 54, 72, 119, 122, 123, 124, 148, 152 of and 4th Schedule to the Constitution. Provision for the election of the both, the President and the Vice-President, were to hold office for a term of

DOI: 10.4324/9781003363002-5

five years. No person was to hold office as President or Vice-President for more than two terms; whether or not the terms were consecutive.

The Amendment, therefore, sought to democratize the executive but it carries no importance. Now for the 12th Amendment which reverted the governmental system to a parliamentary one has made all its provisions ineffective.

### *Political View of the 9th Amendment*

On 9 July 1989 in the House, Prime Minister Mr. Moudud Ahmed termed the ninth amendment bill as a pragmatic step to further strengthen the democratic set up in the country. (The Bangladesh Observer, 10 July 1989. See the parliamentary debate of 9 July 1989.) Prime Minister Moudud Ahmed said the bill was designed to democratize and improve the constitution and it would remove the leadership crisis. 'The passage of the bill will help consolidate the national independence and sovereignty,' he added (See the Parliamentary proceeding of 10 July 1989 published in the Bangladesh Observer on 11 July 1989)

Following this, Mr. Mizanur Rahman Chowdhury, former Prime Minister and General Secretary of Jatiya Party said that the ninth amendment would set up an unprecedented example of democracy in the third world. Describing the ninth amendment bill as 'epoch-making event' he said that it would make the presidential form of government fully democratic where the Vice-President would be a running mate of the President in the election like the system in the United States. (See the parliamentary debate of 10 July 1989. see also the Daily Ittefaq of 11 July 1989)

### *People's Interest on the Application of 9th Amendment*

The appointment of Chief Justice Shahabuddin Ahmed as Acting President on 6 December 1990 after the fall of autocratic President Ershad in the face of mass upsurge prematurely put the provision of Ninth Amendment in operation. However, after the introduction of Twelfth Amendment to the constitution, ninth amendment, with regard to the provision of Vice-President and direct election of President, ceased to exist. However, in spite of absence of peoples' interest and participation in the ninth amendment, it may be said the amendment was made to make the constitution more democratic and systematic no doubt.

## Tenth Amendment—Balancing of Power

When the constitution was made in 1972, through various article the rights of women were safeguarded and ensured under the specific fundamental rights and values of equality. The constitution ensured political equality as a fundamental right that does not differentiate any gender, religion, age, or socio-economic background. The normative theory of democracy considers that women are equal citizens; therefore, they should participate equally with men in public decision making.

In general, women's engagement in politics is essential for the nation's democratic growth and the empowerment of women. The tenth amendment did not only increase reserved seats in the Parliament, but it also enhanced the equal participation of women in the economic, political, legal development.

The tenth amendment was passed through Act No.38 of 1990. It amended, among others, Article 65 of the constitution, providing for reservation of thirty seats for the next 10 years in the Jatiya Sangsad exclusively for women members to be elected by the members of the Sangsad. Constitution (Tenth Amendment) Act, 1990, Act No.38 of 1990, made to amend certain provisions of the Constitution of the People's Republic of Bangladesh. Whereas it is expedient to amend certain provisions of the Constitution of the People's Republic of Bangladesh for the purposes hereinafter appearing;

> Therefore, the following Act is herewith made:
>
> 1. Short title—This Act shall be called Constitution (Tenth Amendment) Act, 1990.
> 2. Amendment of article 65 of the Constitution—For clause (3) of article 65 of the Constitution of the People's Republic of Bangladesh (henceforth referred to as the Constitution) shall be substituted with the following clause, namely:
>
> '(3) Until the dissolution of Parliament occurring next after the expiration of the period of ten years beginning from the date of the first meeting of the Parliament next after the Parliament in existence at the time of commencement of the Constitution (Tenth Amendment) Act, 1990, there shall be reserved thirty seats exclusively for women members, who shall be elected according to law by the members aforesaid:
> Provided that nothing in this clause shall prevent a woman from being elected to any of the seats provided for in clause (2).'

It is essential to focus on the history of women's participation in politics globally and nationally to understand the necessity of the amendment and also the socio-political aftermath of the amendment.

## *Women's Participation in Politics in The Indian Subcontinent During Early 19th Century*

Women's participation in the Parliament has always been under-represented. At any socio-political level, this scenario remains the same. Although each nation has its unique features in politics, one aspect is common everywhere it is inconsistent and not conducive to the participation of women. Since the early 19th century women had been fighting for equal rights globally and especially for the right to vote and political participation. Even in the western parts such as Europe and

America, men and women had roles to fill the different spheres of society. Men were expected to live a public life and women had domestic life. In the early 19th century, women demanded equal opportunity for education, work and vote. In the West, women started to get access to education but for Southeast Asian countries such as Pakistan, India, or Bangladesh Women's education was a luxurious thing and was only accessible to the elite class family. Equal political rights were an unimaginable concept for uneducated women in this subcontinent in the early 19th century. When colonialism stared in India, women's roles were pushed more to the traditional way of life. The 19th-century social reform movement did help in removing prejudices against women's education and provided a secular space for women in the public realm in India. National organizations like Women's Indian Association (1917), the National Council of Women in India (1920), All India Women's Conference (1926) which went on to organize 12 women's conferences till 1937 and Federation of University Women in India (1920) were established with the sole objective of stimulating the interests of women in civic and public life and the removal of disabilities of women whether legal, economic or social and the promotion of social, civil, moral and educational welfare of women and children throughout India. Gandhi legitimized and expanded Indian women's public activities by initiating them into the non-violent civil disobedience movement against the Raj. In the decades that followed, women showed active participation in freedom movement paving the way for some women centred organizations. When Gandhiji brought India's freedom struggle to the mass, women were very active participants throughout the struggle and a large number of women were coming and participating. After the partition of India and Pakistan, women participation in politics took different ways separately.

## *Role of Women Organization in The Reformation of Law and Politics Before Independence*

In a masculine dominant society, women's participation in politics did not come in practice overnight though equal political rights were established through the fundamental rights and as a democratic normative theory.

Women empowerment in politics should be analysed from a historic perspective to appreciate a century-long struggle of various women organizations and many political movements to establish their constitutional right in politics. Different initiatives have been taken by these women's rights organizations to end patriarchal practices against women, such as violence against women, dowry, children and women trafficking, unequal pay, abuse of female workers, access to credit, and unequal political and social rights. The Era of active women politics started in Bangladesh even before the independence Through organizations such as, All Association of Pakistan Women, Federation of Business and professional women's club University Women and Karachi. Many specialist women's organizations later came into being, but almost all of these groups were focused on welfare and social knowledge within themselves dealing with issues such as education for children, skills growth and income generation and baby caretaker centre. However, the All Pakistan Women's Association did play a significant role in implementing the Family Laws Ordinance of 1961 and in fostering women's seats in national and regional legislatures. But since APWA (All Pakistan Woman Association) was associated with the then government, its operations were unable to highlight the women's demands for greater involvement in politics.[1] Organizations such as United Front for Women's Rights also failed to highlight women's demands for creating their greater participation in politics because of their specific motive for women empowerment. Political agitation during 1968-69 for the anti-Ayub movement also gave birth to an organization like e East Pakistan Mahila Sangram. Their objective was an election of sovereign parliament, direct election for the reserved seats for women, equal wages for the female workers, establishment of mother/child centres and Child hospitals, etc. The role of Bangladesh Mahila Parishad (Bangladesh Women's Council) is undeniable in promoting the protection of women's rights and empowerment and in raising awareness of equal rights for men and women under the law and in practice, and in creating a democratic, secular, non-discriminatory family, society and state. Bangladesh Mahila Parishad (Women's Council of Bangladesh) started its journey as a human rights organization in April 1970. It emerged initially as the East Pakistan Mahila Parishad with the initiative of poet Begum Sufia Kamal, the competent successor of Begum Rokeya and the pioneer dreamer of women's emancipation of the subcontinent. The organization was formed through conversation in the backdrop of mass movement and upsurge of 1969 in former East Pakistan. All the founding members worked as organizer and actively took part in the war of liberation of Bangladesh.[2] The organization was renamed as Bangladesh Mahila Parishad after the liberation of the country in 1971.

The organization started its operation with the key principles of promotion of women's empowerment, development and solidarity with an aim for secular, democratic and progressive women's movements in the country. The specific objectives of the organization were to stop violence against women; promote political empowerment of women; ensure women's' human rights; establish peace and democracy; ensure women's development and equality through policy intervention; and establish a Lobby and Advocacy agent. In materializing the goal and objectives of the organization, Bangladesh Mahila Parishad's diversified activities were implemented through its 12 units—Organization, Resist Violence against Women and Legal Support, Rehabilitation Center (Rokeya Sadan), Movement, Research, Training and Library, Publication, Mass Media, Health and Environment, Social Welfare, Project and Development, and Networking. Registered locally as a legal entity in 1976, it also became the member of Economic and Social Council of United Nations (ECOSOC).[3]

Military Regime in Bangladesh and Islamic Fundamentalism resulted in the fall of Women empowerment when Bangladesh started to get on its feet as a newly emerged war-torn country. For the first time, the 1972 constitution recognized the equality of the sexes in the social and political sphere. It also safeguarded women's equal socio-political participation through various articles including 10, 19, 27, 28 and 65. The original 1972 Constitution of Bangladesh incorporated a provision for secularism. The 1979 Fifth Amendment deleted the principle of secularism and incorporated Bismillah-ar-Rahman-ar-Rahim (In the name of Allah, the Beneficent, and the Merciful). After the main constitutional feature of secularism was deleted, a process of state-sponsored Islamization began. This eventually made a declining effect on all the safeguarding articles that promoted women's equal participation in politics as the Islamic ideology has different kind of restriction for women.

In 1982, the army chief of staff, Lieutenant General Hussain Muhammad Ershad came into power. He proclaimed martial law, made himself chief martial law administrator and dismantled the structures of democratic government that the administration of the late president General Zia had carefully tried to build during the previous five years. Ershad suspended the Constitution, disbanded Parliament, prohibited all political activities, and deprived the president, vice president, and cabinet ministers of their offices. His government policy withdrew the fundamental rights and democratic policies that eventually resulted in a fall of equal social and political rights of women. When the military government passed the Eighth Amendment Bill in 1988, Islam was established as Bangladesh's state religion. Two famous women's organizations, the Women's Forum and Naripokko (Women's Side), filed a petition before the Supreme Court opposing the legitimacy of the amendment. The petition claimed that as Islam does not approve of a woman as a head of state, the eighth amendment discriminates against women in social and political arena. In other fields of social advocacy, non-party women's organizations had been active in developing women's rights in other fields.[4]

## *Socio Economic Changes In Women's life in 90s Through NGO*

In the past three decades, women's socio-economic conditions have improved significantly. Their condition was totally different than present time. In 1990 patriarchal societies, women of Bangladesh used to earn a smaller portion of household wealth. As a consequence, they faced reduced resources for jobs, access to medical services and nutrition. One of the key reasons for poverty was that poor people were neglected from accessing funds to allow them to have benefit from financial resources to increase their level of income and livelihoods and boost their economic status to get out of poverty. In 1985, Grameen Bank provided micro finance products specifically to avail credit facilities to the poor and small enterprises. Micro credit was established by Professor Dr. Yunus (economist) via the Grameen bank in 1985. Microfinance and the democratic restoration, education and empowering women are considered essential instruments for the adoption of successful and sustainable anti-poverty policies. In addition to reducing poverty, the micro-credit scheme has also helped poor women to turn into entrepreneurs, enhanced women's engagement in politics, helped the poor to access education and medical care and increased women's decision-making in communities and society. To facilitate the acquisition of credit and other financial resources, Bangladesh's microcredit programs target women more often than men. Over the years, females have received over two-thirds of the loans. Women's shares were the highest in Grameen Bank (89%) and ASA (84%) in 2011. One particular strategy in tackling poverty that has caught the attention of many aid donors and non-government organizations (NGOs) is the provision of small loans through microcredit programs. Bangladesh, one of the poorest countries in the world, is the cradle of this 'microcredit movement.' Grameen Bank in Bangladesh enjoys international fame and its model has been replicated in countries all over the world. Likewise, the Bangladesh Rural Advancement Committee (BRAC) is showing success as one of the largest NGOs in the world. Both have generated an international wave of interest and have been the main source of inspiration for the Microcredit Movement, which was launched in 1997 as a 'global movement to reach 100 million of the world's poorest families, especially the women of those families, with credit for self-employment and other financial and business services by the year 2005.' The micro-credit institutions in Bangladesh have implemented a method of granting loans only to women. The key aims were to introduce women into business activities by offering small loans by start-ups and being independent rather than relying on men. In Bangladesh, microcredit began to influence women to become entrepreneurs and potential active citizens of the country by proving their skills and knowledge. Economic independence led women to be politically independent.

## *The rise of Women's Political Leadership*

Women's participation in politics started to become prominent from 1991 when Former Prime Minister Khaleda Zia and her party BNP won the election after eight years of Ershad's presidency. She served as Prime Minister of Bangladesh in the years from 1991–1996 and 2001–2006. Bangladesh's current structure was a Presidential form of government until the 1991 election. There was a strong demand that the presidential system would be replaced by the parliamentary system. Immediately after the election, she introduced the landmark 12th constitutional amendment bill in the Jatiya Sangsad (the Parliament) on 6 August 1991, to introduce the parliamentary form of government by replacing the presidential system. And on 19 September 1991, Khaleda Zia took oath as the Prime Minister of Bangladesh under the new parliamentary system. Her political background was influenced by her own husband former President General Ziaur Rahman. After her husband was assassinated in 1981 by military officers, she became politically active, and in 1984 she assumed the leadership of the Bangladesh Nationalist Party. Khaleda Zia was arrested repeatedly during the dictatorship of Hussain Mohammad Ershad in the 1980s, but in 1991 she led the opposition to victory and became Prime Minister. She was not only the first women Prime Minister of the country, but she also reintroduced the democratic parliamentary system after a decade of the military-based authoritarian government of General Zia and Ershad.

Sheikh Hasina is a politician and leader of the Awami League political party, who twice served as prime minister of Bangladesh (1996–2001; 2009–present). Sheikh Hasina is the daughter of Bangabandhu Sheikh Mujibur Rahman, the principal orchestrator of Bangladesh's separation from Pakistan in 1971. During his confinement by the Pakistani government, she started to get actively involved in the political process and acted as her father's political liaison. In 1975, her father (former President and Father of the nation) and other family members were assassinated in their own home by several military officers. During that time, Sheikh Hasina and her sister was traveling to West Germany and subsequently spent six years in exile. She got elected to the leadership of the Awami League during that time. In 1981 she returned to Bangladesh and became a prominent and outspoken advocate of democracy. As she was advocating democracy bluntly during military rule, it resulted in her placement under house arrest on numerous occasions. When she secured a seat as leader of the opposition in the Parliament, she began to protest against military violence and demanded basic fundamental and human rights for the citizen. In 1990, in response to an ultimatum issued by Sheikh Hasina and widely accepted by the people of Bangladesh, Gen. Hussain Mohammad Ershad resigned. In 1991, Hasina failed to obtain the majority of the seats in the Parliament but later she got elected as the Prime Minister in 1996. After almost a decade she again got elected as a Prime Minister in 2009. She again got elected in the 2014 election, but the fairness of the election was left still questionable as the main opposition party BNP boycotted the election. In anticipation of the 2018 polls, these issues remained in force, while BNP agreed to contest the elections that year. Khaleda, the then BNP leader, was jailed earlier that year on charges of embezzlement and graft and was not permitted to participate. As a leader, Sheikh Hasina showed many bold moves and economic progression. A big success of Sheikh Hasina is the bold move to bring the war criminals of 1971 to justice. Another success that can be attributed to Sheikh Hasina is that her government is engaged in a persistent operation against religious militancy. She has shown zero tolerance for religious fanaticism and fundamentalism, and Sheikh Hasina has triumphantly protected the Bangladesh Constitution's basic principle of secularism. By the time Bangladesh marks its 50th birthday in 2021, Hasina's goal is to increase the annual economic growth rate from the present 7% to almost 10%.[5] Bangladesh has emerged as one of the world's fastest-growing economies in the last decade. Its per capita income has doubled. The group 'least developed nations' is all ready to exit. Another tremendous achievement of Sheikh Hasina is the empowerment of women. This is the first time in Bangladesh that the high offices are occupied by a significant number of women. Bangladesh ranks ahead of India in both gender equality and empowerment indices, according to Nobel laureate Prof. Amartya Sen. A national policy on women's empowerment was introduced by the government of Sheikh Hasina and dramatically altered their social and legal status by the enforcement of the policy.[6]

## Necessity of the 10th Amendment

### Democratic Value

Article 10 of the Constitution calls for the introduction of steps to ensure women's participation in all fields of the national life as the gender, race, religion or socio-economic background of a person cannot be differentiated when it comes to the equal treatment given by the state. Moreover, Article 19(1) says that the State shall make every effort to ensure equal opportunities for all people. Also, the Article 27 specifies that all citizens are equal before the law and are entitled to have equal protection of the law. Article 28 (1) provides that the State shall not discriminate against any citizen on the grounds of religion, race, caste, sex, or place of birth. More explicitly and categorically in Article 28(2), it has been said that in all aspects of the State and public life, women shall have equal rights with men. This provision defines that all the rights specified in the Constitution, such as the right to life, the right to personal liberty, the right to land, freedom of speech, freedom of movement, the right to practice a career or occupation, are equally applicable to women in Bangladesh.

Even though the constitution has granted equal rights for women, the real scenario about participating in the political arena from 1972 to 1990 showed a different image. In the 90s, in every sector of life, a woman's status was much lower than a man. Women were associated with domestic life when politics was seen as a traditionally masculine and male-dominated public practice. The change in article 65 was not only about implementing the constitutional right, but it was also more about encouraging women to be a part of the policymaking process. This helped women to be more empowered and make an overall change in society. The fact has already been established that national development cannot be achieved without ensuring women's development.

### Economic Value

In 1990, when the democratic rule was reinstated, vast economic reforms were made. Re-establishing democratic rights and equality in the social and political arena was a necessity to reinstate democracy. In 1990, the total population was 106,188,642 of which, half were women. It was important to encourage them to be part of the social reformation to establish democracy again. Increasing the parliamentary reserved seat for women was a part of the equality treatment to ensure women's empowerment in politics and decision making which could lead the county toward socio-economic growth later on. The statistics of poverty has declined from 60 to about 30% over the few years after re-establishing democratic system. GDP growth rate accelerated to 4.5% in the first half of the 1990s and to 5% in the second half of that decade.[7] One of the most prominent and visible changes in our country's biggest economic development came through the RMG sector where 90% of the workers are female.[8] Where women started running the biggest sector of our economy, there was an imbalance when it was about being a parliamentary member and their equal participation in politics.

To reduce the disproportionality in order to ensure democratic rights given to women, increasing reserved seats in the Parliament was another elevator to ensure the fundamental right.

### *International Obligation*

Bangladesh has become a signatory party of The Convention on the Elimination of all Forms of Discrimination Against Women (CEDAW) in Nov 6, 1984. The government has to maintain a constant accountability with the UN for being a signatory party to The Convention on the Elimination of all Forms of Discrimination Against Women (CEDAW). This convention encourages the participation of women in the public services in general and decision-making in particular.[9] Also in International Covenant on Civil and Political Rights Article 7 states that, all UN party States have a duty to ensure that their laws and policies allow women to take part in civic and political processes such as voting and running for political office.[10] As a state party to this treaty Bangladesh cannot discriminate any women when it is about being part of a political process or running for political office. Bangladesh needed to encourage women to be part of the policymaking process to match with the international growth in favour of promoting equal rights and opportunities for women around the world.

**Social Change:** Empowering women through increasing parliamentary seats did not only make an overall impact in the economy but also made a positive social impact. During this decade, gender discrimination in primary school education was also reduced drastically. Bangladesh has been cited as a success story for growth, including on women's rights. The UN quoted the 'impressive' reduction of poverty in Bangladesh from 56.7% in 1991-1992 to 31.5% in 2010.[11] According to the UN, Bangladesh achieved gender equality when enrolling in primary and secondary schools. Between 2001 and 2010, maternal mortality dropped by 40%. It was visible that the women empowerment in the socio-political arena can develop a country's situation drastically.

## Eleventh Amendment—Rise of a New Autocrat

The eleventh amendment of the constitution happened on 10 August 1991 through the constitution's eleventh amendment act, 1991.[12] The constitution amendment bill had been passed to remove the barrier for the acting president to go back to the previous position after finishing his job. The Acting President was now allowed to go back to his original post of chief justice after the transfer of power and this was the first step towards the caretaker government system.

There are some political reasons which had taken the constitution to the eleventh amendment. Before discussing the amendment, it is needed to have an overview of the time when General Ershsad started his rule illegally. Hossain

Muhammad Ershad stayed in power for a long time and by this period his activities created anger among different class of people. In January 1990 the 'Anti-Ershad' movement begun in the country but the preparatory phase started before this time when he came to power in 1982. At that time, students protested from the front against his illegal way of ruling the country.[13] On 17th September 1982, the student political organizations made a silent procession during the celebration of education day and the police arrested three students from University of Dhaka on the charge of putting posters around the campus. The protest had raised further and the police, with other paramilitary forces, came to the campus to stop them. The police had beaten students indiscriminately.[14] After the incident, the Chatra Samgram Parisad was formed and a three-point demand was formed. The first demand was realizing of full democracy and basic human rights, the second demand was the abandonment of proposed education policy and the final one was the release of all political prisoners and end of political repression. After few months, in January 1983, the political parties released joint statement about the action of the police on the students.[15] The other political organizations also joined and this statement was the beginning of the unified protest against the regime.[16] The protests of this phase carried the movement further and created a situation for Ershad to leave the power. Also, it created a place for democracy. As a result, in the latter period, the concept of neutral government for election had grown and made way for the eleventh amendment by accepting the condition of Chief Justice Shahabuddin Ahmed.

At that phase, in an event General Ershad commented some sarcastic things about the language movement day which was noticed by the political parties and public. At the same time, police fired in a student rally and killed a number of students. The police arrested some political leaders for protesting against it. These incidents had taken resulted in the formation of the fifteen party alliances by the main political organizations with a unified student body. BNP was not part of this and took initiative to form the seven-party political alliance. Though these alliances were separate but adopted many similar political agendas like five-point demand for the restoration of democracy.[17]

In 1990, the protest against Ershad government grew more and came into the final phase. At that time, the scenario of the movement featured strikes, large demonstrations and fight of the police and the paramilitary forces. Awami League with its eight-party alliance and BNP with its seven-party alliance were taking different protest against the government. The seven-party alliance called for the boycott of all the elections under the Ershad regime. On the other hand, Awami League and eight party proposed to boycott only the presidential election under Ershad government. In this situation, the opposition parties seemed ti collapse and could not get together. The subaltern forces also took position against the opposition leadership.[18] The movement shifted from opposition parties to the hands of the field workers. Also, the subaltern social groups were fighting, organizing and dying for the movement. As a result, the opposition got the fear of being left behind and to stay in the movement they followed the way of the subaltern groups.[19]

The oppositions got unity in the streets and the discussion of the caretaker government got a new path. Also, the nature of future government and election under Ershad regime took a new turn. Though there were few disagreements between opposition parties, at the end, they agreed on some points like, they would boycott and resist election under Ershad government and the Ershad government would hand over the power to a caretaker government through resignation. Also, the caretaker government would ensure a free, fair election and it must hand over the power to a sovereign parliament after completion of election.[20]

To remain in power, Ershad approached some last strategies. The public was very active in the streets against Ershad at that time. So, Ershad's aim was to divert the public attention from this matter so that he could control the opposition parties. With that aim in mind, he created communal hatred against Hindu in many parts of the country. Many businesses of Hindu people got destroyed and many of them also got killed. The opposition parties condemned that they could not come together. A peace procession was also proposed but Awami League leader, Sheikh Hasina, refused to share the stage with Khaleda Zia. Afterwards, the workers got together and raised strong voice against this communality. As all the options failed, the President made another strategy. He released the serious criminals from the prison and gave them weapon to attack the rallies.[21] After this he adopted another strategy by declaring state of emergency and imposed curfew. People went against it and came on the streets. The residents of Mohammadpur took the first attempt to break the curfew. Later the Dhaka University students called many rallies and the next day, VC and Pro-VC of Dhaka University resigned. The radio station and the TV artists refused to go work. Also, the government workers of secretariat building said that they would not work until Ershad resigned from his presidency. Lastly, seeing no other options, Ershad agreed to leave the power.[22]

It is the public who had taken a drastic step to force Ershad to leave his presidency. Without their contribution, it would not be possible for the political parties to force Ershad to leave president office. This is the general people who were enraged with the autocratic rule and wanted democracy in this land. This is the desire of democracy that brought forth the eleventh amendment. After a long rule of autocracy, a fair election was needed for ensuring democracy. The election was required to take place under a neutral government where person like Justice Shahabuddin Ahmed was present. People did not care about the legality of appointing and getting back to the previous service, they wanted a fair election even if it required a violation of law, but the state had to make sure that no violation occurred. With this reason and many more in mind, Justice Shahabuddin Ahmed finally legalized everything he wanted by the parliament.

The parties came into some consensus about caretaker government. They agreed on two conditions that any person who had opposed the liberation war and was somehow directly or indirectly related with Ershad's regime would not be eligible for being the President.[23]

It shows that the failure of these two conditions could mislead the country.

The nation was facing crisis and that created the necessity of a clean imaged person who would hold the position of the neutral caretaker government. The parties were looking for a person who had no relation with politics but had a record of sensibility and also acceptable to them.[24] They were searching among government officials, media personality, judges, academicians, army officers and among other professions.[25] While the opposition parties got signal that Ershad would step down from his power, three alliances came together in a joint meeting presided by BNP leader, Major (Retd) Majedul Huq and nominated incumbent chief justice Shahabuddin Ahmed. Latter people from three alliances Rashed Khan Menon, Mr. Mujahidul Islam Salim and two others gave the name of their nominee and also handed a copy of their choice to the chief Justice Shahabuddin.[26] It is also said that BNP and the eight party alliance proposed the name of retired air vice marshal A.K Khondoker as the head of the neutral government but Awami League was against this proposal. After all these debates, finally they agreed on Justice Shahabuddin Ahmed and offered him to play role of acting president for arranging a fair election.[27]

The Vice President, Moudud Ahmed resigned on 6 December 1990 and appointed chief Justice as the Vice President. On the same day, Ershad had resigned from his office of president and in the absence of the President, the Vice President, Shahabuddin Ahmed got the position of Acting President.[28]

The Chief Justice said that he would accept the offer only if he could get back to his previous office of judiciary. The election happened under the Acting President Shahabuddin Ahmed which was consider as one of the most successful elections in the history of Bangladesh. In this election, BNP got 133 seats and made a coalition government with Jamat-e-Islam. This election later turned into a role model for future elections. Even now, people give examples of this election under Shahabuddin government for a demand of fair election.[29]

The appointment of Justice Shahabuddin as the Acting President had a connection with the election culture of Bangladesh. To understand the appointment of a neutral person and the process of giving validity to the appointment through eleventh amendment, it is necessary to look back on the past incidents of the election. On 7th March, 1973, the Awami League secured 292 seats among 300 seats which were very much expected by the people as it got huge popularity and also the election commission had that capacity to do a free and fair election. Though allegations were made that the ruling party captured polling centres and got out the opposition from the booths, the election was considered as a free and fair one.[30] In the next decades, a huge change happened in the country which impacted the fall of the democracy. On 15 August 1975 Sheikh Mujibar Rahman was brutally killed along with his whole family and Khondokar Mustaq took the power. He suspends the constitution and proclaimed the martial law. Few months later he was removed from the office and Chief Justice Sayem took over the presidency. Later, Major General Zia came and arranged referendum which was unknown to Bangladesh constitution and claimed that 99% people showed confidence on him which was questionable. In 1979, the second parliamentary election took place and General Ziaur Rahman formed BNP. In the election, BNP got 207 seats among 300 seats.[31]

After the assassination of General Zia, Ershad ousted Sattars's government and followed the path of General Zia. He, later, also introduced his party and arranged referendum. He claimed of getting a huge number of votes but that was not true. It was later affirmed by independent, local and foreign observers that the statics was of maximum twenty per cent voters. Ershad arranged third parliamentary election in 1986 claimed of getting 51% of the total number of seats and it was found that only 42% of votes were casted. This election was also alleged of being not fair. This election broke the all records of the past. Ershad's party captured many polling stations and terrorized the voters. In 1988, fourth parliamentary election took placed without any major opposition. Ershad's party got 251 seats but that election was not considered as an election by the people of Bangladesh.[32]

If all the elections are observed carefully, it can be clearly perceived that except the first parliamentary election, all the other elections were questionable. It also shows that the election is always controlled by the ruling government and the independent election commission has no power in real to do fair election. This is the reason of choosing a person in 1990's election who has record of sensibility and of havinf no relation with politics. When Ershad agreed to leave the power, the parties started to find a person who could fulfil those requirements for ensuring free and fair election. The parties gave nominees but they all came to agree that Justice Shahabuddin is right person and for that his condition of getting back to his job after the election was also accepted. As a result, after the formation of the Parliament, the parties had to come up with the eleventh amendment for his returning back to the previous office and legalize all the actions during his period.

The process was not so smooth because, differences on the party's consensus had grown after the election, especially between the two major parties, Awami League and BNP. They had forgotten their commitments to Shahabuddin Ahmed and Awami League was not ready to see someone in the position of the President from the side of BNP. As Awami League had lost the election, there was a possibility of the party to getting into trouble. On the other hand, Shahabuddin Ahmed did not want to stay in the president office and also wanted to go back to his previous position in the judiciary. The Acting President reminded the political parties of their commitment to make constitutional amendment for him to get back to his previous position.[33]

The offer of becoming the head of the government on the condition of returning back to the judiciary seemed unconstitutional to many people. The reason is that the constitution does not permit an incumbent Justice to take the charge of the highest executive and also did not permit to re-join the judiciary after serving.[34]

To remove the frustration and bringing public attention to the matter, Shahabuddin Ahmed gave public speech on 5th June 1995 for an immediate settlement on this issue. He states that the Parliament has to take necessary constitutional measures in the coming budget session to solve the problem and provide ways to leave his position. He also said that he took the responsibility of the President on the basis of consensus among the political parties which did not exist anymore and therefore, he wanted to quit the position.[35]

All this chaos concluded on 2nd July, 1991when Mr. Mirza Golam Hafiz, Minister of Law and Justice, introduced the constitutional Amendment bill in 1991 on the eleventh amendment for appointment of chief justice as a Vice President facilitating to return to his office in the judiciary as a chief justice after the election. The bill was passed by 278 votes and 28 members abstained themselves from casting the vote. This amendment included a new paragraph in the constitution in paragraph 21 after paragraph 20 in the fourth schedule with sub-paragraphs. In the first sub-paragraph, it had made valid all the actions of the Acting President in the period between 6th December 1990 and 10th October 1991. The two sub-paragraphs permit the President to join previous office as chief justice.[36]

The appointment of Justice in the position of the President had happened in past as well when Justice Abu Sayed Choudhury, Justice Sadat Mohammad Sayem and Justice AFM Ahsanuddin Choudhury were appointed by violating Bangladesh constitution. They did not raise questions of validity on their appointment and neither of them wished to go back to their previous services. But Justice Shahabuddin Ahmed wanted to do so and did it with some struggles. The reason might be that he did not want to lose his reputation which he had earned through his lifetime. His demands got more reasons because of the increasing temperature in politics after the election.[37]

Though the appointment procedures can be criticized, the contribution of Justice Shahabuddin Ahmed to make an end of political chaos before the election cannot be ignored. Moreover, his contribution will be remembered for opening a new door for democracy. Justice Shahabuddin Ahmed was not only ideal to the politicians but also had achieved trust and got to the acceptance of the general people. The controversy can be debated on but the respect he had earned it is praiseworthy.

Another thing needs to be mentioned that the parties generally claim their leaders have the best quality to lead and run the country but in a critical situation like this, they cannot stand together, rather oppose each other. Also, the justice should get acclamation because he understood the necessity of this amendment and without this. He would have been criticized more. Now, the criticism is less because of his active role during the caretaker government period. It can also be presumed that Justice Shahabuddin Ahmed went to the President's office knowing that he could make his appointment legal later with the legal procedure. Though the amendment was made after the caretaker government came into being, it can consider as the first step towards it. The amendment may seem to relate with only one person but directly or indirectly, it made the way for the thirteenth amendment regarding the caretaker government. Also, the fifteenth amendment where the caretaker government was abolished can be somehow connected with the eleventh amendment. The eleventh amendment which made the path of the beginning of caretaker government had later suffered mixed experiences. The future elections under the caretaker government had also resulted in being fair but still, those are not above the questions. Lastly, with many controversies, the court declared the caretaker government illegal and with the fifteenth amendment, the system had been abolished. Along with other impacts of the eleventh amendment, the growth of the caretaker government was influenced because the promise of the eleventh amendment to Justice Shahabuddin Ahmed gave opportunity to see that how much it was effective to protect the democracy.

At that time, the political parties were in protest against Ershad government and did not want to do election under his authority. Everyone wanted a person who had record of neutrality and can create equal opportunity for all political parties. At the end, everyone agreed that Justice Muhammad Habibur Rahman would be perfect for this position. The problem arose with an Article of the constitution that the acting president could not go back his previous position of work. Justice Habibur Rahman was the chief justice at that time and for that the change was made that the appointed person could go back to his previous position after finishing his job. Later he became the Vice President and after resignation of President Ershad, Justice Habibur Rahman hold the position of Acting President. It is said that the election that had happened under his government, was the fairest and most transparent election in the history of this country. In an interview, Dr. Kamal Hossain said that the eleventh amendment happened in an interesting way. At that time, parties, especially Awami League and BNP, were giving objection to each other's nominees for the post. The time was running out for appointing in the post and at the last moment, everyone agreed on Justice Mohammad Habibur Rahman. The moment it was informed to him, he said that he could not leave the job of Chief Justice as he had time for his tenure. He further told that he could accept the proposal only if he was allowed to get back to his position after finishing his new job. Everyone accepted the condition and quickly made change in the constitution through the eleventh amendment.

### *The Impact of the Eleventh Amendment*

Justice Habibur Rahman was made the chief advisor and under his authority, a new election took place. This election was known as the transition from authoritarianism to democracy in Bangladesh. The election opened a new door to practice democracy. Before the election, there were lots of question about the fairness of the election. Later, it turned out to be one of the fairest elections in the history of Bangladesh. The major credit belonged to Justice Habibur Rahman and it may not have been possible to process a fair election without him.

## Twelfth Amendment—Distribution of Parliamentary Power

The Twelfth Amendment reintroduced the Parliamentary system of government in Bangladesh making path for a fresh start of constitutionalism. With the 12th amendment, the parliamentary system of government was restored for the second time after continuous existence of the dictatorial presidential system for 16 years. The Twelfth Amendment shares similarities with the Fourth Amendment in terms of spirit and language though there are some Articles which are different. The followings are fundamental changes to that end introduced in the constitution:

A. President's Position

1. As per the provisions of Articles 48 and 55 of the amended Constitution, the Prime Minister is the chief executive whereas the President is the titular head of the state. No post remained for the Vice-president and Deputy Prime Minister as it has been abolished.
2. In the original Constitution, the selection process of the President was by a poll. The members of the Parliament elected the President by the secret ballot as provided for in the Second Schedule of the Constitution. However, Second Schedule was not restored by the Twelfth Amendment. Nonetheless, after this Amendment, as per Article 48, the selection process of the President is in accordance with the law. It means that the members of parliament may by law make provision for election by open ballot. This process actually hinders the exercise of personal freedom of members of parliament in the process of electing the President.
3. The Fourth Amendment t introduced he provisions under which the number of terms in office was not specified for the President. The Twelfth Amendment restored the democratic provisions of the original constitution by abolishing these undemocratic provisions. In Article 50(2), it is provided that the President shall not hold office for more than two terms. It does not matter whether or not the terms are consecutive.
4. Under the original Constitution, only one function could be exercised the President independently. But now, under Article 48(3) of the Twelfth Amendment, two functions can be exercised independently by the President.

    i. to appoint the person who appears to him to command the support of the majority of the members of parliament as Prime Minister; and
    ii. to appoint the Chief Justice. The extended power which is present in the twelfth Amendment unlike in the original Constitution i.e., appointment of Chief Justice is a healthy provision in the sense that if it were to be appointed on the advice of the Prime Minister then political consideration would have hindered in the appointment procedure in the judiciary.

5. The Twelfth Amendment, in comparison to the original Constitution, has imposed double check on the power of the President to prorogue, summon, and dissolve parliament by inserting a new proviso to Article 72

'… … provided further that in exercise of his functions under this clause the President shall act in accordance with the advice of the Prime Minister tendered to him in writing' meaning that now the president shall not prorogue, summon and dissolve parliament not without the written advice of the Prime Minister. The purpose of imposing this double-check is to prevent undue and whimsical exercise of power by the President to dissolve parliament that can make a directly elected government unworkable, instances of which it had been observed several times in Pakistan.

6. Article 141A has been amended to the effect, as to the declaration of emergency, that the proclamation of emergency shall require the countersignature of the Prime Minister for its validity before the emergency is proclaimed. Thus, the Prime Minister virtually holds the whole power of declaring emergency. The purpose of inserting this double-check has also been with the same view i.e., to bar the possible misuse of power that the President could do. The politics of united Pakistan left bitter experiences with us as examples of such abuse of power by the presidents for their selfish reasons rendered the governmental system unworkable in the past.
7. Another double check, under Article 141C, the abolishment of enforcing fundamental rights during emergency, has been inserted with the same purpose that the President shall postpone the enforcement of fundamental rights during emergency by the written advice of the Prime Minister.
8. Regarding the impeachment and removal of the President, the revival of the provisions of the original Constitution can be seen i.e., the cases related to the initiation of motion and the passing of the resolution, both require simple Majority and two-thirds of the majority respectively.[38]

B. The 'Prime Minister' and the Cabinet

By keeping similarities with the provisions of the original Constitution, the cabinet led by the Prime Minister, has been reintroduced.

1. In Article 55, it has been provided that the cabinet shall be collectively responsible to parliament. Also, the executive power of the Republic shall be practiced by or on the authority of the Prime Minister.
2. The member of the Parliament, who appears to command the support of the majority members of the Parliament, shall be appointed as the Prime Minister by The President. Other ministers shall also be appointed by him after consultation with the Prime Minister (Article 56).
3. In comparison to the original Constitution of 1972, the Twelfth Amendment has introduced two changes regarding the cabinet.

   i. Ministers were allowed to be appointed from outside the Parliament according to the original Constitution under Article 56 on the condition that such an external minister must have to be elected as a member of the Parliament within six months of being appointed as a minister. But after introduction of the Twelfth Amendment, it is possible to appoint one-tenth of the total number of ministers from outside the Parliament and they need not be elected as parliamentary member unlike the provision in the original Constitution; but they must the qualification required for being elected as members of the Parliament.

It is worth mentioning that this provision for the appointment of ministers outside the Parliament is not recognized in a true parliamentary system. But this can be justified on the ground that it allows the government to realize the utility of the service provided by the technocrats. In most of the developing countries, there is a lack of capable and skilled people among the parliamentary members.

ii. Regarding the issue of tenure of the Prime Minister's office, the original provision concludes that the Prime Minister shall either resign from his position or ask the President to dissolve the parliament if he fails to hold the support of a majority of the parliamentary members. Later a new condition was imposed through the Twelfth Amendment that if the President is satisfied that no other member of the Parliament commands the support of the majority of the parliamentary members, only then he shall dissolve the Parliament [Article 57(2)].[39]

C. The Situation of Floor Crossing and Ministerial Responsibilities
To prevent floor crossing, more stringent measures have been introduced by the Twelfth Amendment though it was different according to the provisions of Article 70 as it stood before the amendment. Article 70 has been extended by adding two sub-sections. Forming any dissident group is prevented by section 70(2) within the party. Also, it is provided in section 70(3) that a party member will come under the preview of anti-defection provisions if an independent member joins any political party.

D. The intervening gap between two sessions of parliament were reverted to that of the original Constitution from the provisions as it was provided for in Article 72. Therefore, the role of parliament has been strengthened.

E. The Twelfth Amendment revived Chapter III which dealt with the provisions of local government and was Part IV of the Constitution though it was omitted by the Fourth Amendment.

F. In respect of international treaties, the Fifth Amendment and the Twelfth Amendment have improved the power of the parliament compared to the original Constitution. According to the new Article 145A, which has been added, it is provided that the the President shall lay all treaties with foreign countries before the parliament. However, on the ground of national interest, the President could refuse to lay any of such treaty before the parliament.

In true parliamentary form of government as it is practiced in UK, India and Australia, it needs to be pointed out that It should be pointed but that the King or President excersies the power of dissolution at his direction. The power is exercised in accordance with long practiced traditions and conventions of the parliamentary system. However, this discretionary power of the President had been misused, as mentioned earlier, during the Pakistan period that resulted in cabinet instability and failed government. To prohibit the arbitrary act of the President, the framers of the constitution of Bangladesh has provided for strict provisions, after learning from bitter instances of Pakistan, that do not leave any scope.

Also, it is noteworthy to mention here the power of the President has lost its its importance due to the barricade created by Articles 70 of the Constitution though the conventional features of a parliamentary system, as far as the powers of the President to dissolve parliament are concerned, are restored by the Twelfth Amendment.

It is time to ensure democracy and good governance, as it exists in most of the developed countries, to fulfil the desire of the people by and large so that they can co-exist peacefully with each other in Bangladesh. Bangladesh became independent from Pakistan after the great liberation war of 1971. In 1975, the murder of Bangabandhu Sheikh Mujibur Rahman, the father of the nation, created a great political crisis during which the Military took over the power. The scope for direct and indirect military rule was made limited by the 12th Amendment of Bangladesh Constitution. The first constitution of Bangladesh in 1972 adopted the Westminster model of Parliamentary democracy.

However, this model saw multiple hurdles such as one-party system authoritarianism, and personal rule. In spite of these hurdles, the power was taken over by mostly accepted elected form of governments since 1991.[40] Since 1972, 16 amendments have been made to the Constitution of Bangladesh. In the process, the Westminster model of Parliamentary Democracy was repealed by the 4th Amendment and it introduced Presidential form of government. Onn the other hand, the 12th Amendment reintroduced parliamentary form of government and repealed the 4th amendment of the constitution. On 6th August 1991, the Twelfth Amendment of the constitution was passed. This was a landmark in constitutional development in the country and it amended articles 48, 55-60, 70, 72, 109, 119, 124, 141A and 142.

After this amendment, the position of the Head of the State was held by the President of Bangladesh and the Prime Minister held the position of the Executive head. The post of Vice-President was abolished by this amendment and it held the Cabinet which is headed by the Prime Mister is responsible to the Parliament for exercising their powers, actions, and functions. However, all executive actions shall be taken in the name of the President. This amendment also ensured that the impeachment authority of the President is vested to the Parliament and the titular President (elected for not more than two terms) shall be elected by the members of the Parliament. Moreover, direct democracy was introduced by this amendment in the local government bodies. To resist the protest of the political parties

(15 party alliance lead by the Awami League, 7 party alliance lead by Bangladesh Nationalist Party and Jamat-e-Islami) against Martial regime, a parliamentary election on 26th April 1986 was announced by the then President Hussein Mohammad Ershad. in order. To challenge the opposition political parties, a political party called the Jatiyo Party was formed by Ershad.

However, both the opposition political alliances did not agree at the first phase to take part in the election arranged by the military regime. Nonetheless, on 21st March, Awami League, the mainstream opposition political party, decided to participate in the election whereas alliances formed by the Bangladesh Nationalist Party refused to take part in the election arranged by the military regime. As Awami League broke the grand alliance, it allowed Ershad to remain legally in power for four more years after. Jatiyo Party secured 153 seats, Awami League secured 76 seats, Jamat-e-Islami secured 10 seats, Communist Party of Bangladesh secured 5 seats, Muslim League secured 4 seats, Jatiyo Samajtantrik Dal (JSD-Rob) secured 4 seats, Krishak Shramik Awami League secured 3 seats, Jatiyo Samajtantrik Dal (JSDSiraj) secured 3 seats, Workers' Party secured 3 seats, National Awami Party secured 2 seats, and independent participants secured 32 seats In the parliamentary election of 1986. However, the Jatiyo Party further gained upper hand after the election when 23 out of 32 independent members of parliament joined in Jatiyo Party and obtained 30 more seats which were for women.[41]

This election, to some extent, reflected Ershad's promise of civilianizing his martial regime and the desire of the people for the end of Martial rule. The first session of the parliament after the election was boycotted by most members of the opposition parties. They claimed that martial law and democracy cannot go together. This happened because Hussein Mohammad Ershad was the then Chief of Army Staff. Therefore, a presidential election was declared on 15th October 1986 by General Ershad. Ershad, after his retirement from Army, became a full-fledged politician and occupied the position of the chairman of Jatiyo Party. In the presidential election, 12 candidates competed for the position but Ershad won the election by securing 83.57% votes. On 23rd October 1986, Ershad took his oath as a president after winning the election. After becoming president in a seemingly legitimized way Ershad called for the second session of the Parliament on 10th November 1986. There, he passed the 7th Amendment of the Constitution which validated the martial law regime.

Though parliamentary democracy was reintroduced by the 12th amendment of the Constitution, the ruling party seem to always bypass the parliament and they also try to pass law through promulgation. On the other hand, the nature of the opposition parties is reduced to boycotting the parliament thereby enabling the ruling party to pass any law without any fruitful debate. So, Anti-Terrorist Bill (1994), Ganges Water Sharing Treaty with India (1996), Chittagong Hill Tracts Peace Treaty (1997) and Anti-Terrorist Bill (2000) which were prominent ordinances turned into bills. In the recent past, the poor attendance of the Prime Minister was also observed apart from the tendency to bypass the parliament.

The members of parliament from opposite political parties continuously tried to put the ruling party under pressure by following the strategy of boycotting the parliamentary sessions whereas they were supposed to attend every parliamentary session to facilitate constructive discussion to stop passing autocratic decisions of the ruling party. Therefore, the nature of the opposition political parties was not parliamentary rather they were preferring street politics.

Moreover, the opposition parliamentarians claimed that the time slots allocated for them to deliver their speech in the Parliament is disproportionate to the time allocated to the members of the governing party. Three basic characteristics among the parliamentarians, in respect of their behaviour, are seen. These were personality cult, abusive speech and blame game among the politicians.

In addition to that, the ruling party always complained that the attitude of the opposition party towards the government was conspiratorial, vindictive, false and unconstitutional. Interestingly, the debates centre on the same issues such as the government is curtailing the freedom of the media and of the judiciary and the government is using different apparatus like Special Power Act in order to oppress the opposition. However, no political party in the near past showed any interest in resolving these disputes rather they blame each other for not resolving these issues. The mechanism and the administration of the parliament are the issues of continuous debate among other things. It is always pointed out that the Speaker is always partial in treating the members of the parliament because more time is allotted for the ruling party's MPs. Accountability of the government which is a vital part of parliamentary practice is not often ensured. In the parliament, Prime Minister as well as Ministers deliberately bypass to the questions asked to them. Moreover, the prescribed parliamentary rules and regulations are not properly followed by the secretariat. The office of Ombudsman has been made questionable and paralyzed since it is created. It barely has the power to scrutinize the administrative actions taken by the government.

Three basic factors are responsible for the dysfunctionality of the parliament. Firstly, the nature of the political culture of Bangladesh is characterized mostly by aggression and violence. Historically, such violence and aggression had contributed to the political demand of the party. As Secondly, ideals and philosophy are replaced by the whims of an individual. Therefore, the decision of an individual becomes the supreme command of the party. Finally, the lacking of democratic practices among the political parties are also responsible for dysfunctional nature of parliament.

Two types of tools are specifically used by the political parties to fight each other. These are Direct and Indirect Democratic Tools. Voting rights cancellation, incorporation of one party system, the military regimes and ban on religion bases political parties are include in the Direct Democratic Tools. On the other hand, financial corruption, political corruption and misuse of democratic rights are included in Indirect Democratic Tools. Among them, financial corruption refers to money laundering, bribing during election, corruption on the governmental projects and bribing for tender and auction. On the contrary, fake voter roll making, political discrimination among government officers, legalizing military regimes, making constitutional amendments hastily and without considering the view of the mass people and giving care taker government a political flavour are the constituting elements of political corruption. However, the true concern for Bangladesh is the political corruption. It is because the country has a history of ensuring punishment for financial corruption but there is rarely any instance of ensuring punishment for political corruption. Blame game and misuse of democratic rights are some of the common practices of the political parties of Bangladesh.

Rather than participating actively in the parliament, undemocratic measures like—meetings, processions, blockades and strikes are preferred. The blame games which are commonly played by the two mainstream parties (Bangladesh Awami League and Bangladesh Nationalist Party) in Bangladesh can be presented in a set of binaries such as secular vs. non-Secular, pro-Liberation vs. anti-Liberation, anti-Pakistan vs. pro-Pakistan and Bengali vs. Bangladeshi.

Democracy is very much appreciated and democratic government is most desirable form of government all over the world. Though democracy is practiced in the developed countries, the existing democratic system in developing countries requires vast scrutiny. In Bangladesh, the bureaucracy is highly politicized in nature and the parliament is often dysfunctional. The political parties believe in the motto of 'winner takes all.' On top of that, Election Commission has been used for the benefit of the ruling party from time to time.is observed to be functioning as an agent of the ruling political party.[42]

The dysfunctionality of the Parliament and the lack of governmental accountability are not uncommon. By incorporating and cancelling the provision for the care taker government, the current political crisis is made. Though judicial orders should always be welcomed by the parliament, it is not the case in reality. Judiciary has nothing but judicial orders and the power of implementing and the responsibility of implementing judicial orders are vested upon the executive. However, the separation between legislature and executive can barely be seen in the Westminster model of parliament. If there is unwillingness on part of the legislature and executive in terms of respecting the judicial orders, would the general people go? World Bank identifies voice and accountability are the markers of good governance. However, the scenario is completely different in Bangladesh. The people of Bangladesh do not have a voice rather they only have the option to choose their representatives once in every five years. Sometimes, that option is also curtailed. Accountability can neither be seen nor assured in the governmental level due to the failure of the parliament and the highly politicized nature of the bureaucracy. The freedom of press and media is often times restricted in Bangladesh. The government threatens all endeavours to raise voice. Therefore, Non-Governmental Organization (NGOs), which function often try to raise the voice of the people and speak about the freedom of press and media, are threatened. The independence and impeachment of judiciary as well as appointment are far from the expected level. Though political stability always remains a vital apparatus for good governance, it is still a myth for Bangladesh. Good governance and democracy complement each other. Examples of the coexistence of good governance and democracy can be seen in developed countries and it is also observed that democratic practices improve good governance. Though democracy and good governance coexist in Bangladesh theoretically, the story is far from true in reality. In It can be said, from the above discussion, that it is clear from empirical point of view that good governance and democracy barely coexist in Bangladesh.[43]

To fulfil the desire of the people of Bangladesh and to form a strong government, both good governance and democracy are necessary. To ensure proper democratic practices in the country, Bangladesh had to go through a lot of hardships. Some prescriptions, to good governance and ensure democracy in the government, are given below:

1. Among the political parties, democratic practice should be ensured as it is necessary.
2. Politicization of the office of the Election Commission should not be done so that it cannot used for political purposes. Also, it should be invested with the power to scrutiny the financial status of any member of any political party.
3. The political parties should welcome the constructive criticism by civil societies rather than restricting their voice.
4. The politicization of bureaucracy should be stopped and the accountability of the government should be guaranteed by practicing democracy.
5. Press and media should be made totally free in terms of their independent. Also, the politicians and people at large should welcome the constructive criticism of press and media.
6. Judiciary should be made independent. Also, impeachment of judiciary and transparency in the appointment process should be assured.
7. People from opposite political parties should not be harassed intentionally because of their political ideologies and statements.
8. The ruling parties and oppositions should ensure parliamentary from of democracy. Boycotting the parliament by walking out should not be the preference.
9. Punishment should be ensured for political corruption, like that of financial corruption.
10. Direct access to the governmental bodies by people should be ensured. Government officers should uphold the sentiment that they are in office to serve the people. Moreover, the Right to Information Act 2009 should be updated and made accessible to all so that people's right to information is ensured.

The amendment of a country's constitution, at times, becomes necessary to adapt to the changing needs of national development; to overcome difficulties which may be encountered in future working of the constitution and to realize any popular demand for changing the political system. The amendment of

Constitution should only be resorted to in cases of serious repercussions or emergent circumstances or a special contingency. However, in Bangladesh, the amendments of the constitution have often been used to achieve political purposes rather than for strengthening constitutionalism. Moreover, multiple and multifarious amendments undermined the sanctity of the Constitution as an organic instrument and created confusion and crisis of constitutionalism. For example, the 2nd and 4th Amendments of the Constitution which effected vital changes in the Constitution, have undermined foundations of rule of law and acted as strategies used by the Awami League Government to enhance its monolithic control over the state.

The procedure of amendment, instead of being rigid, has proved to be too flexible, and as many as fifteen amendments have been made so far in the Constitution of Bangladesh in 42 years span of its life. There is no separate constituent body for amendment and Parliament, the ordinary legislative body of the state performs the functions in its capacity as a legislative body enacting and repealing the ordinary laws of the state.

The fact that many amendments have been made just to amend the constitution for political gain justifies the conclusion that on some occasions, the Parliament has acted in a hasty and casual manner. In this respect Parliament lost its credibility in such a manner and to such extent that the judiciary was forced to import the concept of 'unamend ability of basic structure.'[44]

## Thirteenth Amendment—Establishment of the Non-partisan Caretaker Government

The Thirteenth Amendment of the Constitution of the People's Republic of Bangladesh, in 1996, introduced the Non-Party Caretaker Government (NCG) system in Bangladesh with a view to holding free and fair elections for the national Parliament. Three elections had been successfully carried out under the NCG system (1996, 2001 and 2008). The unique form was brought into effect due to extreme distrust between the ruling and the opposition political parties. Complicated and convoluted constitutional questions often jeopardize political processes and impede the operation of government entities. Many procedural defects hampered the operation of the established caretaker governments in the 13th amendment.[45] The framework of caretaker government had been greatly influenced by internal causes such as political instability, lack of military professionalism and institutional pitfalls. Bangladesh's people were mostly satisfied with this system as NCG performed its duties successfully.

However, the NCG was abolished by the Parliament in 2011 on the basis of an adverse decision of the Supreme Court. The political Parties (ruling and main opposition) were, then, engaged in a confrontation over whether the elections will be held under NCG or under the current political Government. Thirteenth constitutional Amendment could have served well if a non-partisan president had objected to it. The thirteenth Amendment changed Article 61 of the constitution giving full authority to the President over the nation during the term of the caretaker government. Such control was the characteristic of a presidential system of government and not of a parliamentary one.[46] The reform, thus, gave the President absolute power, an authority not accorded in compliance with the constitution to an elected government. The President thus became an unreasonable dictator who was not elected by the people directly.

The Non-Party Caretaker Government (NCG) system was introduced in Bangladesh as a progressive concept. It was brought into effect through the Thirteenth Amendment of the Constitution in 1996. Three elections (1996, 2001 & 2008) have been held under NCG successfully and the power to govern the country's people has been transferred to the winning party peacefully. In earlier times, ruling parties tried to dictate the outcomes of elections by terrorizing their oppositions, especially when the elections were held under the partisan Governments. Thus, Bangladeshis had lost their faith in elections. Over the period of 1971-2001, five elections were held under political Governments, where almost all ruling parties were alleged to have used force to win the elections. The excesses of ruling Parties made oppositions search for a mechanism that would bring neutrality in elections.[47]

> *On 24th November, 1995 the government dissolved the 5th parliament and the 6th Parliamentary Election was scheduled on 15th February, 1996. But since the government did not pay any heed to the demand of caretaker government by the opposition, all the opposition parties boycotted election. The ruling party BNP proceeded to contest the election with sudden hand-picked parties as the military director Ershad did. The announcement of the result of the election added fuel to the fire-like opposition movement. All the opposition parties launched their country-wide non-cooperation movement and demanded the fall of the government as well as the dissolution of 6th parliament. The whole politico-economic condition of the country was leading to a complete civil war. Lastly finding no other the way-out BNP government introduced the Caretaker Government Bill (the 13th Amendment of the Constitution) on 21st March at the first session of the 6th parliament. The Bill was passed on 26th March, then the 6th parliament after 7 days of its life was dissolved on 30th March and Justice Habibur Rahman was appointed, as the Chief. Adviser of the Caretaker Government as envisaged in the 13th Amendment of the Constitution.*[48]

The Caretaker government, in political science, is not a new concept. The concept is observed in many developed democratic nations when outgoing Governments choose to perform their duties as Caretaker Governments. Caretaker Governments are found in European democracies, when the incumbent government rules the country until power is transferred to newly-elected Government through elections.[49] European countries regularly have Caretaker Governments, partisan or non-partisan when no Party has a majority in the newly-elected Parliament. In such a case, Parties carry on coalition negotiations which can take months. During this period, a non-Party or technocratic Government is often appointed to keep the State operating while there is no permanent Government. As many as 24 technocratic Governments were in power in EU nations between 1945 and 2012.[50]

During this period of Caretaker Government, there actually is no Government but the President or King will appoint persons to act as Ministers or instruct the current Ministers to stay in their positions, 'as caretakers,' meaning they will not change policies or make any non-urgent decisions. Belgium recently had a caretaker Government for 590 days after the 2010 elections.[51] Even Britain has experienced non-political or 'grand coalition' Governments in emergency situations which have carried out free and fair elections. A coalition Government of Prime Minister Churchill's Conservative Party and its opposition Labour Party was formed by Churchill to deal with the crisis of German bombing, blockade and expected invasion during World War II in the years from 1940 to 1945. This coalition Government conducted the 1945 election which saw the Conservatives thrown out and the election of the first Labour Government with a majority in the Parliament.[52]

Precisely, a Caretaker government should not introduce any new program or start new policies. A Non-Party Caretaker Government can be defined as 'a Government which has very short tenure, and does not have so much authority to introduce any changes in structure, rules and policies of the existent government.' Generally, the Government which takes the responsibility to run the administration during the interim period is called a Non-Party Caretaker Government.[53] Such a Government cannot make any new policy, write new legislation or make any commitment to introduce new and large expenditures.

This Amendment was passed with 268-0 votes on 26th March, 1996 and it became a law on 28th March. The Amendment added a new Chapter (Chapter IIA: Non-Party Caretaker Government) in part IV of the Constitution with 5 new Articles (58A, 58B, 58C, 58D and 58E). It also introduced amendment Articles 61, 99, 123, 147, 152 and the Third Schedule of the Constitution.

Under such political turmoil, the sixth parliament enacted the thirteenth amendment to the Constitution. The amendment inserted the new chapter IIA and the new article 58A in the Constitution. It also amended the articles 61, 99, 123, 147 and 152 and also the Third Schedule of the Constitution. The amendment contained provisions of keeping some articles 48 (3), 141A9 (1) and 141C (1) ineffective during the period of the caretaker government. The salient features of the amendment and the caretaker system were as follows:[54]

**Entering upon Office:** There shall be a Non-Party Care-taker Government during the period from the date on which the Chief Adviser (CA) of such government enters upon office after the Parliament is dissolved or stands dissolved by reason of expiration of its term till the date on which a new Prime Minister enters upon his office after the constitution of the Parliament.

**Responsible to:** The Non-Party Care-taker Government shall be collectively responsible to the President.

**Executive Power:** The executive power of the Republic shall, during the period mentioned in clause (1), be exercised, subject to the provisions of article 58D (1), in accordance with the Constitution, by or on the authority of the CA and shall be exercised by CA in accordance with the advice of the Non-Party Care-taker Government.

**President's Power on Defence Services:** The supreme command of the Defence Services of Bangladesh vests in the President and the exercise, thereof, shall be regulated by law and such law shall, during the period of Non-Party caretaker government, be administered by the President.

**President's Power of Declaring Emergency:** The Thirteenth Amendment to the Constitutions allows the President to issue a proclamation of emergency without the advice of the CA.[55]

**Composition of the Caretaker Government:** The caretaker government will be composed in the following way:

Non-Party Care-taker Government shall consist of the CA at its head and not more than ten other Advisors, all of whom shall be appointed by the President.

The CA and other Advisers shall be appointed within 15 days after the Parliament is dissolved or stands dissolved; and during the period between the date on which Parliament is dissolved or stands dissolved and the date on which the CA is appointed, the Prime Minister and his cabinet who were in office immediately before the Parliament was dissolved or stood dissolved shall continue to hold office as such.

The President shall appoint as CA the person who, among the retired Chief Justices of Bangladesh, retired last and who is qualified to be appointed as an Adviser under article 58C of the Constitution. Provided that if such retired Chief Justice is not available or is not willing to hold the office of CA, the President shall appoint as CA the person who, among the retired Chief Justices of Bangladesh, retired next before the last retired Chief Justice.[56]

If no retired Chief Justice is available or willing to hold the office of CA, the President shall appoint as CA the person who, among the retired Judges of the Appellate Division, retired last and who is qualified to be appointed as an Adviser under the article 58C of the Constitution. It was also provided that if such retired Judge is not available or is not willing to hold the office of CA, the President shall appoint as CA the person who, among the retired Judges of the Appellate Division, retired next before the last such retired Judge.

If no retired Judge of the Appellate Division is available or willing to hold the office of CA, the President shall, after consultation, as far as practicable, with the major political parties, appoint the CA from among citizens of Bangladesh who are qualified to be appointed as Advisers under article 58C of the Constitution.

Notwithstanding anything contained in this Chapter, if the provisions of clauses (c), (d) and (e) cannot be given effect to, the President shall assume the functions of the CA of the Non-Party Care-taker Government in addition to his own functions under the Constitution.[57]

**Eligibility of the Advisers:** The President shall appoint Advisers from among the persons who are-

Qualified for election as members of the Parliament;

Not members of any political party;

Not, and have agreed in writing not to be, candidates for the ensuring election of members of the Parliament.

Not over 72 years of age.[58]

**Appointment of the Advisers:** The Advisers shall be appointed by the President on the Advice of the Chief Adviser.

**Resignation of CA and Advisers:** The CA or an Adviser may resign his office by his own hand-written letter addressed to the President. The CA or an Adviser shall cease to be CA or Adviser if he is disqualified to be appointed as such under article 58C of the Constitution.

**Status of CA and Advisers:** The CA shall have the status of and be entitled to the remuneration and privileges of a Prime Minister and an Adviser shall have the status and be entitled to the remuneration and privileges of a Minister.

**Dissolution of the Caretaker Government:** The Non-Party Care-taker Government shall stand dissolved on the date on which the Prime Minister enters upon his/her office after the constitution of the new Parliament.

**Functions of Caretaker Government:** The Caretaker government shall discharge the following functions:

The Non-Party Care-taker Government shall discharge its functions as an interim government and shall carry on with the routine functions of such government with the aid and assistance of persons in the services of the Republic; and, except in the case of necessity for the discharge of such functions, it shall not make any policy decision.

The Non-Party Care-taker Government shall give to the Election Commission all possible aid and assistance that may be required for holding the general election of members of the Parliament peacefully, fairly and impartially.[59]

Bangladesh has a long history of political unrest, military rule, autocracy and a glorious struggle for democracy. The introduction of a constitutional, nonpartisan and neutral caretaker government to oversee future elections was hailed as a milestone in Bangladesh's political history. Under the constitutionally recognized caretaker system had already witnessed three parliamentary elections during period 1996 to 2008. Many at home and abroad believed that Bangladesh's success with the system can serve a model for the developing countries facing problems similar to Bangladesh.

The idea was to allow an interim authority to take over the election process once the incumbent party steps down three months prior to the election. In the constitutional development of Bangladesh, the 13th Amendment of the constitution, in a sense, is a positive step for the following reasons.[60]

Firstly, the fundamental basis of formation of government in democracy is election. If this election is not free and fair, the formation of government cannot be said to fulfil the norms of democracy; and in this case the most celebrated maxim of democracy 'alt power belongs to the people' becomes a mere farce. More the election process will be free and fair, more the people will see their voting right, in other words, right to elect representatives meaningful. The most important positive merit of the 13th Amendment is that it has paved the way for making the elections free and fair, particularly free from government influence.

> *'Secondly, it has been a common trend in the politics of almost all developing countries that during the election period the manpower makes the worst abuse of public purse and properties to get victory in their favour.*[61] *This manipulation in the election process virtually creates an insurmountable stumbling block to the development of some important democratic institutions like the Election Commission, press, media and political party etc. Since the 13th Amendment provides interim separate caretaker government and no party government can continue in power during the general election, there remains no scope of manipulation of public purse and properties by the party in power.'*[62]
>
> *'Thirdly, coming to power every government now will have to think that once parliament is dissolved or its term is ended, it will automatically find itself out of power and then the public will have the fullest opportunity and atmosphere to exercise their right to elect representatives and of government. On the other hand, no government now will be in a position to think for manipulation in the elections; rather it will think for doing material benefit to the people. There is therefore, possibility that the government will now be more responsive than in the past.'*[63]

Supporting the 13th amendment of the constitution Justice Md Abdul Wahhab Miah in his judgment on the Constitution (Thirteenth Amendment) Act 1996 has argued that the 13th amendment is intra vires but not ultra vires to the Constitution.[64]

Though caretaker government system is hailed by people in home and abroad, from the beginning of the introduction of the caretaker system, however, scholars, observers and political leaders identified its structural deficiencies, limitations and some contradictory features.[65]

The thirteenth amendment altered the basic structure of the Constitution/ government of the country. Bangladesh, as a parliamentary democracy, normally practices a system where the PM enjoys the confidence of the Parliament and acts as the executive chief of the country and the President works as a titular head. But the thirteenth amendment empowered the government. As a result, the titular President becomes a 'real' President when the caretaker government takes the charge of the state affairs. The President was vested wider power in matters of President. A provision of the Constitution categorically mentioned that,

> The Non- Party Care-taker Government shall be collectively responsible to the President. During the tenure of the caretaker government the system of government took a completely different turn and the parliamentary form of government became an interim presidential form of government.

The thirteenth amendment conferred some real and absolute powers to the President who is not entitled to have all these powers under the Constitution. In exercising these powers, the President is beyond the reach of the caretaker government. The thirteenth amendment thus transforms the figurehead President to an all-powered President, effectively introducing an interim presidential form of government during the tenure of the caretaker government. It has created two separates but potentially conflicting sources of governmental power: The President and the caretaker government. These are affirmatively inconsistent with and repugnant to the basic structure of the Constitution.[66]

In normal time the President acts, except appointing the PM and the Chief Justice, as per the advice of the PM. During the tenure of the caretaker government, the President did not need to act in accordance with the advice of the CA. He enjoyed more freedom in his actions. The thirteenth amendment gave the President power to administer the defence services. It also empowered the president declare emergency without the concurrence of the CA if he is satisfied that a grave emergency exists in which the security or economic life of Bangladesh, or any part thereof, is threatened by war or external aggression or internal disturbance.[67]

The President's enhanced power aroused strong criticism from various corners. BNP supported this move by presenting since he was the only elected office holder during the period of interim government. Many observers found a different reason for BNP's decision to give the President such a wider power. According to them, the BNP government gave the president such power with an ill-motive to influence the elections.

The idea of giving additional power to the President had also been criticized from the points of the President's institutional capacity. Normally the President is a ceremonial head. He maintains his office with a lean staff. But when the President exercises his enhanced power, he depends on the government's infrastructure. One scholar pointed out that the ceremonial President with more power is a paradox; he lacks institutional support, and his exercising of the enhanced powers implicates the entire government.[68]

The thirteenth amendment prescribed that executive powers would be exercised by the CA. On the other hand, the amendment gave some powers to the President which he would exercise without the advice of the CA. It had been termed by many as a contradiction. There was thus a risk that the system of government may become diarchic if the President and the CA fail to agree to work together and/ or to collaborate with each other.

As per the **article 58C** of the Constitution if the President had to choose a CA from among parties. Though the provision mentioned that the President would appoint the CA 'after consultation as far as practicable' but how this consultation would be held and what did the consultation mean—either by agreement among the parties or by consensus—were not clearly mentioned. It was a vague and ambiguous provision.

The caretaker government was an interim government. But how long it had to remain in the office was not specified in terms of days or months.

**Article 58B** of the Constitution read:

> There shall be a Non-Party care-taker Government during the period from the date on which the Chief Adviser enters upon office after Parliament is dissolve or stands dissolved till the date on which a new Prime Minister enters … after the constitution of the Parliament.

In absence of the specific time-frame, some tried to interpret that the Constitution allowed an indefinite period for the caretaker government.[69]

The constitutional provision allowed the President, as the last option, to assume the functions of the CA of the caretaker government in addition to his own function. This provision had been considered as something directly opposing the idea of caretaker system. The President is a political person elected from a political view. So a partisan person cannot be the chief of a non-party government. The President as Chief Adviser makes a mockery of the constitutional and accountable government and perhaps destroys the caretaker government as an institution.

The caretaker provisions were applicable to national elections only. Local government polls are indispensable to ensure the grassroots democracy. It had been argued that by ignoring elections and local government polls, caretaker provisions left a major arena open for electoral corruptions.

It has been said and expected that the members of the caretaker government and the CA would be non-political and they would have no previous link with any political party. These non-political persons were given to manage the most political event, the national elections. It was also a paradox. 'There is thus,' one scholar has apprehended, 'a risk that a lack of experience of the NCG (Non-Party Caretaker Government) in handling party political matter may make it insensitive to politicians' problems and priorities.'[70]

In Bangladesh most of the appointments in HC are made from political considerations. Political manoeuvrings are very much active in the higher judiciary. As per the provisions of the thirteenth amendment, it was emphasized that the CA and other members of the caretaker government would be taken from the judiciary. Many observers were critical about the negative impact of involving the judiciary with the demand of the caretaker government. Eminent jurist, Ishtiaq Ahmed, mentioned that handling party political matters may make it insensitive to politicians' problems and priorities. He also said that the demand for a caretaker Government, a little later, became a demand for a 'non-partisan government composed of 'nominated' persons. Later, it was improved by the demand of the having the Chief Justice to head such a government. As time passed, this demand was amended further by including, in the list after him, the immediate past Chief Justice and lastly, in that order, an eminent citizen. The supreme judiciary was being drawn into politics. Whether it was the appointing Chief Justice or the immediate past Chief Justice, the role of political chief executive of the republic contained the danger of distorting the constitutional scheme in which the Supreme Court exists and exercises its powers and jurisdiction.[71] Apprehensions were also made to the extent that higher judiciary might be over-politicized. The incumbent government can make plan to influence the coming caretaker government by appointing a Chief Justice of their choice through the politically elected President. According to a scholar,

> The Constitution does not require the government of the day to consult the Chief Justice while making appointments to the HCD (High Court Division) and AD (Appellate Division). On the other hand, the President, who can appoint the Chief Justice without any consultation with the PM, may in effect be influenced in his decision by the party in power as he is elected by (party) MPs. In other words, by exercising control over the appointment and promotion of the judges of the SC, the government of the day might hope to influence the formation of the NCG in the long run and, ultimately, the election process.

It was observed that in a country where the courts are inherently politicized, finding a former chief justice, supportive or sympathetic towards a particular party, would not be hard. Hypothetically, the scheme might also be used by party government to plan in advance the appointment of politically motivated judges to the Supreme Court and have them prematurely retired before an election. Thus, such a party could have one of its own allies chosen as the head of an NCG. In such an event, the entire edifice of neutrality would fall apart.

The demand of forming a caretaker government for holding free and fair elections was, in fact, the reflection of complete mistrust on political leaders. After enactment of the thirteenth amendment, the caretaker government was responsible for holding national elections freely and fairly. Many observers felt that recurrent use of the caretaker government would inhibit the growth of democratic electoral practices and culture. Political leaders would not learn from their mistakes, and no party government would be entrusted with arranging national elections.[72]

Great controversy about the structural deficiencies of the caretaker government had aroused. Under the constitutionally recognized caretaker system three parliamentary elections took place during the period from 1996 to 2001. The seventh parliamentary election was arranged by the caretaker government headed by Justice Muhammad Habibur Rahman. It was a free and fair election although some incidents of malpractices were reported to have taken place. But the fairness of the election and the neutrality of the government were questioned by a section of leaders of the loosing BNP and its political allies JI. Some of them even questioned the validity of the concept of caretaker government.

The Constitution Act 1996 offered for a non-party Caretaker Government which, stand-in as an acting government would provide all potential aid and assistance to the Election Commission for holding the general election of members of the Jatiya Sangsad (National Parliament) serenely, moderately and with detachment. The caretaker government, consisting of the Chief Adviser and not more than 10 other advisers, would be communally accountable to the President and would stand on charge on the date on which the Prime Minister entered upon his office after the charter of the new Sangsad (Parliament).

The Supreme Court in its historic ruling on 10 May 2011, held the 13th Amendment of 1996 introducing the caretaker government prospectively void and unconstitutional. The ruling did not apply retrospectively to nullify past elections under the caretaker governments and next two elections were allowed to be held under the 13th Amendment.

The apex court repealed the 13th Amendment in the Constitution, but said that the next 10th and 11th parliamentary elections may be held under the system to avoid any chaos. The apex court, however, observed that the Parliament, meanwhile, is at liberty to amend the law under which the chief justice or any other judges of the Appellate Division of SC are not involved in the non-party government system in the next two elections. The non-party caretaker government of Bangladesh is a form of government system in which the country is ruled by a selected government for an interim period during transition from one government to another, after the completion tenure of the former, Xinhua news agency reported. 'The Constitution (Thirteenth amendment) Act 1996 (Act 1 of 1996) is prospectively declared void and ultra vires the Constitution,' said the SC order.

Former Chief Justice ABM Khairul Haque had signed the 342-page judgement in the Supreme Court on 13 September, 2012. He was the top judge who headed the seven-strong benches that delivered the verdict on 10 May 2011. Justices Mahmud Hossain, Sinha and Mozammel Hossain agreed with him. Justices Wahab Miah and Sultana differed while Justice Iman Ali left the matter for the Parliament to decide. In its short verdict, the apex court also observed that the rescinded system may be practised for another two parliamentary terms. The bench, which heard the petition from 1 March to 6 April also heard the views of eight senior lawyers as 'amici curiae.'

The Parliament was also asked by the court to make Constitutional amendments to ensure that the former Chief Justices or any other judges from the Supreme Court are not selected to head the caretaker governments if the system remains valid for two more parliamentary elections. For the first time, mixed languages—Bengali and English were used to write a verdict. Usually, verdicts are written in English by the court. Unlike the usual process, the main part of the verdict was written in Bengali by Justice Khairul Haque. 150 pages of the verdict was written by Justice Ali.

The idea that all parliamentary acts are, as a matter of fact, legitimate as these acts are enacted by the elected representatives is essentially problematic because of the perception that our parliament is the sovereign law-making institution like that of the British Parliament. However, Bangladesh Parliament, unlike that of the British Parliament, operates under a specific written constitution where Article 7 provides that a law should not be enacted if it is repugnant to or inconsistent with the Constitution. The SC, as the custodian of the Constitution, can declare any parliamentary act illegal if the act is is repugnant to or inconsistent with the Constitution due to its judicial review power. Such instances are numerous. It is very common in most places of the world that judicial review power is exercised by apex judiciary under written constitutions, starting from Marbury v Madison (US SC 1803). In case of Anwar Hossain Chowdhury in 1989 and in the cases of 5th and 7th amendments in recent times, the SC of Bangladesh has exercised this power. There is barely any difference between the 5th, 7th, and 13th amendments as far as their constitutional consistency is concerned. The SC has a responsibility to tidy up the constitutional mess which is created by those amendments which serve sectarian interests by making the supreme law of the land self-contradictory and incoherent. Those people/parties who got benefited from this mess consider this power of the SC controversial. But must be respected because it is dignified constitutionalism.

Dr. Kamal Hossain, as Amicus Curiae, provided his valuable opinion on the constitutionality of the Thirteenth Amendment.[73]

He opined that it destroyed the Republican character of the Constitution (which was a basic feature). The dreams which were woven into the constitutional demands were those of a democratic political order in which power would truly belong to the people (Article 7), to be exercised through a sovereign parliament, composed of representatives elected on the basis of universal adult franchise. The elected parliament would bring about social and economic transformation. It was clearly expected that the true representatives of the people elected through free and fair elections (free from manipulation by money and muscle) would be totally committed to end exploitation by implementing programs for fundamental economic and social change.

The petitions call for an interpretation of the provisions relating to the basic features of the Constitution. The grounds urged would tend to suggest that the Thirteenth Amendment is repugnant to the Constitution and 'destroys' certain basic features (referred to as the grounds). This approach itself is misconceived, since the validity of a Constitution Amendment, which was made based on consensus of major political parties (and sections including civil society), and had been acted upon by them in each of the successive elections, should not be the subject matter of a challenge going to the root of its constitutionality. On close analysis, it appears that the grievances are in fact about the manner in which the provision has been applied in specific cases/events, in particular, the mode/manner in which the Chief Adviser discharged his responsibility in 2001 and, the manner in which the Chief Adviser was appointed and a number of actions taken by him in 2006 have raised questions about his role.

It was also submitted through his opinion that the approach which the apex court should adopt is to recognize that the Thirteenth Amendment was made in the context of the situation created in 1996 when the election held by the outgoing government had been rejected by the Opposition as neither free nor fair. The results were announced showing a larger turn out when it was widely perceived to have been participated by less than 5% voters and all the opposition parties had refrained from participation. They had been offended by the malpractices in the Magura bye-election. This created a situation where there was a demand for fresh election. The question was who would conduct the election. There was only the precedent of the election which was conducted by Chief Justice Shahabuddin Ahmad in 1991 in the very special circumstances when General Ershad had been compelled to resign and there was need for an acceptable neutral administration to conduct the election. The alternative which was being projected was a martial law proclamation, which would have totally undermined the constitutional order to protect the Constitution. There was a proposal to establish a Caretaker Government by having an amendment adopted by the Sixth Parliament whose constitutionality itself was not free from questioning. In the end the adoption of the Thirteenth Amendment was, rightly thought to be the best alternative.

Again, Dr. Kamal Hossain opined that it destroyed the democratic character of the Constitution. The absence of a long title in the bill in 1996 was unwarranted inasmuch as this requirement was not part of the original Constitution and was itself introduced under the cover of martial law. It was, therefore, not a basic feature of the Constitution and the amending bill itself is evidence that such a requirement was not recognized when the amendment was enacted. The other two grounds, namely, dyarchy as a result of Article 61 and dictatorial powers are both tendentious and show lack of understanding of a constitutional mechanism adopted by consensus to meet the widely-shared concern to supplement the Election Commission's capacity to ensure free and fair elections. The alleged inconsistency with the principle of democracy is misconceived. The foundation of democracy, that is, government by the people, for the people and of the people, is Article 7 of the Constitution together with fundamental rights provision (Chapter III).[74]

Next, he submitted that it destroyed the Independence of the Judiciary. He observed that The Thirteenth Amendment was in the Constitution when it was expressly said by the Hon'ble Court that there is no provision in the Constitution which curtails independence of the judiciary. Without prejudice to the foregoing, the question is asked: has anything happened since Mazdar Hossain case so that the above finding can be questioned. The possible argument is that the incumbent governments as part of election strategy seek to appoint and promote judges or retire judges by a pre-determined plan with a view to gaining undue advantage by appointment of a preferred judge to head the caretaker government to ensure that he occupies the position of immediate past Chief Justice and possibly of the expectation of certain judges to be manipulated, may create instability within the highest judiciary.

Lastly, Dr. Kamal Hossain submitted that Article 58C (6) created dictatorial powers for the Government. He also observed that there is a national consensus supporting electoral reforms to ensure a free and fair election. For ensuring truly free and fair election and to ensure that citizens could make informed choice, they need to be protected from manipulation of money, muscle and media which is owned and controlled by powerful interests. The suggestions set out above are intended to strengthen the constitutional provision made in Part VII relating to the Election Commission. The measures suggested would provide for supplementing the Election Commission to discharge its constitutional mandate.

He also recommended that the Government of Bangladesh should be forward thinking aiming to further strengthen the Election Commission and to cure the defects (if any) in the system of Caretaker Government towards the goal of ensuring 'effective participation of all the people in a more free and fair election.' We should not do the opposite by removing the Caretaker Government and revert back to pre-1996 position. The Caretaker Government was introduced following broad social and political consensus (which is the change brought about by the people to protect their rights to have effective participation in a free and fair election process) to facilitate and make the hands of the Election Commission much stronger; to encourage the Election Commission to nurture an enabling environment to hold the elections in a manner perceived by the people as free and fair through effective participation of all the voters and contestants in a healthy democratic atmosphere.

Awami League-led grand alliance welcomed the Supreme Court verdict that declared the constitutional provision for the caretaker government illegal. The leading political leaders of this part expressed that the caretaker government system was introduced to meet a special need and it cannot be a permanent solution. By calling the decision as 'time worthy,' they also recommended that all political parties should reach a consensus through discussion on how or under whom the general elections should be held in future. They suggested that a civil society member, a former bureaucrat, an eminent educationist, a former minister or a former lawmaker might head the caretaker government in future in line with the apex court verdict.[75]

## Fourteenth Amendment—Enforced Parliamentary Gender Neutrality

The allocation of seats reserved for women was provided by the 14th Amendment. This amendment was passed on 16 may, 2004. The extension of 30 reserved seats for women members in parliament passed by 10th amendment was expired in 2001. 14th amendment reintroduces reserved seats for women member that have been increased from 30 to 45.

The 14th Amendment did not only increase the number of women's seats reserved, but also made it mandatory to place portraits of the Prime Minister in government offices, and raised, among other provisions, the retirement age of Supreme Court judges was that increased by two years.

### *The Original Provisions of the Act Were*

> 65(3): Until the dissolution Parliament occurring next after the expiration of the period of ten years beginning from the date of the first meeting of the

Parliament next after the Parliament in existence at the time of the commencement of the Constitution (Fourteenth Amendment) Act, 2004, there shall be reserve 45 seats exclusively for women members and they will be elected by the aforesaid members in accordance with law on the basis of procedure of proportional representation in the Parliament through single transferable vote.[76]

## *Introduction of a New Paragraph in the Fourth Schedule*

23. Temporary special Provision regarding women members in the Parliament.

1. for the residual period of the Parliament in existence at the time of the commencement of the Constitution (Fourteenth Amendment) Act, 2004 there shall be reserved forty-five seats exclusively for women members and they will be elected by members of the Parliament in accordance with law on the basis of procedure of proportional representation in the Parliament thought single transferable vote.
2. During the period mentioned in sub-paragraph (1), the Parliament shall consist of the three hundred members mentioned in clause (2) of Article 65 and the forty women members mentioned in sub-paragraph (1) of this paragraph.

8th Parliament did not only pass act for the 14th Amendment to increase reserved seats for women in parliament but also there was another controversial political implication by BNP. Thirty reserved seats for women in parliament was expired on 2001, reserving women seats in parliament was a much-needed steps to re-establish democratic value in parliament in support of article 10–19(1), 27, 28(1), and 28(2) of the constitution. But other provisions of the 14th Amendment have more political implications than actual ones. The Fourteenth Amendment was generally regarded as a partisan decision that supported the interests of the ruling party since it increased the retirement age of Supreme Court judges from 65 to 67.

## *Political Reason and Aftermath*

Although Bangladesh is formed with a democratic framework, practically it has been a hotchpotch with military-based government many times after independence. In October 2001, when BNP led four-party alliance came to power through the caretaker government, the election was recognized and accepted nationally and internationally.[77] But they lost citizens' acceptance for corruption, misdeed, and Islamic foundationalism over five years of their time. They further tried to manipulate the next upcoming election in 2006 through the 14th amendment. Conducting an election under the caretaker government was legally possible under the 13th amendment.

BNP started to lose citizens' trust in the first year of their power due to various terrorist activities in different universities under their banner, looting, and taking control of different industries by illegal armed cadres. During a visit to Bangladesh, Secretary General of Amnesty International, Irene Khan, shared her deep concern about the country's severe human rights abuses.[78] There was a disparity between crime and justice. Different diplomats criticized about the lawlessness throughout the country. In 2002, Awami Leauge Chairperson's car was attacked by terrorists and different AL leaders were arrested randomly. While AL was protesting against BNPs failure to give justice and misconduct, BNP started to blame AL for terrorist activities.[79] Bangladesh was ranked as the most corrupted country in 2002.[80] Repeatedly, Bangladesh ranked the first position as the most corrupted country in 2001, 2002, 2003, and 2004 by Transparency International.

When the economy and the citizens were going against BNP, they started losing people's faith. That was the time when they started fearing about losing the next election. They needed to take a smart move to ensure the victory in the next election by manipulating it under a new caretaker government. K.M. Hasan was appointed as Chief Justice of the Supreme Court on 22 June, 2003 by the Government. On 2004, the 14th Amendment was made to ensure K.M. Hasan to be the chief advisor of the upcoming caretaker government to manipulate the election. If the retirement age had not been increased, KM Hasan would not have been the first choice to head the NCG. The four-party coalition had been calling for K. M's nomination. After increasing the retirement age of judges, KM Hasan would be the last retired chief justice before the next parliamentary election and, in accordance with previous practices, he could be appointed as the head of the NCG from the 13th Amendment where the president would select the chief adviser from among the recently retired Chief Justices. K.M Hasan was the caretaker government's Chief Adviser. Oppositions claimed that this move of increasing the age of Supreme Court judges is a move to ensure the appointment of Chief Justice K.M Hasan as he was in the past a leader of the ruling BNP. After the 13th Amendment, the chaotic political situation could not be halted following the institutionalization of the Caretaker Government. Ruling party, BNP, made it a fragile and thrustless institution among political actors by its constitutional status, structure, functions, and manipulations. The ruling party's move was seen as an attempt to install its people in the Caretaker Government in order to manipulate upcoming elections for the party's advantage. The 14th Amendment was a visible unconstitutional and biased move to appoint the head of the Caretaker Government. Right after the 14th Amendment, the opposition, Awami League, declared that they would not be taking part in any election under Justice Hasan's Caretaker Government. Along with the opposition party, Awami League, thousands of people started to protest throughout the country against the manipulative ill move by BNP. In this chaotic situation, former Chief Justice KM Hasan refused to become Chief Adviser to the next Caretaker Government. Because of the dynamic political situation and massive protest, Justice Hasan told BNP policymakers straight away that he was not interested in being the Chief Advisor.

On 29 October 2006, President Iajuddin Ahmed, in addition to his presidential duties, assumed the office of chief advisor to the non-party Caretaker Government. President Iajuddin Ahmed took on the role of Chief Adviser to the Caretaker Government fter two days of violent protests throughout the country. One month later, Awami League President, Sheikh Hasina, said after a meeting with her politician that the President's neutrality as the head of the Caretaker Government is questionable. Awami League and 14 party leaders mutually agreed on one fact that the President Iajuddin Ahmed should be removed from the post of the chief adviser of the Caretaker Government. Parliamentary election was planned to be conducted on 22nd January 2007 under Iajuddin led Caretaker Government. The Awami League party and its allies announced that they were boycotting the vote because they presumed that it was not going to be fair. President Iajuddin Ahmed also quit as interim leader and postponed a planned 22 January election under his Caretaker Government, saying that it was 'not possible' to hold it on schedule.[81] The moves were followed by months of violent protests amid claims by a political alliance that the vote is being rigged. The President declared state of emergency before he resigned. Military was deployed to control the chaotic and violent situation in the country. One day later, central bank governor, Fakhruddin Ahmed, was sworn in as the head of a new interim government. The 14th Amendment eventually proved ineffective for the BNP as it paved the way for a military-backed NCG headed by Fakhruddin Ahmed. Headed by Fakhruddin Ahmed, the military-backed Caretaker Government appears unlikely to relinquish power until at least the end of 2008. It adopted a campaign against corruption that had threatened the usual democratic elites. The reins of power had oscillated between Khaleda Zia and Sheikh Hasina since the return of democracy in the 1990s. The nation was riddled by widespread corruption. While there were regulations to counter corruption, they were not sufficiently enforced, nor were the relevant organizations successful. When Fakhruddin came into power along with actions against corruption, he introduced electoral changes, including the issuance of national ID cards and actions against Islamist militants. BNP has lost its popularity and peoples trust over the time for corruption and political unrest.[82]

Khaleda Zia became the first women Prime Minister of Bangladesh and came into power in 1991 as the chairperson of the Bangladesh Nationalist Party (BNP). The country's long-standing political deadlock began in 1994, when Sheikh Hasina Wajed's Awami League (AL) party began boycotting the Parliament to protest alleged corruption in Begum Zia's BNP government. The AL and the BNP differ little on domestic policy; their disputes often reflect the personal animosity between Hasina, the daughter of Rahman, and Begum Zia, the widow of a military ruler who was allegedly complicit in his assassination. The AL boycotted the February 1996 elections and then forced Begum Zia's resignation in March and triumphed in elections held in June. The BNP also marked its time in opposition by boycotting the Parliament and organizing periodic nationwide strikes.[83] The AL was voted out of power in October 2001 in elections marred by electoral aggression and coercion. With 214 of the 300 seats in the Parliament, a new BNP-led alliance that featured two Islamist parties took control again. The AL originally declined to recognize the outcome of the election and resorted to parliamentary boycotts, widespread hartals (general strikes) and other forms of opposition to pressurize the government on different topics. In August 2004, a series of grenade explosions at an AL rally in Dhaka nearly killed Hasina and left 22 people dead and hundreds injured. Although the government appointed a commission to investigate the attacks, its impartiality was called into question, and the perpetrators remain at large. In January 2005, another grenade attack at an AL rally killed five people, including a senior party leader.[84]

General lawlessness had increased in recent years, partly due to bombings and other attacks by Islamist extremist groups. Two of the largest—the Jamiat-ul-Mujahideen Bangladesh (JMB) and the Jagrata Muslim Janata Bangladesh (JMJB)—were banned in February 2005, and following an escalation of violence in late 2005, a government crackdown yielded the arrest of JMB leader Sheikh Abdur Rahman and JMJB head Siddiqul Islam (popularly known as Bangla Bhai, or 'Bengali brother') in March 2006. Around 800 members of the two groups were also detained. In May 2006, these two men and several other JMB leaders were sentenced to death for the 2005 attacks and six of the seven convicted militants were executed in March 2007. The threat of Islamist violence subsided after the 2006 crackdown, but it had not disappeared altogether.[85] From November 2006 to January 2007, political violence continued in Bangladesh,[86] resulting in the death of approximately 45 people.[87] In January 2007, an alliance of opposition parties led by the AL declared that it would boycott the elections scheduled for 22 January 2007. The January 2007 state of emergency reportedly allows military and law enforcement authorities to make arrests without warrants (AHRC n.d.). People arrested under Emergency Powers Rules (EPR) for crimes including cases of corruption, deemed a threat to Bangladesh's national security and therefore, were not permitted to seek bail (OANA 18 Sept. 2007; Reuters 22 Mar. 2007).[88]

According to Odhikar, a Bangladeshi human rights organization and election monitor, in the first month of the country's state of emergency, over 52,000 persons were arrested and 29 were killed by law enforcement authorities. In September 2007, Human Rights Watch reported that as many as 200,000 people may have been arrested under the state of emergency.

Other measures implemented under the state of emergency include restrictions on political party and trade union activities, ban on rallies, processions and meetings and a suspension of news broadcasts from private television channels. In addition, newspapers and electronic media may not publish material that criticizes the government. Persons violating the security measures could face prison terms of two to five years as well as fines.[89] In September 2007, the Caretaker Government announced a partial lifting of the ban on political activities. The ban was apparently eased only in Dhaka in order to allow political parties to discuss electoral reforms with the Election Commission. In addition to imposing a state of emergency, the Caretaker Government of Bangladesh also launched a drive before the next election to clean up graft in politics. Several lists of people, including political figures, accused of being engaged in illegal practices, had been issued by the caretaker administration. According to a report on 4 March 2007 in the Daily Star, based in Dhaka, the authorities of Bangladesh have seized the passports of individuals who are suspected of corruption, as well as those of the members of their families so that they cannot leave the country. An anonymous source quoted in the article noted that police may also arrest family members in order to compel suspects to surrender. Many persons have reportedly left the country for fear of being investigated and arrested.

The arrested politicians included former ministers of the BNP and AL. Tarique Rahman, and Khaleda Zia's uncle, who was the BNP leader and former Prime Minister, was arrested on corruption charges in March 2007. Similar charges were also brought two months later against Begum Zia's second son, Arafat Rahman.[90] AL chief Sheikh Hasina Wajed and 'dozens' of her associates were charged with murder in April 2007, as well as with other crimes reportedly committed during the violent demonstrations in October 2006. Matiur Rahaman Nizami, leader of the Jamaat-e-Islami which was a Islamic fundamentalist party and a part of the BNP-led administration, was also charged with murder. The government had barred Sheikh Hasina, who was outside Bangladesh when the charges were raised against her, from returning to the country. During the same month, BNP leader Khaleda Zia was allegedly exiled by the Caretaker Government. However, controls on the two leaders were relaxed after international criticism of the actions of the caretaker administration. Nonetheless, AL chief, Sheikh Hasina, was arrested on corruption and assassination charges in July 2007. News sources revealed that after a raid on her house by 'hundreds' of policemen, she was detained in Dhaka. The accusations were refuted by Hasina, describing them as politically motivated and a ploy to bar her from taking part in future elections. The BNP chief and former Prime Minister, Khaleda Zia, was arrested on corruption charges in September 2007. Arafat Rahman Koko, Begum Zia's son, was also arrested for similar charges. Like Hasina, Begum Zia refuted the allegations, saying that the case against her was 'fabricated' and 'conspiratorial' and one of her attorneys stated that the detention was a way to drive her out of politics. Since both women had been held under the Emergency Powers Rules (EPR), they were allegedly not entitled to request bail.

## Fifteenth Amendment—Tectonic Shift in Approach to Transition of Power

Many important parts of the Constitution were changed by the Fifteenth Amendment. These changes resulted in many debates and controversies among the general mass, intellectuals and the politics of the country. The 15th Amendment was formed on 30th June 2011 in the Constitution. It had been done to bring back the essence of the original constitution of 1972. This amendment had added both good and controversial effects to the Constitution. This amendment transformed the preamble of the Constitution through few changes. 'Bismillah-ar-Rahman-ar-Rahim' was inserted at the beginning of the preamble. Then a sentence was added by the amendment, 'a historic struggle for national liberation' instead of 'a struggle for national liberation' and the four principles of the original Constitution were restored which are nationalism, socialism, democracy, and secularism. Among many controversial characteristics of this amendment, one is that it allowed the practice of religion-based politics which was not present in the original Constitution. The amendment Article 38 read along with 2A affirms the permission to form faith-based political parties subjected to some restrictions. On the other hand, this amendment categorizes nationality and citizenship with two new definitions of two different identities for the people. It states that the people of Bangladesh would be termed as 'Bangalees' when the nation is concerned and the citizens will be known as 'Bangladeshis.'[91]

Article 7A is another controversial thing that included constitutional sedition. This Article criminalizes the abrogation, repeal or suspension of the Constitution by means of force or use of force or by any other unconstitutional means. It banned the amendment of the preamble and its basic structure and some other important articles. There are more than fifty articles where the scope of doing amendment has been curtailed. In article 150(2) of the Constitution, a new thing was inserted which many people see as partisan. It says that the portrait of the father of the nation, Bangabandhu Sheikh Mujibur Rahman, must be displayed at the offices of the President, the Prime Minister, the Speaker, the Chief Justice and in head and branch offices of all government and semi-government offices, autonomous body, other specified places of the country and outside of the country as well. The amendment added another clause for the safeguard of the environment. It would preserve, protect and develop the environment for the present and future generations. There were some other changes in the Constitution that had come with this amendment but lastly, the most important and controversial part was the abolishment of the caretaker government. **In further discussion we will see the background scenarios and the impact of this amendment among the people of this country.**[92]

The provision of the caretaker system was abolished from the Constitution. All future parliamentary elections would be held under the incumbent cabinet. Islam as the State religion was kept and '*Bismillah-Ar-Rahman-Ar-Rahim*' was retained above the Preamble. 'Absolute faith and trust in Allah' were removed from the Constitution.

This amendment restored secularism and revived freedom of religion. The religion-based politics was now allowed. The indigenous people would be termed as tribal and ethnic minorities. The people of Bangladesh will be known as Bengali as a nation and citizens of Bangladesh will be known as Bangladeshis. Articles 7A and 7B were inserted in the Constitution to end the takeover of power through extra-constitutional means. Some basic provisions of the Constitution were made 'unamendable.' For example, the legality of trials of war crime suspects, who were not part of any armed force or auxiliary force in 1971, cannot be challenged in any court.

The election will be held within 90 days in the case of dissolution of the Parliament. The number of women reserve seats was increased to fifty. The Supreme Command of the defence services will vest in the President. The Chief Justice will be appointed through the President. On the other hand, the other judges will be appointed by the President in consultation with the Chief Justice. The portrait of Bangabandhu Sheikh Mujibur Rahman will be displayed at different national and international offices. A new Article included that the state will take initiatives to preserve the development of the environment as well as wildlife. The State will take steps to protect and develop the unique local culture and tradition of the tribes, minor races, ethnic sects, and communities.

## Abolishment of Caretaker Government

The abolishment of the Caretaker Government system is a very important and most controversial part of the Fifteenth Amendment. The purpose of the Caretaker Government was to ensure proper election and give the power to the elected government through a fair election. The Caretaker Government system came into existence on 28th March 1996 through Thirteenth Amendment of the constitution. On 30th June 2011, the Caretaker Government system was abolished after 15 years.[93]

## The Background Behind Abolishment of Caretaker Government System

The abolishment of the Caretaker Government system shocked many because this system got a reputation through good governance, reformation in areas like election administration, human rights and anti-corruption. Though its function and transparency were not above questions still it had a great acceptance among people. The reasons behind this abolishment were much more political rather than the welfare of the people. It can be clearly understood if we evaluate the history where political parties used this system for their benefit. They wanted it when it was advantageous for them and opposed it when it went against them. In the past, before the establishment of the Caretaker Government, the Awami League wanted the Caretaker Government system while the government of that time rejected the proposal by saying that it was illogical and unconstitutional. Now that Awami League came to power therefore it changed the whole system.[94] However, despite having the political implication, it is also true that the Caretaker System was manipulated by the BNP led government and that created the opportunity to take advantage by third parties to rule the country other than due democratic political process.

The government always gives the excuse of the judgment of Appellate Division on the Thirteenth Amendment where it directs to make changes in the Caretaker Government system. In January 2000, a lawyer filed a writ petition in the High Court Division of the Supreme Court by challenging the Thirteenth Amendment on the grounds that it was 'violative of democracy, a basic and fundamental structure of the Constitution.' In 2004, the High Court Division of the Supreme Court upheld the Thirteenth Amendment on the grounds that it had 'not affected or destroyed any basic structure or feature of the Constitution' because the NCG provision did not negate democracy, in fact, it was an aid to democracy because it allowed for free, fair and acceptable elections. Then it was appealed and the appellate division gave its judgment by saying that the two general elections could be done under the Caretaker Government and in the meantime, the parliament is at liberty to bring necessary changes by excluding the provision of appointing chief justice or other justices of the High Court Division.[95]

The reason why the appellate division directed that two general elections must be held under the Caretaker Government system is the old maxim that it is necessary and safe for the people and the state. It indicates that the appellate division thinks that the Caretaker Government needs to be abolished but not so early. The government can change this system by taking some time and by this the other electoral institutions would be empowered and an environment of fair election would be ensured. The government did not follow this judgement fully and abolished the Caretaker Government through the Fifteenth Amendment. The government always said that they did not abolish the Caretaker Government system unnecessarily or because of any political benefit. They said that it is the highest court of the country which says the Caretaker Government is unconstitutional. After the verdict of the court, they have taken steps to abolish it from the constitution. It is very sad that they always referred to the fragments of the judgment to give validity to their actions but never justified other parts where the court suggested abolishing it in a slow process.[96]

## *The Impact of Abolishment of Caretaker Government Among People*

The abolishment of the Caretaker Government system made a huge impact on the people' lives especially before the election of 2014. The opposition party BNP wanted the Caretaker Government system back and for that, they started protests. The protests turned into violence and many people died. BNP boycotted the election but the election happened with the participation of other parties. Acceptance and fairness of the election without the Caretaker Government system was a matter of dispute among many people. In many countries of the world, fair elections happen under an incumbent government but it arguably very difficult to ~~get~~ conduct fair elections without a neutral government in countries like Bangladesh.[97]

We also have to remember that nothing must not be done outside the constitution. Though the Supreme Court judgment suggested that two elections could happen under the Caretaker Government, it was essentially against the Caretaker Government system. There is scope to examine the word 'could' here. Was this 'could' mean to be a 'must' or 'may.' Furthermore, doctrine of necessity justifying extraconstitutional actions as well. However, further it mentioned that the Caretaker Government was unconstitutional. So, respecting the judgment and to ensure constitutional supremacy, if the government abolished the Caretaker Government system then it cannot be said that it was wrong and it created an obstacle in the process of ensuring ordinary people's right to practice democracy.

## The Recognition of Minority People in the Constitution

In the 15th Amendment, Article 6(2) substituted that the people of Bangladesh will be known as Bengalis and the citizens of the country will be known as Bangladeshis. This distinction in the constitution is baseless and makes confusion. On the other hand, Article 23(A) addressed the minority groups in different names but they are not called indigenous though it had been a demand of the minority people to be recognized by it in the constitution.

## The Background of not Recognizing Indigenous Identity in the Constitution

There is a tendency of avoiding indigenous identity from the beginning of the constitution. The logic behind this, the nation was born with the identity of Bengali nationalism and for that whoever lives in this country will be known as belonging to Bengali nationalism. On the other hand, there was a strong view that we should consider them as indigenous people because there are several international conventions and declarations of the United Nations where the use of the word 'indigenous' has been prohibited. It is perceived as a constitutional obligation to give respect to international law. In that case, it would be against our constitution if we reject their identity.[98]

The demand for constitutional recognition as indigenous people has started since the year 2000. Then it got stronger in 2007 when the United Nations gave a declaration. According to many scholars, this demand for recognition is not very old. In previous cases, they never demanded to be recognized as indigenous, aborigines or sons of the soil. In 1957, ILO organized a convention on Convention Concerning the Protection and Integration of Indigenous and Other Tribal Populations in Independent Countries where some proposals were given and Bangladesh ratified it. The aim of the convention was to assist tribal people to achieve equality along with other citizens. Later this convention was repealed and in 1989 a new convention was held on Convention Concerning Indigenous and Tribal Peoples in Independent Countries where some new proposals were brought up but Bangladesh did not ratify it. One of the features of this convention was that the tribal people of a particular area will be known as indigenous people but whatever so ever is proposed in this convention, Bangladesh has no obligation to follow them as it did not ratify it.[99]

The protection of sovereignty or geographical integrity is the main priority of a state because without them the existence of a state is in danger. If a state stands then the other functions of the state will go smoothly in the name and ideology of that state. The problem is to give recognition of different nationalities in a single state because it can create threats to the sovereignty and geographical integrity of the state. Considering this, many states have not ratified the ILO Convention 169, because if they do so then they will have to give recognition to those nationalities which may cause threats for the sovereignty of the state.[100]

In the ninth parliamentary election, the Awami League government gave an election manifesto where it promised that it would give indigenous recognition to the hill tract people. On the other side, the historical hill tracts peace accord 1997 happened at the time of the power of Awami League Government. There was a great expectation that if the Awami League Government came into power, the recognition would be given to the tribal people. Unfortunately, that did not occur and in 2011 the Fifteenth Amendment came into existence where these people are recognized as a tribe, minor races, ethnic sects and communities but not as indigenous people. The people of Chittagong hill tracts still wanted the recognition and they were struggling to achieve it. One of the leaders of the indigenous people, Santu Larma said with agitation that 'Bengali people are also an ethnographic group but they are a large ethnographic group. If people call them with this name then how would they feel?'[101]

## *The Impact of not Recognizing as Indigenous Identity in the Constitution*

The distinction between nationality and citizenship made a distinction among people. The distinction refers to the notion that every citizen of this country will be known as a Bangladeshi but then again, their identity is Bengalis as they are the people of this country. Now, other people may accept this distinction but people who belong to indigenous groups having their own, separate cultural identity and are known as non-Bengali have to accept this identity without giving consent to it. On the other side, it is Article 23A of the constitution that gives another identity of the indigenous people by saying that 'The State shall take steps to protect and develop the unique local culture and tradition of the tribes, minor races, ethnic sects and communities.' So, this makes it more problematic and insulting for indigenous people to have three different identities where their self-identity by which they want to be recognized is missing. The indigenous people consider themselves as a nation who have been staying in this region for thousands of years and have their own language, cultures, and customs. They have almost everything that a different nation should have. So, calling them as tribal people is an insult to them. On the other hand, the Bangla meaning of the word tribe is *Upojati* which is known as a branch of something; comparing these people with a branch is again an insulting thing for them because they want to express and recognize their identity as a single race.[102]

A group of people who have their own language, culture and customs have total liberty to decide how they will be recognized. No one can force them but we have to remember that a particular group or community is staying in the territory of a state. So, the states also have the right to decide the inevitability or validity of their identity.

## Constitutional Sedition

In the fifteenth Amendment, another important inclusion is the punishment and recognition of constitutional sedition. In Article 7(A), it was inserted that if any person, by show of force or use of force or by any other unconstitutional means, abrogates, repeals or suspends or attempts or conspires to abrogate, repeal or suspend this Constitution or any of its articles, or even if he subverts or attempts or conspires to subvert the confidence, belief or reliance of the citizens to this Constitution or any of its article, his act will be considered as sedition and will be guilty of sedition. Then again, Article 7(A) (2) said if any person abets or instigates any act mentioned above or, approves, condones, supports or ratifies his act will also be liable for the same offence. The person who commits the offence will be sentenced with the highest punishment prescribed for other offences by the existing laws.[103]

## The Background of Inclusion Articles Regarding Constitutional Sedition

The inclusion of this part has significance and controversial reasons. After independence, two military governments came into being, suspended the constitution and ruled illegally for a long time. This was not expected from a country which got birth by having belief in democracy and also where the original constitution included democracy as a fundamental principle just after independence. The Awami league government has suffered a lot because of the military rule. The Prime Minister Sheikh Hasina said before the amendment that the amendment is 'necessary for upholding democracy and for blocking the way for usurpation of state power through the imposition of martial law in future.' Also, it was said that the supreme law of the land was damaged through martial law proclamations in the name of amendments.[104]

This gives a clear idea that the Awami league government did not want to have a scope for military people to back in power but this inclusion gave a vague idea. The reason is that whenever a military government came through a coup, it did not consider the legality of the government. It was always known by them that their activities will be illegal and the courts will not give support in future but they continue their power. Now, if in future the situation arises when the military comes into power, they will not consider this inclusion that the constitution forbade or not allow them to come into the power. They again violate the constitution and try to stay in power illegally.[105]

So, military people will not value this part that by show of force or use of force or by any other unconstitutional means if the military government abrogates, repeals or suspends or attempts or conspires to abrogate, repeal or suspend this Constitution or any of its article and try to stay in power, will be considered illegal. Yes, again it can be said that this inclusion may create some difficulties and give a message to everyone that the people of this country want to run this country through a democratic government, not by an authoritarian or an unelected one. Also, it has given an extra emphasis on the value of ordinary people's rights on democracy.[106]

If we see this article carefully, we will understand the first part where words like show of force or use of force do not indicate the ordinary citizens. The act can only be done by a certain group of people or a military authority. If we take the language like by any other unconstitutional means to subvert the confidence, belief, or reliance of the citizens to the Constitution or any of its articles then the ordinary people come under this. The purpose of this part is to restrict the freedom of speech of ordinary people.

### *The Impact of Inclusion of Constitutional Sedition Article*

The columnist, writer, news presenter and others will not express anything independently in the fear of it being used against them on the charge of casting ideas that subvert the confidence, belief or reliance of the citizens to the Constitution. The words like show of force, use of force, unconstitutional means are subject to interpretation, contest and debate. There is no clear definition about them. For this, the government can use this power arbitrarily to anyone for criticizing the Constitution. In a transparent way it can be said it gives the government scopes to stop anyone who is against the government. This limited people's one of the fundamental rights, that is freedom of speech. It may always be said that the amendments have been done for the welfare of the people but this part of the amendment indicated that it was done for the welfare of the government.[107]

### *Prohibition on the Amendment of the Preamble, Basic Structure of the Constitution, and Other Important Articles*

The fifteenth amendment inserted Article 7(B) with the assertion that the preamble, all articles of Part I, all articles of Part II, the provisions of Part IXA all articles of Part III, and the provisions of articles relating to the basic structures of the Constitution including article 150 of Part XI cannot be amenable by way of insertion, modification, substitution, repeal or by any other means. The power of amending has curtailed more than fifty Articles of the constitution.[108]

### *Impact of Making Certain Articles Non-Amendable Among Ordinary People*

The future elected parliamentarians who will represent the people of the country had lost power to amend many parts of the constitution. In future, if it is needed to add anything for the betterment of the people on the unamendable part of the constitution, the parliamentarians will not be able to insert them. We should remember one thing that law changes with the time and necessity of the people. If it is restricted for lifetime, it will affect the situation when there is a necessity of changing law or need to give strength to the constitution and as well as people's fundamental rights that will be deprived. Even though we should not forget that all the power belongs to the citizens of this country. This has an inflicting meaning that the people's benefit has to be given the first priority. If the future parliamentarian's power is curtailed to amend the constitution, the question arises how much these amendments might contribute for the welfare of the ordinary people of this country.[109]

## *Conflict among Secularism, State Religion, and Religion-based Politics*

The contradiction between secular and religious character of the state is another important part of this fifteenth amendment. At first, in the starting of the preamble, the amendment inserted 'Bismillah-ar-Rahman-ar-Rahim.' In Article 2A, it added that the religion of the state is Islam but the state will ensure equal right and equal status in practice of all the religions.[110] Then in Article 12, it is said that the state will not give any political status in favour of any religion or abuse of any religion for political purposes. This is again a contradiction with Article 42 which is also added through this amendment that gives permission with four restrictions to form association on the basis of religion. The permission to form religion-based politics has an indirect fundamental right which can be enforced through the court. Now, this is self-contradictory because one of the fundamental principles of the state is secularism and again with all of these provisions it gives the state an identity of religion and as well as permission to do politics on the basis of religion.[111]

## *The Tradition of Using Religion in Constitution*

In Bangladesh politics religion is always a factor for politicians. If we observe carefully, in the past, religion had been used two times in the Constitution. First, Major General Ziaur Rahman inserted *'Bismiliahir Rahmanir Rahim'* in the beginning of the Constitution. Later, Hossain Mohammad Ershad declared Islam as a state religion. Both of them had done this for gaining political benefit. The people of Bangladesh are very religious and anything related to Islam make them feel sacred out it. The military chiefs were aware of that and used religious sentiment to gain popularity. Also, another reason is that Muslim allies would be a factor for them to stay in the power. After inclusion of religion in the constitution, the relations with Muslim countries improved and funding of dollars had started to come from the Middle East.[112]

## *The Background of Inclusion of Religion in the Fifteenth Amendment*

The intention of the Awami League government was clear about using religion in the constitution. It is not something that happened suddenly. When the parliamentary committee was being reviewed under the light of the court's decision, the Prime Minister Sheikh Hasina said that her party would want to have Islam as a state religion. Also, she gave a statement that the party was not against banning religion politics but would want to specify some restrictions. The moment the bill came to the Parliament, the Workers Party, Jatiya Samajtantrik Dal, Ganotantri Party and National Awami Party opposed the proposal. It was the Jatiya Party who had also supported not to ban the religion based political parties. Finally, the Awami League government, with more than three fourth majority, without any threat, achieved their purpose.[113]

It was understood that the previous rulers used religion because of having other political views and ways of coming to power. The shocking thing was that a party like Awami League who has secular ideology also used the religion for political purposes. It was expected that having the most of the majorities in the Parliament and secular ideology, it would go back to the original Constitution. In order to adopt the 1972 constitution, a lot has accommodated but any change with regards to religion had been avoided carefully. The Awami League realized that excluding religion from the Constitution is a threat to their power as the majority population in Bangladesh are Muslim. It would be easy to get popularity and vote in the upcoming elections by inserting religion in the constitution. Despite being a secular party, it could not deny the importance of religion in this country for staying in power.

## *The Impact of Contradiction Between State Religion and Secularism Among Ordinary People*

The amendment made an indirect classification among citizens. In Bangladesh, there are people of other religions like Hindu, Buddhist, Christian and as well as indigenous people. When the Constitution is saying that Islam is the state religion, it gives an automatic classification where these people would consider as a second-class citizen. It can be argued that the latter part of this cleared that the state will ensure equal status and equal right in the practice of other religions but again confusion, contradiction and vague clarification prevailed. People of other religions are very few in number and this ambiguity makes them feel deprived and discriminated against.[114]

## *Display of the Portrait of the Father of the Nation*

The Constitution declared Bangabandhu Sheikh Mujibur Rahman as the father of the nation through the fifteenth Amendment. In its new inclusion, it said that the portrait of the father of the nation, Bangabandhu Sheikh Mujibur Rahman, will be displayed at the offices of the President, the Prime Minister, speaker, chief justice and other offices in the country and as well as abroad. This is also known for many people as a partisan act of the government. There is no doubt that the birth of Bangladesh might not have been possible without Bangabandhu Sheikh Mujibur Rahman and considering the historical reasons, he can rightly be titled as the father of this nation. The placement of this historical matter in the Constitution gives extra significance to accepting this matter. The Awami League government knew this and they made it in a way that prohibits the amending of this part forever so that no one can claim to change this in future. It is very clear to this government that if anyhow BNP came to power in future, they would definitely try to change it and therefore, this prohibition had been given. Though it is doubtful to presume the significance of this restriction when the power would be in the hands of some other party, it is obvious that bringing a change to this would not be very easy. This change has given scope of confrontational politics in future.[115]

### *Preserve and Protect Environment for the Present and Future Generations*

The best part of the fifteenth amendment is the inclusion of a new clause for the protection of the environment. It said that the state will protect natural resources, biodiversity, water bodies, forest and wildlife; and preserve and develop the environment for the present and future generations.[116] The protection of environment clause was included in part two of the Constitution which meant that it would be treated as a fundamental principle of the state policy. This is a good thing but still the environmental activists think that this would be better if the protection of the environment was mentioned as a fundamental right in the Constitution. It had been done intentionally because giving protection of the environment as a fundamental right would give a lot of scopes for the high court division to interfere in different environmental matters. Many decisions would be made which would harm many businesses. The development of businesses and the environment are related. So, somehow it gives protection to the particular group of people by not recognizing it as a fundamental right. Still, recognizing environmental protection as a fundamental principle bound the state to take initiatives to protect the environment for present and future generations.

## Sixteenth Amendment—'Independence of the Judiciary?'

The Constitution is the guide which leads a nation to prosperity. A modern state cannot be thought of without it. So, after nine-month long blood-shedding battle in 1971, Bangladesh achieved her long-awaited independence and therefore, took an instant effort to formulate a constitution rapidly based on the ideological spirit of the war of independence. However, to accommodate the demands and will of the people and even to fulfil the narrow interests of the rulers sometimes,

Bangladesh Constitution had been amended several times. The 16th Amendment is one of them. Except a few cases, almost every amendment has a great political impact in the constitution. The most aspired and comprehensive sixteenth Amendment induced a great debate among the political parties, intellectuals, constitution experts and masses.

A cutting-edge state can't be thought of without a Constitution. The whole legal, official and authoritative elements of the State are managed and guided by the Constitution. In 1972, the main constitution of Bangladesh was drafted that enabled the Parliament to evacuate the judges of the Supreme Court (SC). At that point, under the fourth Amendment, this power was vested to the President of Bangladesh. The Fifth Amendment sanctioned the development of a Supreme Judicial Council (SJC). The Supreme Judicial Council, comprising of the Chief Justice and two next senior-most judges of the Supreme Court, was engaged to denounce a decision made on the grounds of demonstrated trouble making or inadequacy. The higher legal executive of Bangladesh isn't thoroughly free from the official while playing out its capacities. Since, under the Articles 95(1) and 48(3) of the Constitution, the President would select judges in the Supreme Court after earlier counselling with the Chief Justice and on exhortation from the Prime Minister. After the arrangement, the Supreme Judicial Council additionally was vested with the ability to maintain the residency of office and conditions of unfortunate behaviour because of which equity can be denounced. Nonetheless, the Parliament got back the intensity of indictment of Supreme Court and made a decision by sixteenth amendment. As per the changed Article 96(2), the Constitution had re-established the ability to indict the judges of the Supreme Court to the Parliament pursued by a request of the President. Article 96(3) had engaged the Parliament to direct the method by law. The crucial idea of reprimand was straightforward. Under Article 94 and 95 of the Bangladesh Constitution, judges are named and they held their workplaces amid great conduct. Under Article 96 of the constitution, they were arraigned.[117]

## *General Discussion on Sixteenth Amendment of the Constitution of Bangladesh*

Before moving on to the detailed discussion of several important points of Sixteenth Amendment of the Constitution of the People's Republic of Bangladesh, we need to look at the relevant provision from Sixteenth amendment which is about the impeachment of Justices of Supreme Court. In accordance with the Article 96 of the existing Constitution of Bangladesh,

> Until he attains the age of sixty-seven years, a Judge shall hold office. That is subjected to the other provisions of this article.[118]
>
> Without the order, which must be passed pursuant to a resolution of Parliament and supported by at least two thirds majority of the members of

> the Parliament, of the President and unless the misbehaviour or incapacity of a judge are proven, he shall not be removed from office.[119]
>
> The procedure may be by law regulated by the Parliament in relation to a resolution under clause (2) and for investigating and proving the misbehaviour or incapacity of a Judge.[120]
>
> By writing under his hand that must be addressed to the President, a Judge may resign his office.[121]

In the Article 96 of the 1972 constitution, a provision was there regarding impeachment of Supreme Court judges. It said that the impeachment. It suggested that the impeachment could be done by an order of the President by having two-thirds majority in parliament upon proven misconduct and incapacity. However, a new provision was incorporated, during the presidential system of government, in the constitution that stipulated that any judge of the Supreme Court may be impeached by an order of the President.[122] According to the provision which is mentioned above, a judge can be removed from office before providing him or her scope of answering show cause notices that mention actions against them on the grounds of misbehaviour and incompetence. But, in 1977 and 1978, another provision was inserted in the constitution where the authority of impeachment of Supreme Court judges were given to the President, on the grounds of misconduct and incapacity, following recommendations of the Supreme Judicial Council which is formed by the Chief Justice and two other senior judges of the Supreme Court. This provision went against the basic principle and democratic spirit of the constitution, the objective says.

The principle of accountability of the judges of the superior court, like other organs of the state, lies with the parliament which consists of the elected representatives of the people similar to most of the democratic countries in the world.

Now, this amended article will be analysed from various perspectives and in the light of different methods of Interpretation.

## *Under its Literal Meaning*

If we look carefully at the literal meaning of the above-mentioned Article of the Constitution, it actually shows that,

The proceedings of impeachment of Judges can be initiated by the members of the parliament.

b. A majority of two third of the total number of the members in parliament must be nedded to pass the resolution for the impeachment of Judges.[123] Hence, it is not possible to attain two third majorities if all the members of parliament attend the session.
c. By perusing the provisions of Clause 2 of Article 96, under the said reference, it seems like no matter what the MPs may pass in the session, the ultimate

decision is rested on the hand of the Head of the Executive or to the President to be more specific. In addition to that, it is not clearly expressed anything repugnant in the provision on this regard. That is sya it does not specify what happens if the resolution is not passed within a fixed period by the President.

d. Regarding the Impeachment of Judges, the option of creating the resolution and procedure of investigation is given to the parliament.[124] However, there is no direct law which has been prescribed.
e. The provision for self-resignation by Judges is also availed by it. Though the words impeachment and removal are not similar issues under legal field, both criteria are held in one Article in provisions of the Constitution.

## *In Harmonious Approach*

Under Harmonious Construction, if we try to interpret the Article which is mentioned previously, then the following points appear:

> Appointment of Chief Justice[125] and appointment of Prime Minister[126] are two distinct powers of the President under the provisions of the Supreme Law. However, in the Article 96 of the Sixteen Amendment, another power is availed for the President to pass the order in pursuant to the resolution by the members of parliament specially for the purpose of impeachment of Judges. To be more specific, it does not say anything about consulting the Prime Minister on the regard.

It cannot be said that the amendment is unconstitutional because it confirms the dignity of independent judiciary under the meaning of the following provision: '*The State shall ensure the separation of the judiciary from the executive organs of the state.*'[127]

It would be A violation of Article 22 of the Supreme Law of Bangladesh If the provisions of Article 96 said that the impeachment will be made by the executive of Bangladesh. While the sixteenth amendment allocate the power of impeachment to the parliament, the purpose of Article 22 of the Constitution is served by it in actuality that in reality demands a separate judicial system not from the legislature but from the executive.

## *Drawbacks of Sixteenth Amendment*

A constitutional amendment means modification of the constitution of a nation or state. In many jurisdictions, the alteration of the text of the constitution itself is made; in others no change is made to the text but the effect of it is changed by the amendments. The method which is followed in the process of amending the constitution is included into the constitution itself. Amendment procedures are mentioned in all of the world's active national constitutions.[128] Most of the Constitutions are made in order to provide certain benefits to state or to be more specific to clear ambiguities. But sometimes ambiguities and hassles are created for the state by amendment which has no future observations. There are certain drawbacks of Sixteenth amendment in this regard that that provide an obstacle in relation to an Independent Judicial system of Bangladesh. Some the drawbacks are given below.

For that it can be said that the primary objective of the 16th Amendment Act 2014 is to abolish the principle of Independence of Judiciary. Furthermore, it makes the Judiciary ineffective to protect the Constitution. the principle of Independence of Judiciary is considered as one of the basic features of the Constitution, particularly, from Article 22, Article 94(4), Article 116A of the Constitution as it is shown in the Case of *Anwar Hussain Chowdhury V Bangladesh* (popularly known as the 8th Amendment Case).[129] It is reiterated and reaffirmed in *Masdar Hossain's Case*[130] which is compromised by the 16th Amendment Act 2014 by giving overwhelming power to the executive through Parliament to impeach the Supreme Court Judges. It can be said that all of these are a violent blow on the Judiciary and a blatant effort to down the very fabric of the Constitution and to demolish its structural integrity.

After the sixteenth amendment, though the parliament is empowered to impeach Judges of Higher Courts, the issue is still technically handled by the executives of Bangladesh. It is because the ministers who are part of executive of Bangladesh mostly represent themselves as the members of parliament. Practically, it can be said more clearly that there is no difference between persons belonging to legislature and executives in Bangladesh. Therefore, judiciary is ultimately controlled by the executive in relation to impeachment by the Sixteen Amendment that, prima facie, seems to violate Article 22 of the Constitution of the People's Republic of Bangladesh.

Nevertheless, according the Article 96 of the Constitution of Bangladesh, the President has the power to pass order for the final decision of impeachment. However, the questions arise what would happen if the President does not approve the resolution of parliament and how much value is born by the President regarding the passing of the process of impeachment. These questions because of a similar situation which is described in the process of law making. There it is stated that law will be automatically passed after a certain period even if the President doesn't give his consent. The question is remains in mind though nothing of that sort is stated in Article 96.

Moreover, although decision regarding the impeachment of Judges is solely for the President to make, the President may face a little difficulty to give any descending opinion against MPs resolution because of the power invested on the because of the MPs under Article 52 of the Constitution.

16th Amendment Act 2014 seems contradictory to spirit of the preamble of the Constitution along with our constitutional pledge for a number of reasons. For example, it is stated in the preamble that economic and social justice which are referred to by democracy and socialism shall be fundamental principles of the Constitution. Furthermore, realizing socialist society which will be free from exploitation and where rule of law, equality and justice, social, economic and political along with fundamental human rights and freedom will be secured for all citizens through the democratic process shall be a fundamental aim of the State. Moreover, the preamble mentions that it is our holy duty to safeguard, protect and defend this Constitution and to preserve its supremacy as a reflection of the will of the people of Bangladesh. However, all of these are hindered and restricted because of the amendment that weakens the judiciary which is considered the most important conscience keeper of the State.

Again, article 7B of the Constitution is in conflict with the 16th Amendment Act 2014 in a significant way. It is because Article 7B holds that no provisions regarding the basic structures of the Constitution shall be amended by inserting, modifying, substituting or repealing it since the independence of Judiciary and the separation of it are the most fundamental cornerstone of the basic structure of the Constitution.[131]

## *Advantages of Sixteenth Amendment*

Apart from the issues of the validity of the Sixteenth Amendment of the Constitution of Bangladesh, there are some favourable points of this amendment regarding the effectiveness of the Constitution. These are given below.

By unconstitutional means of Martial law namely the Second Proclamation Fifteenth Amendment) order 1978, the Supreme Judicial Council instead of the Parliament was previously conferred upon the power to remove a Judge of the Supreme Court on the ground of his misbehaviour or incapacity that replaced Article 96 of the Constitution enacted in 1972 by the military ruler. The spirit of Article 7 of the Constitution is violated by the said martial proclamation. Hence, such spirit has been restored by Sixteenth Amendment.

The principle of accountability of the judges of the superior court, like other organs of the state, lies with the parliament which consists of the elected representatives of the people similar to most of the democratic countries in the world. Therefore, the process can also be considered to be under scope of democracy.

Additionally, the theory of separation of power with checks and balances is also reflected by above mentioned issue. This neither violets the essence of Article 22, to be more precise, the Independence of the Judiciary because it does not force the authority to impeach the judge by any of the executive members but only to the MPs elected by the votes of Republics who hold all the power under the scheme of the Supreme Law.[132]

Moreover, this amendment was good move and was also necessary to revive Article 96 of the Constitution of 1972.[133]

## *Comparing the 5th and 16th Amendments*

Before selecting the Sixteenth Amendment, Articles 96 (2) and (3) of the Bangladesh Constitution, an arrangement on indictment done by the Supreme Judicial Council and not by the Parliament was incorporated under Part VI. It concluded two things: (1) Any judge cannot be terminated from the office aside according to the accompanying arrangements done in this article. (2) A Supreme Judicial Council shall be there who is alluded to as the Council in this article, which will comprise of the Chief Justice of Bangladesh and two next senior judges. By an Act of Parliament under this amendment, an exploring or inquisitive expert will be there who shall be very unmistakable and will also remain separate from the Legislature or the Executive organ of the State. Any Judge who would be blamed, will still be completely qualified to guard himself in examination or request, by and large So that remaining in this way, he won't be able to tolerate any preference on any check. Under the fifth change, it was provided that there would be a legal chamber, which would comprise of the equity of the boss and two next Senior judges. The board will endorse the list of accepted rules would be endorsed by the board to be followed by the judges. The board would ask the limit or head of the judges. Depending on any data received from the committee, the President will terminate the judges on the charges of offense, physical or mental insufficiency. The fifth change re-established the autonomous power of the legal executive specifically the established status and sacredness of the Supreme Court. Though the undesirable arrangement provided by the fourth Amendment regarding the arrangement of judges were left untouched, the arrangements for security of residency were re-established which is the first and foremost condition of state of autonomy of legal executive and this was done by providing a solid gadget of the Supreme Judicial Council. Additionally, regarding the control, it was provided that the President can exercise that power after consultation with the Supreme Court; this power included the intensity of posting, promotion and leave permit and order of the subordinate judges and justices that was solely vested in the President under the fourth Amendment, In this way, freedom of both higher and bring down legal executive which was established part was restored.

## *Comparison between 8th & 16th Amendment*

The eighth amendment of the Constitution was corrected by Article 100. A division seat of HCD denied the writ appeal. Such a correction changing the fundamental structure of the constitution was ultra vires and not reasonable in law. The change in the intensity of the Parliament is given by Article 142 under the Constitution. The constitution has some essential columns which could not be revised by its changing force under Article 142. Some fundamental highlights of the Constitution are autonomy of legal executive, partition of forces, and matchless quality of the constitution and so on. The sixteenth amendment hampered the freedom of legal executive and division powers. So, this change disregarded the fundamental structure of the Constitution.[134]

## *Writ against 16th Amendment*

An application under Article 102 of the Constitution of the People's Republic of Bangladesh was made against the sixteenth amendment by *Advocate Asaduzzaman*

*Siddiqui, and others... ... . Candidates, Versus Bangladesh spoken to by the Cabinet Secretary, Cabinet Division, Bangladesh Secretariat, Police Station Shahbag, Dhaka-1000 and others... ... Respondents.* Mr. Manzill Murshid with Mr. Moyeen A. Firozze and Mr. Sanjoy Mandal were Advocates for the candidates Mr. Mahbubey Alam, Attorney General, along with Mr. Md. Motaher Hossain (Sazu), DAG, Ms. Purabi Rani Sharma, AAG, Mr. A.B.M. Mahbub, AAG and Ms. Purabi Saha, AAG, were for the respondent no. 1, Mr. Murad Reza, Additional Attorney-General with Mr. Amit Talukder and DAG for the respondent no. 4

## Grounds of petitioner on the writ

The foundation of the activity to correct the applicable arrangements identifying with the evacuation of the Judges of the Apex Court radiated from a few occurrences which occurred in the on-going past. One of them is that our Parliament passed a law of Contempt of Court in 2013; the High Court Division then pronounced the said law of Contempt of Court of 2013 void and ultra-infection in the Constitution.

An amendment was made in the Anti-Corruption Commission Act of 2004 for the security of local official from the charge of defilement; the High Court Division proclaimed the alteration void and ultra-infection the Constitution.

In a seven-murder case in Narayanganj which was submitted by law upholding offices, a Public Interest Litigation was recorded under the watchful eye of the High Court Division and the High Court Division guided the concerned experts to capture those work force of the law authorizing organizations. From that point a detestable move was taken by the political officials to correct Article 96 of the Constitution through the Parliament.

This move was solidified by the death of the Sixteenth Amendment at the command of the political administrators with the mala fide aim of meddling with the freedom of the Judges of the Supreme Court of Bangladesh in the release of their legal capacities.

In the vast majority of the cases (Writ Petitions), the Government is the respondent; yet the Members of Parliament are crucially inspired by those cases emerging out of the improvement exercises in their neighbourhoods. In addition, in the present setting of Bangladesh, the vast majority of the Members of the Parliament are from business parts and therefore; they have individual enthusiasm for those cases. Against this scenery, the Judges of the Apex Court would *suo motu* be limited from passing any request in the cases in which the Members of Parliament are intrigued.

In perspective of the Sixteenth Amendment, any Member of Parliament can bring a movement against any Judge of the Supreme Court and talk about the equivalent in that and because of this reason, no Judge will have the capacity to play out his obligations fair-mindedly and autonomously. Over the long haul, equity will be disappointed and organization of equity will fall in a matter of moments.

The Sixteenth Amendment is ultra-infection the Constitution as it is worth in direct clash with and opposing to the soul of the Preamble of the Constitution.

Independence of the Judiciary is one of the fundamental highlights of the Constitution as elucidated in *Anwar Hossain Chowdhury and others … Vs. … Bangladesh and others (prominently known as Eighth Amendment Case)* [1989 BLD (SPL) 1] which has been repeated and reaffirmed in *Masdar Hossain's Case* [52 DLR (AD) 82]. The essential goal of the Sixteenth Amendment is to decimate the guideline of autonomy of the Judiciary and to render the Judiciary weak and insufficient.[135]

It is violative to Article 7B of the Constitution as no arrangements identifying with the fundamental structures of the Constitution will be amendable by method for inclusion, change, substitution, and revoke or something else.

The Sixteenth Amendment glaringly devastates the soul and embodiment of the arrangements of Article 22 of the Constitution and along these lines obscures the partition of forces among the distinctive organs of the State and plainly builds up the mastery of the Executive through the Parliament over the Judiciary which will make an incredible lop-sidedness inside the protected bodies and in this way, make the Judiciary a joke and a toothless and sorrowful quiet observer.

The Sixteenth Amendment is additionally ultra-infection the Constitution as by dint of Article 70, the Members of the Parliament cannot express their autonomous perspectives/sentiments against their partisan principal and as a characteristic culmination thereto, the expulsion of the Judges of the Apex Court of Bangladesh will be preferential by its immediate ramifications.

The Sixteenth Amendment is ultra-infection the Constitution as it has undermined the specialist and pride of the Apex Court due to the way that the legitimacy of the procedures in the Parliament cannot be addressed in any Court by the uprightness of Article 78 of the Constitution. In that capacity the Judiciary will be helpless before the Executive through the Legislature and it will not have the capacity to shield itself.

The Supreme Court of Bangladesh being the gatekeeper of the Constitution must not permit any advance upon the Constitution; but rather the Sixteenth Amendment is an advance upon the autonomy of the watchman of the Constitution.

In the Fifth Amendment Case, the High Court Division pronounced the Constitution (Fifth Amendment) Act, 1979 illicit and drained of initio subject to specific conditions. The Appellate Division in the Fifth Amendment Case embraced those conditions with a few changes. According to the judgment of the Appellate Division go in the Fifth Amendment Case, the arrangements identifying with the Supreme Judicial Council were kept unblemished in the Constitution of Bangladesh. So, the sixteen revisions disregard the decision of appealing party division by giving the intensity of expulsion of judges of the Supreme Court, to the Parliament.

In the Supplementary Affidavit dated 27.05.2015, it has been referenced by the solicitors that the Sixteenth Amendment is conflicting with and violative of Article

147 (2) of the Constitution which gives that the compensation, benefits and different terms and states of administration of an individual holding or acting in any office to which this Article applies will not be shifted to the drawback of any such individual amid his term of office. According to Article 147(4) of the Constitution, this (Article 147) applies, among others, to the workplace of a Judge of the Supreme Court. The Sixteenth Amendment has without a doubt fluctuated the expulsion component of the sitting Judges of the Supreme Court of Bangladesh for their unfortunate behaviour or inadequacy to their disservice. Precisely, the Sixteenth Amendment is unlawful and void.

The Sixteenth Amendment will likewise straightforwardly influence the Election Commissioners, Comptroller and Auditor-General, Members of the Public Service Commission and also Members of the Anti-Corruption Commission. By uprightness of this Amendment, they will be evacuated in like way as a Judge of the Supreme Court as per Articles 118(5), 129(2), and 139(2) of the Constitution of Bangladesh and Section 10(3) of the Anti-Corruption Commission Act, 2004 individually. The autonomy of the Commissioners of the Anti-Corruption Commission and the Comptroller and Auditor-General of Bangladesh will be in peril in light of the fact that they won't have the capacity to act fairly and adequately against the wrongdoings of the concerned Members of Parliament who are their genuine supervisors.

One of the fundamental parts of legal freedom is solid assurance against expulsion from office. That worldwide standard on legal evacuation has been stressed in the 'UN Basic Principles on the Independence of the Judiciary' as embraced by the General Assembly in 1985. The Judges of the Supreme Court can't be expelled without demonstrated unfortunate behaviour or inadequacy by a reasonable, unprejudiced, autonomous and unbiased body who is allowed to direct the request and make an assurance all alone from the impact of alternate parts of the State.

The Sixteenth Amendment by method for giving intensity of expulsion of the Judges of the Supreme Court to the Members of Parliament is certainly against the essence of the freedom of the Judiciary. This change has been made in exercise of the subsidiary intensity of the Constitution and this won't consequently make the revision invulnerable from test by method for legal audit. No alteration to the Constitution can be made in practicing subordinate power disregarding the current arrangements of the Constitution and the restrictions forced by it. So, the Sixteenth Amendment is ultra vires the Constitution.

## *Grounds of Respondent Against the writ Petitions*

In the Fifth Amendment Case, all martial law proclamations, martial law regulations, martial law orders made/promulgated during the period between 20th August 1975 and 9th April 1979 which were validated by the Act No. 1 of 1979 was declared illegal, *void abinitio* and ultra vires; but those were provisionally condoned until 31st December 2012 so as to enable the Parliament to make necessary amendment to the Constitution (vide judgment and order dated

11th May, 2011 passed by the Appellate Division in Civil Review Petition Nos. 17–18 of 2011). So, it is totally a misconceived idea that in the Fifth Amendment Case, the Appellate Division of the Supreme Court by its observation favoured to retain or condone the provisions of the Supreme Judicial Council which were introduced by General Ziaur Rahman.

Thereafter the Constitution (Fifteenth Amendment) Act was passed in 2011 which endorsed the system of the Supreme Judicial Council which may be considered as a departure from the original provisions of the Constitution relating to removal of the Judges of the Supreme Court by the Parliament. Finally, it was thought expedient and necessary to restore/revive the original provisions of the Constitution about removal of the Supreme Court Judges through the Parliament which were introduced in Article 96 of the original Constitution and therefore, the Sixteenth Amendment was passed in 2014 reviving the relevant provisions (provisions of Article 96) of the original Constitution.

The Sixteenth Amendment is not intended to dominate the Judiciary by the Executive through the Legislature undermining its independence.

In the instant Writ Petition, no public interest is involved for which the Sixteenth Amendment can be challenged in the form of judicial review of any legislative action nor is the same amenable to judicial review.

The Sixteenth Amendment is not ultra-virus; rather it is intra virus the Constitution which cannot be called in question by way of judicial review in that the same has revived and restored the original provisions of Article 96 of the Constitution (barring age limit) relating to removal of the Supreme Court Judges. As the Parliament has restored the original provisions of Article 96 of the Constitution, the Sixteenth Amendment cannot be subjected to judicial scrutiny. No provision of the original Constitution as enacted and adopted by the Constituent Assembly in 1972 can be judicially reviewed.

By enacting the Sixteenth Amendment, the Government has taken the necessary initiative to maintain the high judicial standard of the Supreme Court Judges and to keep their jobs secured following the best practices of the contemporary world. The system of parliamentary removal of Judges has a long history. It was developed in the 18th century in England to ensure that the King could only dismiss a Judge if both Houses of Parliament passed a resolution or 'address' calling for the removal of the Judge. Parliamentary removal procedure is in place in 33% Commonwealth jurisdictions. The Westminster model of parliamentary removal of Judges as has been reintroduced in Bangladesh through the Sixteenth Amendment is a standard mechanism of removal of Judges of the Supreme Court of Bangladesh for their proved misbehaviour or incapacity.

It is not true that the Members of Parliament have been empowered to perform the functions of all development activities of their local areas and the whole administration is under their control. Though the Government has made them advisers to the Upazilla Parishads, yet it does not necessarily mean that they control the whole of the local administration. The Members of Parliament have no scope to act arbitrarily and illegally. There is not a single instance that exposes the interest of the Members of Parliament in any case where the Judges of the Supreme Court have restrained themselves from passing any order in connection therewith.

It is not correct that by reason of Article 70 of the Constitution, the Members of Parliament cannot express their independent views and opinions against the stance of their respective parties. Every Member of Parliament has the right to express his/her opinion in the Parliament. Removal of Judges is not a political issue; rather it is a delicate constitutional issue that demands a debate in the Parliament among all the members irrespective of their political identity.

The statement made in the Writ Petition that the Sixteenth Amendment has undermined the authority and dignity of the Apex Court because of the fact that the validity of the proceedings in the Parliament cannot be called in question in any Court by reason of Article 78 of the Constitution is quite meaningless and unwarranted. The Constitution itself has given the mandate that the validity of the Parliamentary proceedings shall not be called in question in any Court of law. Being the sovereign law-making body, Parliament's proceedings are immune from judicial interference. This is a universal practice prevailing all over the world.

Had Article 96 of the Constitution not been unconstitutionally and illegally amended by the unconstitutional military regime introducing the system of the Supreme Judicial Council, the Sixteenth Amendment would not have been required to restore Article 96 to its original position of 1972. The Supreme Court is the guardian of the Constitution, but not the supervisor of the whole governmental process. The Sixteenth Amendment is a valid piece of legislation. So, the Rule is liable to be discharged.

## *Opinions of Legal Experts*

The 16th amendment debate is now seriously intense at several levels. It is a conflict between the Judiciary and the Legislature as its powers to remove Judges have been taken away. Many legal experts have given several opinions about the sixteenth amendment. This chapter focuses some expert's opinions regarding the sixteenth amendment.

## *Opinion of D. Kamal Hossain, Barrister*

Dr. Kamal Hossain, who was the Chairman of the Bangladesh constitution drafting Committee and acted in sixteenth amendment case as amicus curia. His supposition is that the sixteenth amendment is ultra-infection the constitution his assessment depends on the accompanying grounds.

The autonomy of the Judiciary is the establishment stone of the Constitution as thought about by Article 22 and it is one of the central standards of State strategy and the importance of the autonomous Judiciary, free from the obstruction of the other 2(two) organs of the State, has been underscored in Articles 94(4), 116A, and 147 of the Constitution and in the Eighth Amendment Case, it has been held that Democracy, Republican Government, Unitary State, Separation of Powers,

Independence of the Judiciary, Rule of Law, Fundamental Rights and so on are essential structures of the Constitution.

The agreement has all the earmarks of being that the established standard of freedom of the Judiciary is proposed to avoid any sort of factional exercise of intensity by the Legislature in connection to the Judiciary, specifically, the intensity of the Legislature to expel the Judges of the Supreme Court of Bangladesh.

Although the freedom of the Judiciary is a fundamental component of the standard of law, yet by establishing the Sixteenth Amendment, the Parliament is inclined to practice command over the Judiciary by method for protecting a privilege to take choices on the subject of expulsion of the Judges of the Supreme Court.

In the first 1972 Constitution, expulsion of Judges of the Supreme Court was endowed to the Parliament on the commence that the Parliament being established by the chose delegates of the general population, when in practicing its capacity, would do as such scrupulously and autonomously, free from any gathering mandate and this is the manner by which it was seen when a comparable arrangement was embraced in the Indian Constitution and both in the Indian Constitution and in the first 1972 Constitution of Bangladesh, the intensity of evacuation of any Judge would just be practiced after a request led by a free Judicial Inquiry Committee; yet H. M. Seervai has communicated his worry in his book 'The Position of the Judiciary under the Constitution of India' (distributed by Bombay University Press) at page 109 that political and party contemplations have become an integral factor in denunciation procedures.

Article 96 of the first 1972 Constitution identifying with the expulsion of Judges was physically influenced by the Fourth Amendment of the Constitution in 1975 which erased Clause (3) of Article 96 and from that point by the Fifth Amendment of the Constitution, the arrangements for evacuation of Judges by the Supreme Judicial Council were presented and eventually the Fifth Amendment was held to be unlawful by the Appellate Division in the Fifth Amendment Case, though the Appellate Division excused the arrangements identifying with the Supreme Judicial Council in Article 96 of the Constitution; however the criticized Sixteenth Amendment implies to abuse the judgment of the Appellate Division go all things considered.

The Judges can't play out their serious obligations except if their autonomy is ensured and secured by anchoring their residency as underlined in the United Nation's Instrument on Essential Principles on the Independence of the Judiciary. The formal necessities of autonomy of the Judges incorporate, among others, their security of residency and reasonable states of administration.

The Parliament, in negligence of the choice of the Appellate Division rendered in the Fifth Amendment Case, has abrogated the Supreme Judicial Council, which unmistakably bargains and debilitates the autonomy of the Judiciary through the Sixteenth Amendment and this Sixteenth Amendment is violative of Articles 94(4) and 22 of the Constitution by method for oppressing the residency of the Judges of the Supreme Court to the impulses and inclinations of the Members of Parliament.

The outcome of the Sixteenth Amendment is that it has rendered the residency of the Judges of the Apex Court unreliable and all things considered the Sixteenth Amendment has made a chance to undermine the autonomy of the Judiciary by making the equivalent defenceless against outside impacts and weights endangering the standard of law in the nation.

As the Sixteenth Amendment is violative of freedom of the Judiciary and detachment of forces, the equivalent is in struggle with Article 7B of the Constitution and by that reason, it is subject to be struck down.

The Sixteenth Amendment has unmistakably changed the expulsion component of the Supreme Court Judges for their demonstrated mischief or inadequacy to their disservice amid their term of office and in this point of view, the Sixteenth Amendment is violative of Article 147(2) of the Constitution.

Article 23 of the 'Beijing Statement of Principles of the Independence of the Judiciary' gives that by reason of distinction in history and culture, the methodology embraced for the expulsion of Judges may vary in various social orders and evacuation by Parliamentary strategies has customarily been received in a few purviews; yet in different wards, that strategy is unacceptable and its utilization other than for the most genuine of reasons is well-suited to prompt abuse and having respect to the socio-political states of Bangladesh, the arrangements identifying with the Supreme Judicial Council for expulsion of the Judges of the Supreme Court are most appropriate.

The American situation of reprimand of the Judges has been condemned as an unacceptable procedure in which 'political and party impact has become an integral factor' and along these lines, the danger of indictment being exceedingly politicized will be considerably progressively prominent in the current political setting of Bangladesh, particularly because of the nearness of Article 70 in the Constitution of Bangladesh and saw from this edge, the freedom of the Judiciary will be jeopardized.

## *Opinion of Mr. M. Amir-ul Islam, Barrister*

Mr. M. Amir-ul Islam learned Amicus Curiae; he was one of the Members of the Constitution Drafting Committee in the post-freedom period in 1972. As indicated by him the sixteenth amendment is unlawful and illicit and violative of the division of intensity. He demonstrated numerous contentions to help his sentiment, these are as discussed below.

There was no other choice for the Members of the drafting Committee however to relegate the activity of evacuation of the Supreme Court Judges to the Parliament and that being thus, the Parliament was endowed therewith by the first Constitution of 1972.

We learn through involvement and experience is the best instructor of an individual and rebuilding of the first Article 96 of the Constitution by the Sixteenth Amendment isn't upheld by experience and in such manner, the Sri Lankan, Indian and Malaysian encounters are not cheerful.

Separation of forces and autonomy of the Judiciary go connected at the hip and the regulation of detachment of forces must be clung to in making the Judiciary totally autonomous of the impact of the Executive or the Legislature and the Sixteenth Amendment, it's implied, is a hit to the freedom of the Judiciary.

The expulsion methodology of the Judges of the Supreme Court is a piece of their arrangement procedure, however sadly in Bangladesh, the arrangement procedure of the Judges of the Supreme Court isn't straightforward, open and open and even following 45 years of our freedom, Article 95(2) (c) of the Constitution identifying with alternate capabilities for arrangement of a Judge of the Supreme Court has not seen the light of the day to the extraordinary disadvantage of open intrigue.

The power of law isn't rationale, however encounter and our experience demonstrate that about 70% of the Members of Parliament in Bangladesh are currently a-days representatives and disputants and for freedom of the Judiciary, they ought not be associated with the procedure of evacuation of the Judges of the Supreme Court of Bangladesh on the ground of demonstrated mischief or insufficiency.

The Parliamentary evacuation system of the Judges of the Apex Court is in vogue in a few nations of the world like the UK, USA, Canada, Australia, India and so forth., yet that has turned out to be out of date and obsolete with the developing sacred statute of the freedom of the Judiciary.

The chronicled point of view combined with our experience and legal perceptions in different cases, to be specific, Masdar Hossain's Case, Eighth Amendment Case, Fifth Amendment Case and so on militate against the Sixteenth Amendment and homecoming of Article 96 (rebuilding of Article 96) is definitely not a conceivable contention in the present situation of Bangladesh.

The guideline of freedom of the Judiciary requests that a Judge ought to be attempted by his companions for his bad conduct/wrongdoing or insufficiency and that will best ensure his autonomy in the release of his legal capacities.

## *Opinion of Mr. Rokanuddin Mahmud, Barrister*

Mahmud Mr. Rokanuddin Mahmud, learned Amicus Curiae on the sixteenth amendment case.

His supposition about the sixteenth amendment case is as follows:

> He does not discover blame with the Sixteenth Amendment, but rather what is of foremost significance is that the law to be encircled according to the revised Article 96(3) of the Constitution must be gone into before he makes any accommodation on the point and except if that law is confined by the Parliament, it is hard to state at this phase regarding whether the Sixteenth Amendment has weakened the freedom of the Judiciary or not.

The Judges of the Supreme Court ought to be attempted by their friends if there should arise an occurrence of bad conduct or inadequacy and that will ensure the freedom of the higher Judiciary without bounds degree and in this regard, the Supreme Judicial Council as presented in Article 96 by the Fifteenth Amendment of the Constitution is the best component.

### *Opinion of Mr. Ajmalul Hossain, QC*

The Sixteenth Amendment has re-established the arrangements of Article 96 of the first Constitution of 1972; it will be a tough occupation for him to pounce upon the defendability of the Sixteenth Amendment.

The arrangements identifying with the Supreme Judicial Council were presented continuously Proclamation (Tenth Amendment) Order, 1977 (Second Proclamation Order No. 1 of 1977) and in the Fifth Amendment Case, the Appellate Division overlooked those arrangements as being increasingly straightforward and protecting the freedom of the Judiciary.

In Civil Review Petition Nos. 17–18 of 2011 by the request dated 29th March, 2011, the Appellate Division by altering its prior choice in the Fifth Amendment Case temporarily excused the arrangements identifying with the Supreme Judicial Council in Article 96 of the Constitution till 31st December 2012 and the Fifteenth Amendment embraced the arrangements identifying with the Supreme Judicial Council in Article 96 and kept up the equivalent; however from there on out of the blue, the Sixteenth Amendment was pushed through bringing doubts up in the brains of the general population about the autonomy of the higher Judiciary.

There is dependably a degree for maltreatment of the intensity of evacuation of the Judges of the Supreme Court by the Members of Parliament on the quality of the Sixteenth Amendment disabling the freedom of the higher Judiciary.

Article 7B of the Constitution ought to have been at the back of the psyche of the Members of Parliament before going of the Sixteenth Amendment and the Sixteenth Amendment is hit by Article 7B of the Constitution as it has influenced the freedom of the Judiciary, one of the essential highlights of the Constitution.

Judicial autonomy envelops both an individual and institutional measurement and the individual measurement identifies with the autonomy of a specific Judge, and the institutional measurement identifies with the autonomy of the Court which he keeps an eye on and every one of these measurements relies upon the target conditions or ensures that guarantee the Judiciary's opportunity from any outside impact or obstruction and the essential assurances are security of residency, budgetary security and managerial freedom.

Judicial freedom has been perceived as 'the backbone of constitutionalism in law based social orders' and the standard of legal autonomy requires the Judiciary to be autonomous both actually and discernment.

The institutional freedom of the Judiciary mirrors a more profound promise to the tenet of partition of forces among the Executive, Legislative and Judicial organs of the State and albeit legal autonomy had generally created as a rampart against the maltreatment of the Executive power, it similarly connected against other potential interruptions, including any from the Legislative organ because of enactment. So as to support up this accommodation.

It is regular information that in our nation, a dominant part of the officials has criminal records; yet in any case they will be engaged with the procedure of expulsion of the Judges of the Supreme Court by dint of the Sixteenth Amendment and this may offer ascent to irreconcilable circumstance representing a risk to the standard of law.

A question must be replied with respect to whether the Sixteenth Amendment has propelled open intrigue or crushed it and he trusts that the Sixteenth Amendment has vanquished it. Mr. Ajmalul Hossain finally presents that the Sixteenth Amendment is a colourable bit of enactment in the realities and conditions of the case and in that capacity the Sixteenth Amendment ought to go.[136]

## *Judgment of High Court Division*

The high court seeks opinions from the following person as Amici Curiae, Dr. Kamal Hossain, Senior Advocate, Mr. M. Amir-ul Islam, Senior Advocate, Mr. Rokanuddin Mahmud, Senior Advocate and Mr. Ajmalul Hossain QC, Senior Advocate. The writ petition was heard on 28.05.2015, 18.06.2015, 02.07.2015, 30.07.2015, 06.08.2015, 19.08.2015, 20.08.2015, 02.09.2015, 03.09.2015, 09.09.2015, 11.11.2015, 01.12.2015, 02.02.2016, 03.02.2016, 04.02.2016, 23.02.2016, 03.03.2016, and 10.03.2016. Judgment was given by the high court division on 05.05.2016. Moynul Islam. J said that, he has no hesitation in holding that the Sixteenth Amendment is a colorable legislation and is violative of separation of powers among the 3(three) organs of the State, namely, the Executive, the Legislature and the Judiciary and independence of the Judiciary as guaranteed by Articles 94(4) and 147(2), two basic structures of the Constitution and the same are also hit by Article 7B of the Constitution. So, he finds merit in the Rule. The Rule, therefore, succeeds. Accordingly, the Rule is made absolute without any order as to costs. It is hereby declared that the Constitution (Sixteenth Amendment) Act, 2014 (Act No. 13 of 2014) (Annexure 'A' to the Writ Petition) is colorable, void and ultra-virus the Constitution of the People's Republic of Bangladesh. However, as per Article 103(2)(a) of the Constitution, we certify that the case involves a substantial question of law as to the interpretation of the Constitution. QUAZI REZA-UL HOQUE J: & MD. ASHRAFUL KAMAL, J: agreed with the judgment of Moynul Islam.

## *Appeal Against Judgment*

Government of Bangladesh and others (appellant) applied an appeal from the judgment and order passed by the high court division in writ petition No 9989 Of 2014 before the appellate division versus Advocate Asaduzzaman Siddiqui and others (respondent).

The appeal was heard on 8th, 9th, 21st, 22nd, 23rd, 24th, 25th, 28th, 29th, 30th May 2017 and 1st June 2017. And the Judgment was passed on 3rd July 2017.

## Judgment of Appellate Division

An Order was passed by appellant division. Since all but one wrote separate judgments expressing their separate opinions, we unanimously dismiss the appeal, expunge the remarks made by the High Court Division as quoted in the judgment of the learned Chief Justice and also restore clause (2) (3), (4), (5), (6) and (7) of article 96 and also approve the Code of Conduct formulated in the main. The 799-page verdict has been written by the chief justice, Surendra Kumar Sinha, and the other six judges of the Appellate Division—Md Abdul Wahhab Miah, Nazmun Ara Sultana, Syed Mahmud Hossain, Muhammad Imman Ali, Hasan Foez Siddique, and Mirza Hussain Haider—have concurred with the views of the chief justice. The full bench of the Appellate Division of the Supreme Court unanimously declared the 16th amendment of the Constitution as illegal, affirming the judgment the earlier decision of the High Court Division. By this trailblazing verdict, the power to impeach a Judge of either division of the Supreme Court remained in the hands of the President, on a report of inquiry of the Supreme Judicial Council as enshrined in article 96 of the Constitution. This decision was based on the doctrine of separation of powers among the three organs of the state namely Legislature, Executive and Judiciary. Our Constitution is largely found upon the doctrine of Separation of Power, which was projected to the whole world by the French Philosopher Montesquieu who, through his theory, had us to believe that assimilation of all three kinds of power in one authority would ensue tyranny. This separation is a prerequisite to ensure independence of higher judiciary as enshrined in article 95 of the Constitution. Moreover, separation of judiciary is a provision of our Constitution under Article 22, as such, a part of the 'Basic Structure' of the Constitution too under art. 7B. consequently, the Parliament, although got power to amend any provision of the Constitution under art. 142, but it cannot make any amendment which withers away any provision of basic structure under art. 7B. People from different corners of the legal arena including intellectuals, practitioners, teachers, students mostly welcomed the verdict.[137] The Government, however, became outstandingly astonished to, and seriously dissatisfied, with the verdict. The key argument placed by the Govt. was centred on the 'Impeachment-Power,' which was vested in the Parliament under the original Constitution of 1972, and subsequently forwarded to the President through the Fourth Amendment of the Constitution in 1975.

## 16th Amendment Case and the Dilemma of Judge's Impeachment[138]

Nine practicing advocates of the Supreme Court, affiliated with a NGO named Human Rights and Peace for Bangladesh (HRPB), filed a writ petition before the

High Court Division of the Supreme Court challenging the constitutionality of 16th Amendment. The High Court Division declared the amendment unconstitutional[139] and the Appellate Division upheld the same.[140] While the constitutional challenge provided significant scope for the lawyers and judges to re-examine the entire fabric of the constitutional system of Bangladesh, the line of submission and reasoning adopted by the petitioners, respondents, amicus curie, the majority and dissenting opinion were disappointing. A thorough reading of the judgments of the High Court Division and Appellate Division in this case reveals that both the bar and bench failed to rise up to the occasion. Most of the arguments were based on a purely literal understanding of key constitutional principles, or were rather polemic, and insufficiently backed by sound constitutional analysis and reasoning.

## *Independence of Judiciary and Separation of Powers as Basic Structures of the Constitution*

At the Appellate Division, Chief Justice Surendra Kumar Sinha endorsed the majority view of the High Court Division by re-stating that 'Under the Constitution, the higher judiciary is entirely separated from the Executive and Legislature and is absolutely independent.'[141] Interestingly, an unusual dimension of the doctrine was considered in the High Court Division when Justice Moyeenul Islam Chowdhury, posed a question regarding the 16th Amendment affecting the independence of judiciary, component of the basic structure of the Constitution, public perception.' According to him:

> .. *[A] billion-dollar question has arisen: whether the Sixteenth Amendment has infringed upon the independence of the Judiciary in public perception? My answer is obviously in the affirmative. In public perception, the independence of the Judiciary has been curbed by the Sixteenth Amendment. We must attach topmost importance to public perception when it comes to the question of independence of the Judiciary. If according to public perception, the Judiciary is not independent, then it cannot be sustained at all.*
>
> *While "public perception" is hard to determine and is never a logical determiner of constitutionality, it is even harder for a judge on the Bench enter an assessment of public perception on a pure legal question.*[142] *Interestingly, Justice Moyeenul Islam Chowdhury concedes at a later stage that courts "do not administer justice by plebiscite".'*

## *Questions into the Suitability and Desirability Of Parliamentary Involvement*

The second question in the case was whether Parliament's participation in the removal of the judges would constitute an infringement of judicial independence.

Seen in this light, the desirability and permissibility of Parliament's institutional participation in judge's removal process was expected to be questioned, supported or tested by the parties and the judges. The case in hand, however, ended in some disappointingly misdirected arguments and reasoning. Firstly, Dr. Kamal Hossain, an important amicus curie in the case has argued that since Parliament is not entitled to reduce the salaries of the judges as per Articles 88 and 89 of the Constitution, it is also not entitled to remove them from their office.[143] Like India, Articles 88 and 89 of the Constitution, consider the salaries and financial benefits of the higher court judges during their tenure, a charge upon the Consolidated Fund and the Parliament is prohibited from changing it to the judge's disadvantage. However, Dr. Hossain failed to explain how this could preclude a parliamentary participation in the removal of a judge who is facing an allegation of misconduct and gross violation of the Constitution. Without much inquiry into the contextual and situation difference between these two cases, the majority opinion in the High Court Division felt 'at one with' Dr Hossain.[144] In the Appellate Division, Barrister Fida M Kamal took up the argument in a similar fashion and the Chief Justice endorsed the point. Secondly, Dr. Hossain argued that transfer of the removal power from the Council to the parliament would constitute a 'disadvantageous' change in the terms of service of the sitting judges and therefore violate the Article 147(3) of the Constitution. This too was 'palpably clear' to the majority opinion in the High Court Division. In the Appellate Division, Chief Justice Surendra Kumar Sinha adopted a similar reasoning. Interestingly, neither Dr. Hossain nor the majority opinion in the High Court Division clarified or explained in what sense a change in the removal procedure of a judge would constitute a disadvantageous variation in the terms and condition of his/her service. Had there been any disadvantageous change in the proposed law in relation to the grounds of removal, right of hearing, self-defence, salaries, amenities, privileges and retirement benefits etc. of the judges concerned, there might have been a possibility of arguing along these lines. It remains arguable as to whether a mere change of procedure is harmful if its substantive entitlements are kept intact.[145] Apart from a generalized mistrust in the Parliament as an institution 'poking its nose' into the judge's removal process, there seems to be no other substantive harm contemplated even by the petitioners and the amicus curie.

Thirdly, as regards the parliament's alleged unsuitability for participation in judge's removal process, the petitioners, most of amici curiae and the majority judges in the High Court Division have drawn heavily upon 'experience rather than logic.' The experiences as emphasized are that around 70% of the members of Parliament are businessmen. They are unmindful of their legislative responsibilities, quality of their legislative performance is of 'low standard,' a lot of them have criminal records, they are severely restrained by Article 70 of the Constitution and partisan directives will rule the show. The experience therefore leads the majority and others to the conclusion that the 16th Amendment would cause a violent blow to the independence of judiciary and separation of power the two important aspects of the basic structure of the constitution.

Likewise, the entire edifice of the Appellate Division judgment is based on exactly the same line of perception as regards Article 70:

> We find no infirmity in the view taken by the High Court Division on construction of article 70; and that in view of article 70, the members of Parliament must toe the party line in case of removal of any Judges of the Supreme Court. Consequently, the Judges will be left at the mercy of the party high command. We find nothing wrong in taking the above view.

It appears that 'experience' based arguments like the above would not stand the test of appropriate and sound legal reasoning expected of any ordinary constitutionality challenge. Primarily, Bangladesh does not yet have any single of 'experience' Parliament removing a Supreme Court judge because of a corrupt motive. Secondly, if we assume the 'experience test' as adopted to resemble something such as the American 'living constitutionalism'[146] discourse, it leads us nowhere. In the U.S. constitutional jurisprudence, living constitutionalism or loose constructionism refers to an interpretative tendency where the court takes a pragmatist approach to constitutional interpretation and claims that sometimes adhering strictly to the original meaning would be unacceptable as a matter of policy. These loose constructionists claim that drastic changes in the socio-legal ecology would often call for an evolving interpretation of the fundamental law of the land.[147]

In the case of Missouri v. Holland, Justice Holmes wrote:

> When we are dealing with words that also are a constituent act, like the Constitution of the United States, we must realize that they have called into life a being the development of which could not have been foreseen completely by the most gifted of its begetters. It was enough for them to realize or to hope that they had created an organism; it has taken a century and has cost their successors much sweat and blood to prove that they created a nation. The case before us must be considered in the light of our whole experience and not merely in that of what was said a hundred years ago. The treaty in question does not contravene any prohibitory words to be found in the Constitution. The only question is whether [252 U.S. 416, 434] it is forbidden by some invisible radiation from the general terms of the Tenth Amendment. We must consider what this country has become in deciding what that amendment has reserved.[148]

To this end, they benefit from the broadly and flexibly drafted texts of the Constitution to achieve the desired outcome.[149] Understandably that is not what the amicus curie and majority opinions were trying to achieve here in Asaduzzaman case. They were, rather, nullifying a system clearly and unequivocally endorsed and adopted by the framers of the original the Constitution as being inconsistent with the original Constitution itself (!) Thirdly, the 'experience test' as used earlier by the Supreme Court of Bangladesh itself in the Thirteenth Amendment case[150] is contextually different, and hence unsuitable to be applied in this case. While nullifying the caretaker government system as introduced through the Thirteenth Amendment, the then Chief Justice A.B.M Khairul Hoque relied heavily on the unpleasant 'experiences' the system caused to the judiciary.[151] Some of the retired Chief Justices leading an election time government led to extreme politicization of the appointment of Supreme Court judges, their elevation to Appellate Division and the ultimate selection of the Chief Justices. Justice Hoque and his colleagues, however, based their decision principally on the undemocratic nature of the caretaker government and its pervasive attack on several basic structures of the original Constitution. The bitter experiences with appointment in the judiciary were rather used as corroborative facts substantiating their basic structure arguments. Unlike the Thirteenth Amendment case, the later experiences unrelated to the specific question in hand (the process of removal of judge itself) are sought to be used as nullifying tools in this case. It is our perception that the focal point of the case lies somewhere else.[152]

## Seventeenth Amendment—Enforced Parliamentary Gender Neutrality, Upgraded

The 17th amendment of the constitution was passed by the parliament on 8 July 2018. This amendment passed that there shall be reserved 50 seats exclusively for women members and they will be elected by the aforesaid members in accordance with law on the basis of procedure of proportional representation in the Parliament through single transferable vote. The 8th Parliament raised the number of seats allocated from 30 to 45 while the 9th Parliament finally increased the number to 50 seats through 17th amendment for next 25 years. According to the Article 65 (3) of the Constitution, 50 seats would be reserved exclusively for women in parliament for the next 10 years from the first session of the 9th parliament formed in 2009. It was confirmed by the 14th amendment in 2004.

Under Article 65(3) of the Constitution, from the first parliament session after the one that passed the 14th constitutional amendment in 2004, 50 seats were reserved exclusively for women in Parliament for 10 years. Therefore, in line with the existing article, the first meeting of a new parliament in 2009, which meant women's seats, was expire next year. The government adopted the 14th amendment to the constitution in 2004 to add the seats reserved and allocate them among the parties with proportionate representation. The number of reserved seats increased in 2011 from 45 to 50 through the fifteenth amendment but the amendment did not expand the quota term. After 17th amendment the parliament now has 350 members total where 300 elected in general elections and 50 MPs from seats reserved for women. Women have lived in a strong patriarchal structure that determines their position relative to males in this nation. All other aspects of their lives are focused on men, so it is usually a low priority for most women to pursue a non-traditional career, like politics. They fall well behind in the two main areas, education and work, which are critical for political participation because of cultural conservatism. The female literacy rate is just 24.2%, and they are not eager to continue education because of the patriarchal society pattern. Also, education and employment rates are not adequate, whereas obstacles such as child marriage have been reduced and education for women is free till high school. Subsistence needs seem to be more important than political power for Bangladeshi women. Thus, variables, such as the socio-economic condition and society, are all intertwined. Not only do they contribute to women's under-representation in parliament, they also hinder their effectiveness. For women who are interested in being involved in politics, the political culture of this country itself is a big obstacle. The corrupt and immoral nature of politics, the lack of democratic practice in electing party leaders, the absolute control by parliamentary party leaders of the views of members in the House, the overlook of election promises, the ignorance of the demands of women's organizations, and the uneven nature of the policy mirror the limited nature of democratic practice in Bangladesh. The social mobility of women and their participation in demonstrations is limited by undeveloped democratic practices. A stronger way to increase the numerical and qualitative participation of women in parliament may be to introduce steps such as a women's quota at all levels of party bodies, a quota for party nominations for general elections and direct elections for reserved seats. Quotas and reserved seats are other problematic areas. Even though it is one of the most efficient strategies for raising the number of women in parliament but for Bangladeshi women, none of these parameters have been effective. In the last seven general elections, elected women without reservation only reached just 2%. Reserving seat is one of the main policies which is ensuring fixed seat in the parliament for women. Reserving women seat in parliament through constitutional amendment is another step ahead to women empowerment. It is impossible to advance the interests of women, with the patriarchal social system strengthened by religious, economic and political norms. Here, political party figures need to play a vital role in carrying forward the women's representation agenda.

### *Sheikh Hasina's Government and Women Empowerment From 2009 to 2018*

It was necessary to amend the constitution for the 17th time, for different needs, for the need of social reformation, for the need to carry on and elevate the democratic norms of equality. The development of women was at the peak when Sheikh Hasina came into power in 2009, and the political unrest was settling down gradually. To match with the rising of women empowerment socially and to maintain equal proportionality at the political and legislative level, the reserved seat of the parliament members needed to increase through the 17th amendment.

Under the leadership of Prime Minister Sheikh Hasina in the last decade, Bangladesh has achieved remarkable success in advancing women. Bangladesh is regarded as an ideal example for the developing country throughout the world for the empowerment of women. The overall development of women by ensuring their equal and active participation in mainstream socio-economic and political activities is one of her prime objectives. From 2009 to 2018 Government has taken necessary policy directives, numerous programs, and projects for the development of women. Bangladesh has improved gender inequality in all aspects the society. Bangladesh was ranked first in gender equality among South-Asian nations for the second consecutive year in 2017 by The World Economic Forum. Bangladesh climbed from lower too high in the 'Gender Gap Index of 2017, rising to No. 47' in the world.[153]

In Women's education, Bangladesh has experienced incredible success from 2009 to 2019. Girl's enrolment rate at the primary schools is 99.4% also 2.7 million girls receiving stipend at the secondary and higher secondary level. Education of girls up to degree level in public college is also free.[154]

## Women in the RMG Sector and Their Contribution In Economy

In their own way, NGOs and women's organizations can contribute to the social and attitudinal shift that we currently need. Since women are legitimate parliamentary delegates, it is difficult to do this without understanding and resolving the issue of women in our society as a whole. The most significant shift in the labour market of Bangladesh is the rise of women's participation. The number has risen dramatically in the last two or three decades. The percentage has risen from 8% to 34% from 1980 to 2016/17.

The Ready-Made Garments (RMG) is an important pioneer in the economy of Bangladesh. It contributes 80% of the total export earnings of Bangladesh. In terms of foreign currency earning, Bangladesh is in second place right after China for exporting garment goods. Around 4 million people work in the garment's factory, 80% of them are women. Among 4 million of the employees working in the RMG sector 3.2 million are women. Females make an enormous contribution to the national economy. Despite noticeable improvement in Bangladesh on a number of key socioeconomic indices, the role of women in the country's labour market remains an issue. On both a statistical and a theoretical point of view, from numerous social and political barriers are the reasons behind the unemployment of women. A large proportion of women with lower levels of education are in the lower rungs of the occupational ladder. In the meantime, women with comparatively higher levels of education face problems seeking jobs as well. So, the problem is hiding behind social and political reformation to the dugout the root issues why women are trailing behind men in the economic contribution. Bangladesh is experiencing an economic transition in which women should be active in setting constitutional norms in all spheres of society, such as equity and democratic participation. Not only can women's inclusion in other work fields in the RMG sector help us towards a world where all barriers are finally torn down.

### Women in Politics

Women and men have worked long and hard for women's right to vote and stand for election, from suffragettes to current day feminists. Progress is clearly visible as women have the freedom to vote in every country in the world. In 1893, New Zealand was the first nation to allow female suffrage, and in 2015, Saudi Arabia was the last country. Yet there is sluggish and inconsistent development. In politics, parliament and public life, women are still underrepresented worldwide. Less than 23% of parliamentarians are women, Beliefs about female politicians are also overwhelmingly dominated by deeply ingrained stereotypes, and such stereotypes can also be used by political rivals to challenge the abilities of women. Women are gradually putting themselves forward for votes, but their numbers are still well below men's numbers, even in developing countries such as the US, where equality has now been known for decades and men and women contribute equally to their society. Countries such as the US also have poor political confidence in women's candidates. The stigma against women is still strong even here in politics. They continue to face challenges that are systemic, socioeconomic, bureaucratic and cultural.

Surprisingly two women, Sheikh Hasina and Khaleda Zia, who dominated the politics of Bangladesh from 1991 to 2020, came into politics from their family not independently. But for other women who wants to be in politics without any political family background is a big challenge. Women are getting more interested to be part of the decision making as they are being more educated and more independent. In 2020 women's participation in politics is not criticized negatively in urban are but in rural area this situation is totally different. Parliamentary position is not only focused on the capital level or divisional level, Political representative should come forward even from the rural level where the safeguard of women's right is must needed. More women are coming in the political sphere now. But this is a result of long term joint hard work of women and women organization who believes in equality and equal participation of women to strongly establish democracy. The role of the Bangladesh Mahila Parishad Woman's Organization (Bangladesh Women's Council) is undeniable in fostering the protection and empowerment of women's rights and in raising awareness of fair rights for men and women under the law and in practice, and in promoting a democratic, secular, non-discriminatory family, society and state. NGO such as Grameen Bank and BRAC also played a vital role for last three decade to change women's economic situation by introducing micro credit loan. Their initiative did not only make women independent financially also provided late age education, awareness of health and provided family planning as well. As Discussed above from 1990 to 2015 Women are the majority in RMG sector and this is transforming this country's economy in an elevated level.

### Necessity of the 17th Amendment

From a democratic point of view, Article 10 of the Constitution calls for steps to be set in order to ensure the equality of women in all aspects of national life as the gender, race, religion or socioeconomic background of a person cannot be differentiated when it comes to the equal treatment given by the state. Moreover, Article 19(1) says that the State shall make every effort to ensure equal opportunities for all people. Article 28(2) says that, in all aspects of the State and public life, women shall have equal rights with men. This provision defines, all the rights specified in the Constitution, such as the right to life, the right to personal liberty, the right to land, freedom of speech, freedom of movement, the right to practice a career or occupation, are equally applicable to women in Bangladesh. Nevertheless, in Bangladeshi culture, inequity towards women remains widespread, but the situation is improving day by day. Structural limitations and attitudinal issues, along with sociocultural barriers, constitute the key hurdles to women's greater inclusion in the democratic sphere. While the Constitution grants men and women equal opportunities in every sphere, although the Constitution offers equal opportunities for men and women in any sphere, Bangladesh's women are still struggling to be equal in the political arena. In the electoral process, the adoption of women's quotas in both Parliament and local government has raised the number of women, but has not yet guaranteed their genuine inclusion in the decision-making process. Both strategies and services would need to be converted into liabilities. At the same time, the government should strive to ensure fair access for women to job trends in Bangladesh, in order to build and improve the ability of women as political leaders, develop public At the same time, the government should strive to ensure fair access for women to job trends in Bangladesh, in order to build and improve the ability of women as political leaders, develop technological training and the access to higher education along with technologically develop rural women to get along with the man in job sector. As per the vision 2021 is to have a digitally developed Bangladesh where technology and ICT is part of the next targeted sector to make big labour force, women should have the access to get trained in district and rural level to be part of the developed Bangladesh.

## Notes

1 Australia: Refugee Review Tribunal, *Bangladesh*, (2005) BGD17686, available at: https://www.refworld.org/docid/4b6fe125d.html (Accessed 30 June 2020).
2 Nibedita Das Purkayastha, 'Bangladesh Mahila Parishad' (Banglapedia, the National Encyclopedia of Bangladesh) (Accessed 19 June 2020).
3 Ibid.
4 S. M. Shamsul Alam, 'Democratic politics and the fall of the military regime in Bangladesh, Bulletin of Concerned Asian Scholars' <10.1080/14672715.1995.10413048> accessed 29 July 2020.
5 *Journal of the Asiatic Society of Bangladesh* (Hum.), 58(2), 2013, pp. 335–362.
6 *The Economic Times*, January 30, 2019.
7 M. Helal and M.A.Hossain. 'Four Decades of Economic Development of Bangladesh: An Assessment. *Journal of the Asiatic Society of Bangladesh*' (2013) accessed 25 July 2020.
8 'Gender Equality and Women's Empowerment in Public Administration' (2012) https://www.undp.org/content/undp/en/home/librarypage/democratic-governance/public_administration/gepa2.html

9 https://www2.ohchr.org/english/bodies/cedaw/docs/CEDAW.C.BGD.6-7.pdf
10 UN General Assembly, International Covenant on Civil and Political Rights, 16 December 1966, United Nations, Treaty Series, vol. 999.
11 https://cri.org.bd/2014/09/01/development-of-women-empowerment-in-bangladesh/
12 Above Note 26, 138.
13 S. M. Shamsul Alam 'Democratic politics and the fall of the military regime in Bangladesh', Bulletin of Concerned Asian Scholars (1995) PL 27, 30.
14 Ibid.
15 Ibid.
16 Ibid.
17 Ibid.
18 Ibid 33.
19 Ibid.
20 Ibid 34.
21 Ibid.
22 Ibid.
23 Ibid.
24 Dr. Md. Morshedul Islam, 'Politics behind the Passage of Eleventh Amendment to the Constitution of Bangladesh' [2015]5(10), p. 1, 1.
25 Ibid.
26 Ibid 2.
27 Alam (n 1), 35.
28 Islam (n 12), 3.
29 M. Jashim Ali Chowdhury 'Elections in "Democratic" Bangladesh.' Unstable Constitutionalism: Law and Politics in South Asia (2015) p. 192, 208.
30 Ibid 204.
31 Ibid 205–206.
32 Ibid 206–207.
33 Islam (n 12), 3.
34 Ibid 4.
35 ibid 2.
36 Ibid.
37 Ibid 4.
38 Amendments of Bangladesh Constitution and Their Impacts – Law Help Bangladedsh.
39 Ibid.
40 12TH Amendment Of Bangladesh Constitution.
41 Ibid.
42 Odhikar, Human Rights Monitoring Report, 2012.
43 Ibid.
44 See *Anwar Hossain Chowdhury V Bangladesh* (the 8th Amendment Case), 1989 BLD (Spl).
45 Nizam Ahmed, 'Non-Party Caretaker Government In Bangladesh: Experience And Prospect' [2004] University Press Limited, Dhaka.
46 Md. Mahbub Alam and Golam Rabbani, 'Abolition Of Non-Party Caretaker Government System In Bangladesh: Controversy And Reality' (2014) 2 European Centre for Research Training and Development UK.
47 Mashiur Rahman, 'Democracy In Crisis' [2010] University Press Limited, Dhaka.
48 Salma Akhtar, 'Amendments To The Constitution Of Bangladesh 1973–2011: Background, Politics And Impacts' [2016] University Press Limited, Dhaka.
49 Mashiur Rahman, 'Democracy in Crisis' [2010] University Press Limited, Dhaka.
50 Duncan McDonnell and Marco Valbruzzi, 'Defining and Classifying Technocrat-Led and Technocratic Governments' [2011] European Studies Association Conference, Baltimore.

51 Geert Bouckaert and Marleen Brans, 'Governing Without Government: Lessons from Belgium'S Government' (2012) 25 Governance: An International Journal of Policy, Administration, and Institutions <http://onlinelibrary.wiley.com/doi/10.1111/j.1468-0491.2012.01579.x/full> accessed 5 September 2020.

52 Masud Al Hasanuzzaman, 'Role of Opposition in Bangladesh Politics' [1998] University Press Limited, Dhaka.

53 Mashiur Rahman, 'Democracy in Crisis' [2010] University Press Limited, Dhaka.

54 Firoj Jalal, *Democracy in Bangladesh: Conflicting Issues And Conflict Resolution,* (Bangla Academy 2012).

55 Nizam Ahmed, 'Abolition or Reform? Non-Party Caretaker System and Government Succession In Bangladesh' (2011) 100 The Round Table.

56 Masudul Haque, 'Revisiting the Role Of The President During Caretaker Government In Ensuring Credible Free Elections In Bangladesh' (2011) 6 Asian Journal of Comparative Law.

57 Nizam Ahmed, 'Non-Party Caretaker Governments And Parliamentary Elections In Bangladesh: Panacea Or Pandora's Box?' (2004) 11 South Asian Survey.

58 Adeeba Aziz Khan, 'The Politics Of Constitutional Amendments In Bangladesh: The Case Of The Non-Political Caretaker Government' (2015) 2015 International Review of Law.

59 Habib Zafarullah and Muhammad Yeahia Akhter, 'Non-Political Caretaker Administrations and Democratic Elections in Bangladesh: An Assessment' (2000) 35 Government and Opposition.

60 Md. Abdul Halim, *Constitution, Constitutional Law and Politics: Bangladesh Perspective* (CCB Foundation 2014).

61 Shahjahan Bhuiyan, 'The Caretaker Government In Bangladesh: An Appraisal of Its Formation' [2020] The American University in Cairo.

62 Shahjahan Bhuiyan, 'The Caretaker Government In Bangladesh: An Appraisal Of Its Formation' [2020] The American University in Cairo.

63 Dr. Md. Aminul Islam, *Bangladesh: The Challenges of The Caretaker Government 1991–2014* (Famous Books 2019).

64 Justice Wahhab, '13Th Amendment Constitutional Necessity' <http://news.priyo.com/judicial/2012/09/20/13th-amendment-const-60262.html> accessed 5 September 2020.

65 Firoj Jalal, *Democracy In Bangladesh: Conflicting Issues And Conflict Resolution,* (Bangla Academy 2012).

66 Po Jen Yap, *The Supreme Court of Bangladesh And Defensive Judicial Review* (Cambridge University Press 2017).

67 Gyasuddin Molla, 'Democratic Institution Building Process In Bangladesh: South Asian Experience Of A New Model Of A Caretaker Government In A Parliamentary Framework' [2000] South Asia Institute Department of Political Science, University of Heidelberg.

68 Abdur Razzaq, '13Th Amendment And Future Of Democracy' *The Daily Star* (2011) <https://www.thedailystar.net/news-detail-189434> accessed 5 September 2020.

69 Manzoor Hasan, 'The State of Governance In Bangladesh' [2013] Centre for Governance Studies, BRAC University & BRAC Research and Evaluation Division.

70 Dr. Aminul Islam and Zuryati Yeasin, 'The Thirteenth Amendment To The Constitution Of Bangladesh (1996): A Critical Assessment' (2019) 8 Asian Journal of Social Sciences & Humanities <https://www.researchgate.net/publication/333674770_THE_THIRTEENTH_AMENDMENT_TO_THE_CONSTITUTION_OF_BANGLADESH_1996_A_CRITICAL_ASSESSMENT> accessed 5 September 2020.

71 Nizam Ahmed, 'From Monopoly To Competition: Party Politics In The Bangladesh Parliament (1973–2001)' (2003) 55 Pacific Affairs.

72 Md. Mahbub Alam and Golam Rabbani, 'Abolition Of Non-Party Caretaker Government System In Bangladesh: Controversy And Reality' (2014) 2 European Centre for Research Training and Development UK.

73 M Saleem Ullah vs Bangladesh and others [2011] Appellate Division, The Supreme Court Of Bangladesh, Submissions of Dr. Kamal Hossain, as Amicus Curiae (Appellate Division, The Supreme Court Of Bangladesh).

74 Law Report, 'SC Sets Aside Caretaker Govt System' BDNEWS24.COM (2020) <https://bdnews24.com/bangladesh/2011/05/10/sc-sets-aside-caretaker-govt-system> accessed 8 September 2020.

75 Ashutosh Sharkar, 'Caretaker System Declared Illegal' The Daily Star (2011) <https://www.thedailystar.net/news-detail-185142> accessed 8 September 2020.

76 *Constitution of the People's Republic of Bangladesh* [Bangladesh], 4 November 1972.

77 Rashiduzzaman, M. "Bangladesh in 2001: The Election and a New Political Reality?" *Asian Survey* 42, no. 1 (2002).

78 *The Bangladesh Observer*, December 31, 2001.

79 Ibid, May 19, 2003.

80 *The New York Times*, August 29, 2002.

81 BBC UK, 12 January 2007.

82 aljazeera, 9 March 2019.

83 Freedom House, Freedom in the World 2008 - Bangladesh, 2 July 2008, available at: https://www.refworld.org/docid/487ca1f1c.html (Accessed 17 June 2020).

84 ibid.

85 ibid.

86 *The Guardian*, 11 January 2007.

87 ibid.

88 Canada: Immigration and Refugee Board of Canada, Bangladesh: Introduction of the caretaker government in October 2006; security measures implemented by the caretaker government; treatment of key political figures of the Awami League (AL) and the Bangladesh National Party (BNP) by the caretaker government, 9 October 2007, BGD102598.E, available at: https://www.refworld.org/docid/474e8953c.html (Accessed 18 January 2021).

89 ibid.

90 BBC, 21 May 2007.

91 Akter (n 26) 55–56.

92 Ibid.

93 Ibid 36.

94 Ibid 106.

95 Adeeba Aziz Khan, 'The politics of constitutional amendments in Bangladesh: The case of the non-political caretaker government.' International Review of Law (2015) p. 1, 7–9.

96 Akter (n 26), 95–96.

97 Khan (n 133) 9–11.

98 'Adibashi Shobdo Poriharer poramorsha Khudo Protikria', *Protom Alo* (Dhaka, 10 August 2014).

99 Maher, Islam, 'Adibashir Antorjatik Sonod ebong Bangladesh', *Protom Alo* (Dhaka, 9 August 2018).

100 Ibid.

101 Islam (n 137).

102 Muktasree Chakma, Adibasider Sangbidhanik Shikriti, *Asak Buletin,* (Dhaka September 2010).

103 Abdul Halim, "The Fifteenth Amendment to the constitution: Concern & Perils of Constitutionalism in Bangladesh." *The Counsel Law Journal*, p. 83, 112–114.

104 Md. Enayet Ullah Patwary 'Caretaker Government and the Politics of Bangladesh' (2014)8, p. 24, 31.

105 Halim (141), 135.

106 Ibid.

107 Ibid 113.

108 Akter (n 26)159.
109 Halim (n 141), 118–119.
110 Ibid 93–94.
111 Ibid 93–99.
112 Jahid Hossain Bhuiyan, 'Secularism in the Constitution of Bangladesh.'*The Journal of Legal Pluralism and Unofficial Law* (2017) 49(2) p. 203, 208.
113 Halim (n 141), 93.
114 Ibid 97.
115 Ibid 125-126.
116 Akter (n 26), 56.
117 Ranu Moni and Muktadir Hasan, "16th Amendment Is the Violation of Basic Philosophy of the Constitution: A Critical Analysis" (Student Research, 2018) <http://dspace.daffodilvarsity.edu.bd:8080/handle/123456789/2848> accessed November 3, 2020.
118 Article 96(1), The Constitution of the People's Republic of Bangladesh.
119 Article 96(2), Ibid.
120 Article 96 (3), Ibid.
121 Article 96 (4), Ibid.
122 Md. Abdul Halim, *Constitution, Constitutional Law and Practices: Bangladesh Perspective*, 3rd Edition, CCB Foundation, 2014.
123 Article 96(2), The Constitution of the People's Republic of Bangladesh.
124 Article 96(3), Ibid.
125 Article 95, Ibid.
126 Article 56(3), Ibid.
127 Article 22, The Constitution of the People's Republic of Bangladesh.
128 Mahamudul Islam, *Constitutional Law of Bangladesh*, 2nd edition, Mollick brothers, 2003, p. 146.
129 *Anwar HussainChowdhury* V Bangladesh [1989 BLD (SPL) 1].
130 13MasdarHossain's Case [52 DLR (2000) 82].
131 Rizvi Hasan, "Critics of Sixteenth Amendment under the Constitution of the People's Republic of Bangladesh" (Student Research Paper, 2016) <https://www.academia.edu/27217001/CRITICS_OF_SIXTEENTH_AMENDMENT_UNDER_THE_CONSTITUTION_OF_BANGLADESH> accessed November 3, 2020.
132 Article 7, the Constitution of the People's Republic of Bangladesh.
133 Preamble, The Constitution (Sixteenth Amendment) Act, 2014.
134 Ranu Moni and Muktadir Hasan, "16th Amendment Is the Violation of Basic Philosophy of the Constitution: A Critical Analysis" (Student Research, 2018) <http://dspace.daffodilvarsity.edu.bd:8080/handle/123456789/2848> accessed November 3, 2020.
135 Ridwanul Hoque, "Can the Court Invalidate an Original Provision of the Constitution?" [2017] University of Asia Pacific Journal of Law & Policy <http://uap-bd.edu/lhr/wp-content/uploads/2017/05/2.pdf> accessed November 3, 2020.
136 Ranu Moni and Muktadir Hasan, "16th Amendment Is the Violation of Basic Philosophy of the Constitution: A Critical Analysis" (Student Research, 2018) <http://dspace.daffodilvarsity.edu.bd:8080/handle/123456789/2848> accessed November 3, 2020.
137 Md Milan Hossain, "Separation of Judiciary in Bangladesh Constitutional Mandates and Masdar Hossain Case's Directions: A Post Separation Evaluation." *International Journal For Court Administration* <https://www.iacajournal.org/articles/10.36745/ijca.310/> accessed November 3, 2020.
138 M. Jashim Ali Chowdhury and Nirmal Kumar Saha, "Advocate Asaduzzaman Siddiqui V. Bangladesh Bangladesh's Dilemma With Judges' Impeachment" <https://www.researchgate.net/publication/336409716_Advocate_Asaduzzaman_Siddiqui_V_Bangladesh_Bangladesh's_Dilemma_With_Judges'_Impeachment> accessed November 3, 2020.
139 Advocate Asaduzzaman Siddiqui v. Bangladesh (Writ Petition No. 9989/2014). Full text of the High Court Division judgment is available at: http://www.supremecourt.

gov.bd/resources/documents/783957_WP9989of2014_Final.pdf (Accessed on November 03, 2020).

140 The case reached the Appellate Division as Bangladesh v. Advocate Asaduzzaman Siddiqui (Civil Appeal No. 06/2017). Full text of the Appellate Division judgment is available at: http://www.supremecourt.gov.bd/resources/documents/1082040_C.A.6of2017_Final_3.8.2017.pdf (Accessed on November 03, 2020).

141 Justice Surendra Kumar Sinha, Bangladesh v. Advocate Asaduzzaman Siddiqui (Civil Appeal No. 06/2017), p. 239.

142 Geoffrey Rivlin, *Understanding the Law* 84 (Oxford, 6th ed. 2012).

143 Dr Kamal Hossain, Advocate Asaduzzaman Siddiqui v. Bangladesh (Writ Petition No. 9989/2014), p. 43.

144 Ibid, Justice Moyeenul Islam at 121.

145 Muhibur Rhaman Manik v. Bangladesh & ors 23 BLD (HCD) 264. See also—Sheikh Hasina v Bangladesh (2008) 60 DLR (AD) 90.

146 Jack M. Balkin, Alive and Kicking: Why no one truly believes in a dead Constitution, (Aug. 29, 2005); http://www.slate.com/articles/news_and_politics/jurisprudence/2005/08/alive_and_kicking.html (last visited November 03, 2020).

147 Missouri v. Holland 252 U.S. 416 (1920) at p. 433.

148 Ibid.

149 Trop v. Dulles, 356 U.S. 86 (1958) at p. 101.

150 Abdul Mannan Khan v. Bangladesh, 26 DLR (AD) 44.

151 Ibid, A.B.M. Khairul Hoque at p. 288.

152 M. Jashim Ali Chowdhury and Nirmal Kumar Saha, "Advocate Asaduzzaman Siddiqui V. Bangladesh Bangladesh's Dilemma With Judges' Impeachment" <https://www.researchgate.net/publication/336409716_Advocate_Asaduzzaman_Siddiqui_V_Bangladesh_Bangladesh's_Dilemma_With_Judges'_Impeachment> accessed November 3, 2020.

153 *The Daily Star*, November 04, 2017.

154 Ibid.

# 6

# CONCLUSION—THE HOPE LIVES ON

A constitution is something which gives legitimacy to the government and defines the powers under which a government may act. As such, the constitution sets limits both to the powers which can be exercised and to the manner in which they may be exercised. Accordingly, the constitution defines the legality of power. This notion is particularly apposite in a country with a written constitution and a Supreme Court which is conferred with jurisdiction to rule on the legality of government action. Under such a constitutional arrangement, it can be said that everything which the government does is either lawful or unlawful depending upon whether or not the contested conduct is held to be 'constitutional' or not.

The inception of the present constitution of Bangladesh can be traced back as early as 1947. After being partitioned by the British Sovereign in 1947, the constituency of Pakistan faced an ongoing dilemma to constitute a favourable constitution for both of its parts. Ayub Khan during his tenure set up a Constitution Commission to make recommendations for the future constitution and the constitution framed by him came into operation on 7 June 1962. This constitution introduced a system which was euphemistically called a presidential form of government where the normal checks and balances to prevent one-man rule were not incorporated in the constitution.

Two elections were held under the constitution of 1962 which clearly demonstrated that the people could not get persons of their choice elected as their representatives. In 1965 Ayub got himself re-elected as the President. The general impression in the country was that the election was rigged. In 1966 Bangabandhu Sheikh Mujibur Rahman started a movement in East Pakistan with his 6-Point programme which reflected the genuine grievances of the people of East Pakistan. Towards the end of 1968, an agitation in political parties gradually gathered momentum and was accompanied by widespread disturbances throughout the country. The Agartala Conspiracy case started against

DOI: 10.4324/9781003363002-6

Bangabandhu Sheikh Mujibur Rahman and others aborted because of massive movement in East Pakistan.

Ayub Khan called a round table conference of political leaders to resolve the political issues which led to the crisis. A solution was near sight, when all of a sudden Ayub Khan by relinquishing his office asked the Defence Forces on 24 March 1969 to step in as, according to him, it was beyond the capacity of the civil government to deal with the then prevailing situation.

The Commander-in-Chief, Yahya Khan, dismissed the Constitution of 1962, dissolved the National and Provincial Assemblies and enforced Martial Law all through the country by a Proclamation issued on 26 March 1969. The Provisional Constitution Order was promulgated by him on 31 March 1969 which significantly followed the motif of the Laws (Continuance in Force) Order, 1958. The Legal Framework Order promulgated by Yahya Khan on the 30 March 1970 and elections were held under its provisions to the National and Provincial Assemblies in December 1970, on the basis of adult franchise. With a good amount of political manipulation, Yahya Khan summoned a session of the National Assembly on 3rd March 1971 in Dhaka. But the session was refused to be attended by Z. A. Bhutto's People's Party and therefore, it was postponed indefinitely by Yahya Khan.

Mujib's Awami League, which had secured almost all the seats in East Pakistan and had a clear Majority in the National Assembly, showed immediate reaction to this act of Yahya Khan and took the charge of the administration in East Pakistan in protest of this action. In order to handle the situation, Yahya Khan held meetings with the major political party leaders in Dhaka and the subsequent events clearly indicate that those were done with manipulative intentions. He, afterwards, began to enforce his military power with brutality by shooting down numerous innocent people in Dhaka and other places of East Pakistan on 25th March 1971 at night when they were all asleep, and this was an act of betrayal for the people of the then East Pakistan. Under such circumstances, the independence of Bangladesh was declared on 26 March, 1971 at the onset of the Bangladesh Liberation War by our Father of the Nation Bangabandhu Sheikh Mujibur Rahman; the following day the declaration was broadcast by Major Ziaur Rahman in the name of Bangabandhu in a radio broadcast. Thousands of people came out on streets to fight back Pakistani Army to make the country free. Independence was proclaimed on 17 April 1971 by the National and Provincial Assemblies members elected in the election of 1970 from East Pakistan. They formed the Government on 10 April 1971 with Bangabandhu Sheikh Mujibur Rahman as the President who was in the custody of Pakistan and Syed Nazrul Islam was made the Acting President until Bangabandhu Sheikh Mujibur Rahman was made free. After a long struggle of nine months, the Pakistan Army finally surrendered on 16 December 1971 and Bangladesh came into existence as a free country.

The Government of Pakistan released Bangabandhu Sheikh Mujibur Rahman and he came back to Dhaka on 10 January 1972. Right after that, he issued the Provincial Constitution of Bangladesh Order, 1972, in his position of the

President of Bangladesh. He provided for a parliamentary form of government in the interim period and formed the Constituent Assembly with the members of National Assembly and East Pakistan Provincial Assembly; these members were the ones elected by the people of East Pakistan for providing the country with a democratic constitution. A constitution was adopted by the Assembly on the 4th of November which came into activation on 16 December 1972, exactly one year after the independence of Bangladesh.

Bangladesh was established as a sovereign unitary Republic by the Constitution with 153 articles, 1 preamble, and 4 Schedules. It formed a government composed of representatives elected by the people which would not be a kinship, that is the rule of one man, or an aristocracy of one class of men. The idea of sovereignty is that Bangladesh will not be subject to any external authority and the term 'Republic' indicates that the Head of the State will not be a monarch, rather an elected functionary. The Constitution confirms that sovereignty remains with the people and the Constitution is the representation and pure expression of the will of the people of the State.

The 1972 constitution was one the truly democratic and progressive constitution at that time. Since the Constitution of Bangladesh came into operation on 16 December 1972, there have been 17 amendments to our constitution under different political realities. From the 17 amendments that have been made to the Constitution thus far, only few among them addressed the pro-people issues, while others can easily be perceived as self-serving efforts that intend to undermine fundamental constitutional principles.

The 1st amendments that were made to ensure justice for victims of international crimes and the 12th amendment which reinstituted parliamentary democracy—aimed at achieving pro-people reforms. A parliamentary form of government was introduced by the Constitution and this government was formed with the President of the Republic as the head of the Constitution who would be elected by the members of the Parliament. The parliamentary members were required to be directly elected on the basis of adult franchise. It will be the task of the President to appoint a Member of Parliament who would again command the support of the majority of the parliamentary members as the Prime Minister and who would also appoint ministers in consultation with the Prime Minister. The Prime Minister would have the executive authority of the Republic who, along with the Cabinet, would be responsible for the ultimate sovereignty of the Parliament and would also ensure it through the Parliament. The Prime Minister and the Cabinet would be able to continue as long as they had the support of the majority of the parliamentary members.

The 4th amendment has different views. Many criticized 4th amendment as this was made to establish a one-party autocratic regime, on the other hand many believed that the intention of 4th amendment was mainly to give a new perspective to the then Bangladesh. Building national unity by bringing all the mainstream political parties together and also by dissolving his own party Awami League to form the Bangladesh Krishak Sramik League or BAKSAL for the interest of the nation was the prime objective of the 4th amendment, described by many. This amendment was also a response to the then political reality by making the constitution to people friendly in a sense to give the constitution a homegrown feeling rather than an ideal and utopian constitution borrowed from developed country context.

The 5th and 7th amendments were orchestrated to legalize rules and ordinances during the period of Martial Law—serving as key examples of misappropriation of the Constitutional amendments. Other radical amendments included incorporation of Islam as a state religion, subsequently causing an awkward co-existence with secularism (8th amendment), denying safeguards to arrest in cases of preventive detention (2nd amendment), repealing of the provisions for non-party caretaker government for conducting free and fair election (15th amendment).

Among other things, the 15th Amendment to Bangladesh constitution has added a provision for protection of environment and biodiversity (Article 18A). This is a rare example of Bangladesh taking into account the emerging constitutional norms of global relevance. In the majority of other cases, however, the discussions and debates on constitutional reforms ignore contemporary constitutionalism on issues such as enforceability of economic rights like right to food and water, environmental obligations and essentials of good governance like objective appointment in the constitutional bodies, and ensuring individual accountability of the members of the cabinet.

The Bangladesh Constitution has authorized the Parliament to further achieve its goals by drafting laws on some important issues, including authorizing lower courts to enforce basic rights (44), drafting requirements for the appointment of superior judicial judges (95), and strengthening parliamentary committees (76), and appointed members of the election committee (118). In the past 50 years, none of this has been achieved.

In addition to the efforts of the parliament, the constitutional provisions can also be promoted and strengthened through the progressive interpretation of the provisions. The Supreme Court was vested with the guardianship of the Constitution. It was bestowed with the power of judicial review. To exercise that power, the Supreme Court, except for some specified situations, could review the actions of the State to ensure that it did not violate any provision of the Constitution or the laws of the land. It could also strike down any law if the charge was inconsistent with any provision of the Constitution including the provisions guaranteeing fundamental rights. In this sense, our success is also limited. In constitutional cases through judicial intervention, our Apex Court has taken progressive initiative by invalidating the martial law system and that brought justice to many. However, in doing so, they sometimes made decisions that lacked judicial insight and objectivity. For example, the widely publicized Fifth Amendment ruling declared that the Fifth Amendment legalized the martial law system, but at the same time retained some of the provisions of martial law, including those that benefit the judges themselves.

For the purpose of self-service, governments under military terms tried to dissolve institutions such as higher judicial institutions, election commissions, cabinets, etc. In many senses Bangladesh is still having a negative impact of such acts. Even after returning to democratic ruling since 1991, we observed many government failed to build national institutions, rather they have used the law's lack of appropriate qualifications for the appointment of high-level judicial bodies, the criteria for the promotion of judges from high courts to the Appellate Division, or the criteria for appointing judges of the Appellate Division, to strengthen their control over the high-level judicial bodies.

This is high time for us to think carefully whether we are going to be governed by fear and by anger or by the rule of law. If we have to live here and live in fear of when undemocratic or extremist political power will rule us. If we are just going to except the system that treats us better if we are rich and powerful then if we are poor and powerless, then we cannot claim to be just. What if we say we are committed to equal justice under the law protecting the rights of every citizen, regardless of wealth, race, religion, or status then we have to end this nightmare for the general people of Bangladesh. We have seen over the years in Bangladesh that in the name of politics or being in the power, Military rulers or political party backed by extremist group has given false hope to the muses and they have ruled the nation by bigotry and bias, and ignored the truth in exchange for being in the power, that's not our constitution promised for our people and this is not justice and that's not right. Hope allows us to push forward, even when the truth is distorted by the people in power. It allows us to stand up when they tell us to sit down. And to speak when they say, 'Be Quite.' The Opposite of poverty is not wealth. The opposite of poverty is justice. That the character of our nation is not reflected in how we treat the rich and the privileged, but how we treat the powerless, the disfavoured, and condemned and that is our constitutional promised and therefore, building more effective, accountable, and inclusive institutions for all is now the demand of time for Bangladesh to fulfil the objective of our Constitution. At the end of the discussion, it is not quite easy to be optimistic. However, in deeper observation, we can keep our hopes high to believe that a better constitutional era is coming. Our Constitution has withstood 50 years of attack by different military regimes and still the high morale of the liberation war still exists. In addition, the people's desire and determination to establish an equal and welfare state has been consolidated for many years. In order to achieve all these, the 1972 Constitution will undoubtedly continue to inspire, enlighten and encourage present and future generations of Bangladesh.

# BIBLIOGRAPHY


Abdul Halim, The 7th Amendment Judgment by the Appellate Division: Judicial Politics or Judicial Activism, *The Counsel Journal* 1, no. 1, p. 19, 27.

Abdur Razzaq, "13th Amendment and Future of Democracy" *The Daily Star* (2011) <https://www.thedailystar.net/news-detail-189434> accessed 5 September 2020.

Adeeba Aziz Khan, "The Politics of Constitutional Amendments in Bangladesh: The Case of The Non-Political Caretaker Government" (2015) 2015 International Review of Law.

Adibashi Shobdo Poriharer poramorsha Khudo Protikria', *Protom Alo* (Dhaka 10 August 2014).

Ahmed, Modud, "Bangladesh: Era of Sheikh Mujibur Rahman", p. 102.

Ali Riaz, *Inconvenient Truths about Bangladesh Politics* (Dhaka: Prathama Prokashan 2012) p. 164.

*Anwar Hossain Anwar Hossain* Chowdhury *Vs. Bangladesh, 1989*, 18 CLC (AD).*Bangladesh* [1989].

Ashutosh Sharkar, "Caretaker System Declared Illegal" *The Daily Star* (2011). https://www.thedailystar.net/news-detail-185142 [accessed 8 September 2020].

Basunia, J. (n.d.). "On Bangladesh Constitutional 8th Amendment Case" (26 09, 2019)

Bhuian Monoar Kabir, "Politico-Economic Limitations and the Fall of the Military-Authoritarian Government in Bangladesh". *Armed Forces & Society* 21, no. 4, p. 554, 561–562 (1995).

CA debates, October 30, 1972, published in *The Bangladesh Observer*, October 31, Collaborators and War Criminals, Bangladesh Genocide Archive.

Dr. Akhter Hussain, *General Ershad and Bangladesh* (The Daily Sun, 2019).

Dr. Aminul Islam and Zuryati Yeasin, "The Thirteenth Amendment to the Constitution Of Bangladesh (1996): A Critical Assessment". *Asian Journal of Social Sciences & Humanities* 8 (2019) https://www.researchgate.net/publication/333674770_THE_THIRTEENTH_AMENDMENT_TO_THE_CONSTITUTION_OF_BANGLADESH_1996_A_CRITICAL_ASSESSMENT [accessed 5 September 2020].

Dr. Md. Aminul Islam, *Bangladesh: The Challenges of the Caretaker Government 1991–2014* (Famous Books 2019).

Dr. Md. Aminul Islam, "Politics behind the Passage of Eleventh Amendment to the Constitution of Bangladesh". 5, no. 10, p. 1, 1 (2015).

Duncan McDonnell and Marco Valbruzzi, "Defining and Classifying Technocrat-Led And Technocratic Governments". European Studies Association Conference, Baltimore (2011).

Firoj Jalal, *Democracy Ii Bangladesh:Conflicting Issues and Conflict Resolution* (Bangla Academy 2012).

Firoj Jalal, *Democracy in Bangladesh: Conflicting Issues and Conflict Resolution* (Bangla Academy 2012).

Freedom House, "Freedom in the World 2008 - Bangladesh, 2 July 2008", available at: https://www.refworld.org/docid/487ca1f1c.html [accessed 17 June 2020]

Geert Bouckaert and Marleen Brans, "Governing Without Government: Lessons from Belgium'S Government". *Governance: An International Journal of Policy, Administration, and Institutions* 25 (2012). http://onlinelibrary.wiley.com/doi/10.1111/j.1468-0491.2012.01579.x/full [accessed 5 September 2020].

Gender Equality and Women's Empowerment in Public Administration' (2012) https://www.undp.org/content/undp/en/home/librarypage/democratic-governance/public_administration/gepa2.html

Gyasuddin Molla, "Democratic Institution Building Process in Bangladesh: South Asian Experience of a New Model of a Caretaker Government in a Parliamentary Framework" (South Asia Institute Department of Political Science, University of Heidelberg 2000). https://d-nb.info/1203740239/34

Habib Zafarullah and Muhammad Yeahia Akhter, "Non-Political Caretaker Administrations and Democratic Elections In Bangladesh: An Assessment". *Government and Opposition* 35 (2000).

M. Helal and M.A. Hossain. "Four Decades of Economic Development of Bangladesh: An Assessment." *Journal of the Asiatic Society of Bangladesh* (2013) [accessed 25 July 2020].

F.A. Huq "Constitution-Making in Bangladesh". *Pacific Affairs* (University of British Columbia 1973).

F.A. Huq "Constitution Making in Bangladesh". *Pacific Affairs* 46, pp. 59–76 (Spring, 1973).

S.S. Islam "The Impacts of the Major Events of 1966 on the Struggle for Independence of Bangladesh". 1.11.2016. *Journal of the Asiatic Society of Bangladesh* (Hum.) 58, no. 2, pp. 335–362 (2013).

Justice Wahhab, "13th Amendment Constitutional Necessity".

M. Kamal *Bangladesh Constitution: Trends and Issues* (University of Dhaka 1994).

Lant Princhett, Kunal Sen and Eric Werker, *Deals and Development, The Political Dynamics of Economic Growth.*

Lant Pritchett, Kunal Sen, and Eric Werker, *Deals and Development: The Political Dynamics of Growth Episodes* (Oxford Scholarship Online December 2017).

M. Jashim Ali Chowdhury, "Elections in "Democratic" Bangladesh". *Unstable Constitutionalism: Law and Politics in South Asia*, p. 192, 208 (2015).

M. Rafiqul Islam, "The Seventh Amendment to the Constitution of Bangladesh: A Constitutional Appraisal". *The Political Quarterly* 58, no. 3, p. 312 (1995).

Mashiur Rahman, *Democracy in Crisis* (University Press Limited, Dhaka 2010).

Masud Al Hasanuzzaman, *Role of Opposition in Bangladesh Politics* (University Press Limited, Dhaka 1998).

Masudul Haque, "Revisiting the Role of The President During Caretaker Government in Ensuring Credible Free Elections in Bangladesh". *Asian Journal of Comparative Law* 6, pp. 1–28 (2011).

Md. Abdul Halim, *Constitution, Constitutional Law and Politics: Bangladesh Perspective* (CCB Foundation 2014).

Md. Mahbub Alam and Golam Rabbani, "Abolition of Non-Party Caretaker Government System in Bangladesh: Controversy and Reality" *2 European Centre for Research Training and Development UK* 2 no. 5, pp. 24–42 (2014).

Nizam Ahmed, "Abolition or Reform? Non-Party Caretaker System and Government Succession in Bangladesh" *100 The Round Table* pp. 303–321 (2011).

Nizam Ahmed, "From Monopoly to Competition: Party Politics in The Bangladesh Parliament (1973–2001)" *Pacific Affairs* 76, pp.–77 (2003).

Nizam Ahmed, *Non-Party Caretaker Government in Bangladesh: Experience and Prospect* (University Press Limited, Dhaka 2004).

Odhikar, Human Rights Monitoring Report, 2012.

Preamble: Constitution of the People's Republic of Bangladesh.

Preventive Detention and Violation of Human Rights: Bangladesh Perspective, Md. Nazir Ahmed.

Preventive Detention, Lawyers and Jurists.

Preventive Detention, Violation of Individual Human Rights: An Overview from Bangladesh Perspective.

Protocol to the agreement between the government of the Republic of India and the government of the people's republic of Bangladesh concerning the demarcation of the land boundary between India and Bangladesh and related matters (adopted 16 May 1974, entered into force 6 June 2015) art2.

Quoted in Carl J. Friedrich, Constitutional Government and Democracy, Oxford & IBH publishing Co. New Delhi, 1974, p. 155.

M. Rashiduzzaman "Bangladesh in 2001: The Election and a New Political Reality?" *Asian Survey* 42, no. 1 (2002).

M.S. Reza "Operation Searchlight in the National Self-determination Narrative". 26 March 2019. https://www.thedailystar.net/law-our-rights/news/operation-searchlight-the-national-self-determination-narrative-1720294?amp

S.M. Shamsul Alam, "Democratic politics and the fall of the military regime in Bangladesh, Bulletin of Concerned Asian Scholars" < 10.1080/14672715.1995.10413048> accessed 29 July 2020.

Salma Akhtar, "Amendments to the Constitution of Bangladesh 1973–2011: Background, Politics and Impacts" (University Press Limited, Dhaka 2016).

Salma Akter, "Amendments to the Constitution of Bangladesh 1973–2011: Background, Politics and Impacts". PhD, University of Dhaka, 2016, p. 1, 44 & 127.

Subhashis Sen, ""Tin Bigha"—Where The People Live Their Daily Life Is Complicated". *Proceedings of the Indian History Congress* 73, 1321–1328 (2012). http://www.jstor.org/stable/44156333 [accessed 27 July 2020].

A.A. Shawon June 7, 1966: Six Points Were Bengalis Charter of Freedom. June 6, 2020. (https://www.dhakatribune.com/bangladesh/2020/06/06/june-7-1966-six-points-were-bengalis-charter-of-freedom).

Richard Sisson. War and Secession, p. 11 & 12.

Summarized from Report of Constitution Drafting Committee, pp. 5–24.

Text of President Ayub's Speech at the Final Session of the Pakistan Muslim League (Convention Group) at Dhaka on March 20, 1966; see *The Daily Ittefaq* (Dhaka), March 21, 1966.

*The Daily Star Forum* 2, no. 9 (October 2007). https://archive.thedailystar.net/forum/2007/october/index.htm

UN General Assembly, "International Covenant on Civil and Political Rights", 16 December 1966, United Nations, Treaty Series, vol. 999

# INDEX

Note: Page numbers followed by "n" refer to notes

For Product Safety Concerns and Information please contact our EU representative GPSR@taylorandfrancis.com
Taylor & Francis Verlag GmbH, Kaufingerstraße 24, 80331 München, Germany

www.ingramcontent.com/pod-product-compliance
Lightning Source LLC
LaVergne TN
LVHW021128300926
849160LV00010B/915

* 9 7 8 1 0 3 2 4 2 4 8 8 0 *